Praise for Book

The book so many of us have been waiting for. Here's a collection
of book lists that will nurture and nourish your own reading life as
a woman. I love this book!

SARAH MACKENZIE
Author of *The Read-Aloud Family* and host of the *Read-Aloud Revival* podcast

As a fellow book girl, I delight in Sarah Clarkson's joyful
compendium of suggestions and reflections for a life filled with
reading. Clarkson's interleaving of personal experiences throughout
Book Girl shows us that books have the power to transform us,
to nourish us, and to sustain us; a good book can be a comfort,
a challenge, or a companion for the journey. Why not join the
merry company of book girls past, present, and future? The book
lists, on a varied range of topics and moods, form the heart of *Book
Girl*; Clarkson's warm and relaxed style and insightful comments
mean that readers will find many new favorites as they peruse the
pages of this charming and valuable guide.

DR. HOLLY ORDWAY
Author of *Apologetics and the Christian Imagination: An Integrated Approach to
Defending the Faith*

I can't imagine a more wise and tender guide to a life of reading
than Sarah Clarkson. Reading *Book Girl* feels like curling up with
a cup of tea in a cozy armchair by the fire, while a soul-friend tells
you passi   ped her,
and how   are about
to get a w

JENN
Autho   *lk Dragon*

Reading is vital for a faith-filled life. From being read to in the womb all the way to her adventures in Oxford, England, Sarah Clarkson takes us on her journey of becoming a book girl. She invites fellow women to allow books to lead us through all the ups and downs of life. Through her story and her wonderfully compiled lists, you'll find encouragement to seek beauty, strength, and companionship in the books we read.

HOLLY PACKIAM
Storyformed.com

Sarah Clarkson's luminous prose incites the very wonder for which she so lovingly advocates, and her *Book Girl* is a wise and winsome guide to the reading life. Crack open the cover and prepare to embark on a lifelong adventure.

LANIER IVESTER
Writer and speaker

I expected Sarah Clarkson's *Book Girl* to be a warm, winsome eulogy to the reading life—and it absolutely is. But it is so much more! In affirming the power of books to shape our vision and our response to life, Sarah's book does exactly what she says good books will do: spark hope, kindle joy, enlarge love, deepen faith. Reading *Book Girl* revitalized not just my love of books but my love of life and my love of God. I came away from its pages with a renewed commitment to live faithfully, courageously, and joyfully right where I am.

K. C. IRETON
Author of *The Circle of Seasons* and *Anxious No More*

A Journey through
the Treasures & Transforming
Power of a Reading Life

Book
girl

SARAH
CLARKSON

TYNDALE
MOMENTUM®

The nonfiction imprint of
Tyndale House Publishers, Inc.

Visit Tyndale online at www.tyndale.com.

Visit Tyndale Momentum online at www.tyndalemomentum.com.

Visit the author's website at www.sarahclarkson.com.

TYNDALE, *Tyndale Momentum*, and Tyndale's quill logo are registered trademarks of Tyndale House Publishers, Inc. The Tyndale Momentum logo is a trademark of Tyndale House Publishers, Inc. Tyndale Momentum is the nonfiction imprint of Tyndale House Publishers, Inc., Carol Stream, Illinois.

For information about special discounts for bulk purchases, please contact Tyndale House Publishers at csresponse@tyndale.com, or call 1-800-323-9400.

Library of Congress Cataloging-in-Publication Data
Names: Clarkson, Sarah (Editor for Whole Heart Press), author.
Title: Book girl : a journey through the treasures and transforming power of a reading life / Sarah Clarkson.
Description: Carol Stream, Illinois : Tyndale House Publishers, Inc., 2018. | Includes bibliographical references.
Identifiers: LCCN 2018015078 | ISBN 9781496425805 (sc)
Subjects: LCSH: Spiritual life—Christianity. | Christians—Books and reading. | Books and reading—Religious aspects—Christianity. | Christianity and literature.
Classification: LCC BV4501.3 .C5274 2018 | DDC 248.4—dc23 LC record available at https://lccn.loc.gov/2018015078

Printed in the United States of America

24	23	22	21	20	19	18
7	6	5	4	3	2	1

To my little book girl, Lilian Joy

Contents

Foreword

THERE ARE MOMENTS when it seems like the clouds of life part and the sun comes peeking through like a warm blanket of grace wrapping around my soul. It feels as if God is tenderly bending down to kiss my cheek to remind me of his affection and grace.

This sunshine invaded my life when I had my first child, Sarah.

I was not prepared to be a *proper* mother. I had never changed a diaper, had only babysat once that I remember, and was totally ill equipped to know what to do. Not being practical by nature, I awkwardly learned how to meet her basic physical needs. But I mainly dreamed of caring for my little one by attentively investing in her mind and soul.

Prior to Sarah's birth, I had lived in Vienna, surrounded by highly intellectual and educated adults from the international community of the United Nations, with diplomats, expats, and people from countless nations and every walk of life coming through the international chapel where my husband and I worked. Though I had a college degree, had studied four different languages in the countries where I'd lived, and had taken theology classes with my husband, Clay, while he was in seminary, I felt keenly the lack of a broad and well-developed education in my own life.

As I rubbed shoulders with these thoughtful and well-read people, it awakened in me a passionate longing to have a deeper well of wisdom born from reading and from the input of people wiser than myself. I yearned to know how to think about a variety of subjects; how to gain insight into history, art, theology, great literature, and philosophy; how to discover the biographies of heroes; how to pursue a soul-satisfying education. But it was only as I was exposed to this new, vast realm of ideas and inspiration that I understood I had been fed on crumbs of knowledge when there was a feast to be enjoyed.

I transferred my own longing for a broader exposure to the best authors, artists, philosophers, and theologians to Sarah and my other children who came after her. I supposed that they, too, had an intellectual potential for growing in these areas, and I made it my mission to read to them as a regular rhythm and habit of our daily lives.

Sarah was a ready companion in all things books. She was born reading, and she read more profoundly than anyone I had ever met. Her enthusiasm pushed me further in my own search for great books. Three more siblings eventually entered our reading community, and reading soon became a daily guide for my children. We journeyed through the pathways of adventuresome tales, mountains of theology, rivers of literary and artistic delight, and mysterious forests of historical odyssey. Swimming in the waters of imagination together gave us a kind of intimate bond with one another that only soul sharing can accomplish. Our souls were shaped and formed on the same stories, experiences, and messages as we grew together.

As I read to my children and watched them grow, seeking out time to spend in our treasured books, I realized that I was beginning to live into my own intellectual potential alongside them. By seeking to explain great ideas to them, my own interest in education and inspiration was satiated. As I taught them, I realized that all people have a capacity to love learning and to seek wells of knowledge, but their "mental muscles," so to speak, must be exercised.

Now one of my greatest pleasures is to meet with Sarah for coffee and to share ideas, to know what she has been reading, to discuss what we are both learning. The deep wells of reading extensively provided her a treasure chest full of knowledge and ideas from which I could also draw as we grew through the years in our own friendship over books. I have even been known to take notes from our times together. The love for learning has only increased in my life, but it has also led me to greater satisfaction as a woman as I have lived into my educational and intellectual potential.

If you are someone who wants to grow intellectually, spiritually, emotionally, and educationally, I know this book will lead you forward in these desires. Following the footsteps of others who are more well read and more broadly educated has given me a pathway to journey forward in my own life. And that is what this book will do for you. It will inspire, encourage, teach, and model the way forward as you expand your own heart, soul, and mind in the great stories and best thoughts found in books from throughout the centuries.

But the best part is that you will feel you have found a friend to guide you, one whose heart is enriched and ready to walk hand in hand with you into an exploration of unmined treasures. Sarah is a companion who will bring you just what you longed for but didn't know how to ask for. Be blessed in the reading of this book!

Sally Clarkson

Becoming a BOOK GIRL

The world was hers for the reading.

BETTY SMITH, *A TREE GROWS IN BROOKLYN*

MY MOTHER SWEARS she read to me while I was still in the womb. I must admit, I used to chuckle at this idea, half skeptical and wholly amused at the mental image of my mother reading dramatically to her newly swelled belly. But I don't laugh anymore. For even as I type this sentence in the quiet of my tiny front room in an old Oxford row house, I'm aware of the kick of my own unborn girl-child and the picture book I have laid nearby for the read-aloud break we will take in a few minutes. It's *Miss Rumphius* this morning, the story of a little girl who discovered that one of her great tasks in life was to "make the world more beautiful" and did just that by planting lupines in rainbow hues throughout the countryside in which she dwelled.[1]

Words like those, and images like that, are the kind to which

I hope my daughter will waken as the story of her own life begins. In speaking them over her unborn little being, I yearn for her already to be formed by a love for the beautiful in a world that often demeans it, by a sense of her own worth and capacity, by the sort of story that will begin to show her the kind of strong, intelligent, loving woman I hope she will become. I understand now, with an ache in my heart that is both my gratitude and my own newborn hope, that my mother desired the same for me in those months before my birth. I almost laugh into the quiet as time seems to expand around me, past and present united in the stubborn and loving wish of two young mothers who hoped to give their coming daughters the beauty of the world and the strength to bear its sorrow, and knew that one of the best ways to do that was through the gift of the reading life.

It's the same gift I hope to pass on to you in the pages that follow.

What's So Good about Being a Book Girl?

That is the question at the heart of this book, and my answer comes in the pages that follow as I explore the gifts I received from being raised as a book girl myself and as I tell the story of my own reading life, the one I yearn to give my daughter as she opens her story in this world. Gifts of learning and wonder, of hope renewed, of the capacity to ponder, of the will to act—these are just a few of the gifts to be explored in the chapters to come as we consider the particular goodness of being a book girl.

The reading life is like one of those potent graces bestowed by fairy godmothers on princesses in old fairy tales, the sort to help a young heroine grow in all good things, to love life in its fullness and beauty, but also to make her strong in resisting the forces of evil stepmothers or wicked fairies already gathered round her cradle. I read aloud to my belly (as did my mother before me) because

I firmly believe that books will help my daughter come into the full strength of her womanhood in all its intelligence and joy, its capacity and grace—and I'm firmly convinced they'll do the same for you.

Those gifts boil down quite quickly to three basic wishes, bright as any in a fairy story. They are the wishes, the hopes that ache in my heart as I read aloud to my little girl, the ones that echo back to me from my mother and shape my prayers for you as this book begins.

I want your heart to be stocked with beauty. To be a book girl is to be formed by a bone-deep knowledge that goodness lies at the heart of existence. The feel of my mother's warmth behind me as she read is one of the first things I can remember—the safe anchor of her body and the music of her read-aloud voice the ocean on which my small consciousness sailed into power through stories of music and brave maidens, feasts and castles, family and home. Before I knew how bad the world could be, I knew that it was wondrously good. I want the same for my daughter and for you. I want your imagination to be shaped by beauty, filled by characters of grace and strength, livened by a sense of wonder in the ceaseless gifts of ordinary life.

I want you to be strong for the battle. The future book girl of mine so merrily kicking my ribs will be born into a world where beauty is under siege and goodness is on the defensive. She will live out her story in this broken place, and sorrow will be her portion long before I'm ready for her to bear it. When my mother walked with me through the nightmares of my girlhood, the dark midnight terrors that plagued my young imagination, I'm sure she knew only bewildered grief. But she taught me how to fight the good fight and to hope with a fierce, creative will by reading me stories that came like lifelines in the night. I can picture her there in the shadows, reading of brave Lucy Pevensie or the staunch Princess Irene, who faced down terrors and fought their way back home. In my memory I see us as held in a circle of light cast from the pages of those stories. It's a light I have found throughout my life in the narratives of great books, the one I yearn for my daughter to discover when her own battle begins, the one I hope will come to you in the stories that cram the pages ahead.

I want you to know you're not alone. A book girl is joined not just to one but to two great fellowships, for the reading life sets book girls in the never-ending companionship of story as well as in the company of one another. To be a book girl is to take up membership in the ranks of women who read and, by their reading, live to the brave and courageous full. I knew this deeply in the reading times I shared with my mom throughout my girlhood and in the ideals I now share with both my mom and sister as we write and chatter back and forth about the novel we've both read or the theological classic we feel will change our lives . . . again.

But I also know it in the generosity of the women who have been my mentors and friends, the ones who stepped into my seasons of discouragement or transition with a novel for the road or a quote to set me back on my feet. I yearn for my little book girl to know this rich camaraderie, to know that when she is hopeless or lonely, there is another book girl who can kindle her courage and steady her soul. I hope that she will know this in person, but if she cannot, I hope she will find it in books that stand with her as companions and friends. I long for her to discover, as I have, the voice of companionship that can reach out from the page of some great novel or memoir to help her to find her faith afresh.

Who Is This Book For?

My desire is that you will find a unique kind of fellowship on the pages of *Book Girl*. Wherever you find yourself in the reading life, I hope that as you turn these pages, you'll discover that you aren't alone. Do you yearn to be a book girl but don't know where to begin? Oh, you are welcome. There's a fellowship of book girls waiting for your presence, and every page here is my way of passing along the gift of reading that I received by pure grace. I can't wait to set it in your hands. Are you a book girl who struggles to find the time to read? Goodness, my friend, we all understand that dilemma in this busy world. Were you once a book girl but seem to have lost your reading stride somewhere along the way? I hope you will remember afresh the joy and wisdom that wait to form you in the books that follow. Do you struggle with loneliness, do you yearn for a beauty you can barely describe, do you hope for friendship, or do you just need some courage to keep fighting the small battles of the everyday? Then pull up a chair, brew a cup of tea, and join the fellowship here as we read our way back to beauty and courage, to laughter and strength, to life in its fullest grace.

In a World Full of Books, Why Read This One?

I'd argue that you should read this book because it celebrates not just the gifts of the reading life but also the rich life of the reading woman, her particular experience and journey, and the wise and joyous fellowship that grows between women who undertake that reading adventure together. This isn't a textbook or a how-to for quick education or a tome on the classics. This is a book that explores in memoir and story what it means to be a book girl, for story to suffuse and shape a woman's experience, for books to walk with her as she navigates the varied seasons of her life. All the chapters and book lists are themed around spiritual or experiential seasons, shaped to encourage and companion the book girl who reads them in regaining strength and vision for her own story.

Book Girl is also my witness to the fact that the reading life is a gift, one I received largely from the wise women in my life whose generosity was expressed in the sharing of the books that taught them to live with humor, humility, and grace. In one of my favorite short stories, "A Jonquil for Mary Penn" by Wendell Berry, there is a beautiful scene that describes "the dance of women laughing," and that image came to my mind countless times as I considered what I wanted to create and offer in this book.

The scene comes near the end of a tale about a young, newly married girl who finds herself woefully underprepared for the farming life to which her marriage has brought her. One winter day she finds herself sick and despairing. She makes it through her chores and crawls straight back, chilled, into bed. But she wakes to warmth—to the creak of a rocking chair, a fire kindled, light streaming in through clean windows. Mary, in a keen, grateful moment, knows that she has been noticed and cared for in her extremity by one of the local women who have claimed and taught her, slowly weaving her into their fellowship. She lies there in bed and remembers the way these women have taught her not only their tricks of gardening and farming but their earthy good humor, their tough grace, their will to endure. The passage describing one such memory is rich in hilarity—how one of them got tangled up in a wire fence and began to chuckle at her own clumsiness, and how they all joined in:

> There on the ridgetop in the low sunlight they danced
> the dance of women laughing, bending and straightening,
> raising and lowering their hands, swaying and stepping with
> their heads back.

What that scene evokes for me is the vibrant, joyous fellowship of women who help each other to that fullness of self, skill, and insight that is the richest gift of friendship. That is what I hope *Book Girl* offers as well. This book is about the dance and joy of women reading, an invitation to that wise laughter, to the grace known by all the book girls of the world who live by the delighted conviction that reading is a vital ingredient in a woman's full engagement with her faith, her creativity, and her capacity to grow in knowledge and love throughout each season of her life.

How Should This Book Be Used?

Consider this book a companion, meant to come alongside you wherever you are in your journey as a book girl. If you are just delving into the reading life and are in need of an overarching vision for what it means to be a reader, you might enjoy reading straight through, exploring each chapter and list as an introduction and an invitation. The following two chapters are especially crafted to be a more practical opening to the reading life, with suggestions on how to begin, how to form reading habits, and how to think about book selection.

But *Book Girl* is meant to last you beyond a first read. By theming the chapters and their accompanying lists to different seasons of experience or growth, I hope you will find this a continuing resource. To that end, and particularly if you are a seasoned reader, I'd say dive straight in and read the sections that speak to you in your particular season of life or describe the sorts of books you are hungry to read in your current phase of exploration.

How This Book (and This Book Girl) Came to Be

With a mother who read to me in the womb, I really couldn't escape engagement with the written word. I loved books from little girlhood, especially stories that fired up my imagination and widened the horizons of what I could dream or hope to become. I grew up in a home crammed with books, in a family who lived by the rhythm of reading—for spiritual sustenance in the morning, for learning or imagination during the day, for laughter and fellowship in the long, starlit evenings. We spoke the language of story to each other, dreaming up adventures like Frodo, wanting to be brave like Davy Balfour, each of us aware of our own lives as stories just beginning. Reading, I realize now, was one of our prime ways of living and loving to the full.

But it wasn't until I was in my twenties, sitting in a conference on modern culture, that I realized how great a gift this reading life was, how purposefully it had been chosen as a heritage for me. I heard a talk on the decline of reading in contemporary life, especially for children, and it brought me to a sudden epiphany. I can still recall my deep and honestly surprised sense of wonder at having been raised to be a reader, at the gift and intention of my parents' investment in books. I sat there in the old church conference hall, sifting through my childhood as I began to examine the way stories had formed my sense of self, the way my parents had used literature to widen my concept of what was possible and to shape my ideas of the good, true, and beautiful.

That was a moment of catalyst for me—the instant in which I took up the identity of a book girl because I realized that the reading life was a gift, one I, too, had the power to give. I left that room determined to understand more about the power of reading, and that led to a decade of research, speaking, and writing about the powerful gift parents can give their children through a childhood formed by great books. I stumbled into full-time work in reading out of sheer enthusiasm, setting studies and other pursuits aside as I researched the way reading expands the whole being of a child. I spoke at parenting events, wrote a guide to children's literature (*Read for the Heart*), then another book (*Caught Up in a Story*) as I began to think specifically about what it means for a child to be "storyformed." My passion for reading was such that I wanted to hand out books to children on the street!

But my own reading adventures were just beginning, and several years ago I found myself not only about to start undergraduate study at the age of thirty but about to realize my dream of becoming a student at Oxford, a desire I'd carried ever since my teenage immersion in the writings of J. R. R. Tolkien, C. S. Lewis, and the rest of the famed Inklings fellowship. I went to England to do a year of theology as a sort of curiosity, a thirtieth-birthday adventure, and then I fell in love with the subject and decided to stay three years, unexpectedly mesmerized by the study of doctrine as I delved into the core tenets of my faith. I also fell in love with Thomas, my adorable Dutch husband, and before my degree was completed, we'd married, moved permanently to the UK, outfitted our first house, and discovered that we were expecting a baby.

As a student, I was immersed in the kind of reading that challenged my whole view of the world, but at the same time gave me a renewed sense of myself as an agent, someone with the power to learn, to discern, to grow, to create. I had been teaching parents about the power of reading to their children for years, but my experience as a student renewed my own identity as a learner. As I read, I saw how deeply I was being formed in my spiritual life, my sense of self, my sense of purpose. The power that came to me both as a reader and as a woman was immense as I discovered my capacity to wrestle well with the doubts and questions I'd always carried about my faith, to face the countless changes that came with marriage and an international move with faithfulness and courage, and to articulate the truth I was discovering to others.

I did all this in the marvelous company of other women who were also avid readers, and of fellow students and dear friends who balanced their lives as learners with their identities as wives, mothers, and teachers. I did this in community with my tutor and mentor, Liz, whose quiet authority and encouragement empowered me to explore; with my sister Joy, also a student, as we wrestled with questions of femininity, theology, and culture together; and with my mother, the first woman who taught me what it means to act in courageous discovery. When my studies finally drew to an end and my mind turned toward the messages burning in my heart, the ideas that had grown in my imagination throughout those intensely formative years, I realized that one of the first things I wanted to write was a book on the gift and grace and radiant power of being a woman who reads.

The idea for *Book Girl* came to me on an autumn afternoon as I sat in my chilly little Oxford living room, the one crammed with Thomas's and my combined libraries (the first thing we bought as a married couple were five extended-height bookshelves), and began to dream. What if I could write a book for other women that would guide them into the same kind of discovery and power that I had experienced afresh at Oxford? What if the gift of a reading life was available to every woman, something as vital for mothers as for their children? What if I could write specifically to women, exploring the way reading can shape and enrich every season of a woman's experience? With those questions, *Book Girl* began.

Now, over a year later, I sit in that same small living room. The book is complete, a manuscript that has grown alongside my belly as my own little book-girl-to-be has kept me company through all the months of writing. As I contemplate the opening of my little one's story, glancing at the pile of picture books I've set ready for her arrival, my eye is caught by a particularly tattered old book, one of the few I've taken the trouble to cart over the ocean from Colorado because it was one of the first my mother read aloud to me. I flip through the pages, savoring the faded illustrations, remembering the cadence of her voice pronouncing the simple, lovely text, pointing out this detail or that tiny beauty on each page. Through the reading life, my mother yearned to give me, in a sense, the whole world. She wanted to outfit her little girl with a wild imagination, a strong will to discover, a curiosity about the world, and the spunk to explore it. My heart soars with thanks . . . and excitement.

Now it's my chance to give that gift. It's the one I'm about to give my daughter, the same one I hope you'll discover in the pages of this book.

So please, my friends, join me in living the gift of becoming a book girl.

Sarah Clarkson
SPRING 2018

CHAPTER 1

On the Crafting of BOOK LISTS

How to Set a Course of Reading through the Ocean of Endless Books

Why are we reading, if not in hope of beauty laid bare, life heightened and its deepest mystery probed?
ANNIE DILLARD, *THE WRITING LIFE*

"OF MAKING MANY BOOKS there is no end," says the rather jaded writer of Ecclesiastes. Nor of the making of book lists, says this slightly wild-eyed but altogether idealistic writer. I still remember when a teenage friend and I were hosted overnight by a family in Boston during a history field trip. The mother asked me to jot down a few of my favorite children's books, so I curled on the couch and set to it as the adults packed picnics and snacks. The house grew curiously quiet (considering the combined presence of twelve children), but I was immersed, culling my best-loved stories from memory until I felt a tap on my arm.

"Sarah," said my bosom friend, Katrina, "it's time to go, and—" she peered over my shoulder before looking at me with a huge roll of her eyes—"thirty-five titles is more than enough. Good grief."

We both should have known my future would involve book lists.

The fact is, I can't keep quiet about a book I love. I want people to understand why this novel or that bit of theology can change the *whole way they see life*. I spent ten years reading classic literature and children's stories before I ever got around to starting a degree in theology (I like to say I took at least a dozen gap years), but once I did, I couldn't stop seeing connections between fairy tales and biblical narrative, doctrine and Victorian novels. I dragged my favorite works of fiction into every theological essay I could. I think I have become known as a bit of a Wendell Berry fanatic here in Oxford, because I've quoted him in essays on the Incarnation, argued against his being an anarchist with my college principal, and made my college small group read his poetry aloud. One of the best bookish compliments I've ever received came when a priest who has been mentor, theological teacher, and marriage counselor to Thomas and me asked for a

Katrina Jones

Katrina has known me since I was eleven years old, and we have been reading novels together (or recommending them to each other), writing letters (we probably number in the thousands by now), and adventuring like good book girls ever since. She is my kindred spirit, my very old and dearly beloved friend, and I couldn't have a book about women readers without a list from her.

My Favorite Books, in No Particular Order (Except the First Three)

- *Les Misérables* by Victor Hugo
- *Jane Eyre* by Charlotte Brontë
- *Redeeming Love* by Francine Rivers
- *The Awakening of Miss Prim* by Natalia Sanmartin Fenollera
- *True Grit* by Charles Portis (I was totally surprised by how much I loved this one. It's not necessary to love Westerns at all to appreciate it—it's just a great story of a tough little girl.)
- *Pride and Prejudice* by Jane Austen
- *Cranford* by Elizabeth Gaskell
- **The Chronicles of Narnia** by C. S. Lewis
- **The Heaven Tree trilogy** by Edith Pargeter

list of novels to take on a spiritual retreat. We showed up at his door with ten possibilities because I couldn't choose just a few.

The thing about my book lists is that they are driven by love—for the story or kernel of truth that lies hidden in the heart of what is written and for the person in whose hands I can't wait to place the book because I honestly believe it will widen and enrich their life. And that's the first thing I want you to know as we open this discussion on the crafting of book lists. The book lists here are formed by love.

The problem, though, is that there really is no end to the number of book lists I could make, the number of absolute favorite titles I want to review in detail, the books I haven't yet had time to read, and the ones I've heard are wondrous. During the months of writing this book, I frantically read as many new books as I could, afraid to miss that one great title or be "behind" on a contemporary classic. I finally had to take a deep breath and remind myself that I have to begin exactly where I am, with the riches I've culled as a reader up to this point in my life.

So before you dive into the lists ahead, a few brief thoughts. First, on *selection*. It's pretty straightforward: I list what I love. Then, *organization*: in other words, how I've arranged these potentially unwieldy lists of beloved titles so that you will know exactly where to go, depending on what kind of book you want to read. Finally, *content*, in which I will briefly discuss the difficult and nuanced practice of discernment and its role in helping me to evaluate the literary quality and worldview of the books I've chosen.

Selection

I can't say it often enough: this book is not meant to be a be-all, end-all list of every modern book you should read or the classics you should cover before death. This is *not* a comprehensive guide to literature. (For that, take a look at the highly ambitious recommended reading list compiled by Mortimer Adler and thank your lucky stars I'll never be as well read as he is.[1] And at least I'm not insisting you read Thucydides.)

Rather, my collective book list is one you could consider a story—a history by book recommendation; a living, delighted record of the books that have most kindled me to life in heart, mind, and soul. The selection process for the lists that follow is pretty basic: every one is a book I have loved. These are the books I press into the hands of my nearest and dearest, the titles I carefully select when those I love are in need of encouragement or freshened vision or comfort.

But I am only one reader who has happened upon a certain stream of books in the great ocean of the written word. The book lists that follow are thus highly individual, even eccentric at points. Of course, I've tried to read widely, dip into the classics, tour contemporary stories, taste some poetry, explore the paths of theology. I honestly think that if you read every title in this book, you'd have a rich exposure to some of the best writers around. But I know I have missed a lot as well. I know some of what I love will resonate with you and some just won't.

My goal in sharing the following lists is to simply open the reading life a little wider to you, set you on your feet, and launch you on your own journey of exploration. "Way leads on to way," wrote the poet Robert Frost, and I hope that you'll discover that book leads on to book and that the titles in these lists will lead you beyond, into the book lists of other writers and the best beloveds of other friends.

Organization

Each chapter is themed around a gift or grace that comes to a book girl through the reading life. The lists that follow are crafted to follow that theme, introducing you to the books that embody and continue the qualities discussed in the chapter. This book is structured specifically to address the different seasons of reading and experiences in the life of a book girl, organized in such a way that you can dip into this chapter or that list and find the resources you need in that particular phase. The lists are shaped to address different needs, varied amounts of time or attention, and different seasons of learning and growth. If you're a mother of toddlers, I'm guessing your reading needs might run toward a restorative novel, while if you're a student in a season of discovery, you'll find the tougher theological titles or cultural commentary to be the meat you need. The lists and chapters are individual, meant to meet you in these varied seasons.

These selections reflect my own reading experience, my deep sense of books as companions that come alongside me to help me to be faithful wherever they find me. During my twenties, during many long, lonely hours, I discovered classic writers on prayer and spiritual formation and spent hours in their brisk and convicting company. At the moment, as I sit here pregnant and overwhelmed by daily life, I doubt I could read one of them without feeling frustrated. Instead, it's a novel I crave, one that helps me to reconnect to ordinary life as a gift and a wonder.

In theming the chapters and lists that follow, I've tried to create the resources and stories I would want to discover in my own various stages of life. My hope for you as a reader is that you will encounter this book as an adaptable companion and resource through many seasons.

Content

Literary Quality

The easiest way to understand what makes a book excellent is simply to read good books. Read a short story by Wendell Berry, dip into George Eliot's *Silas Marner*, throw in a snippet of Narnia and a William Wordsworth poem, and you will be well on your way to discerning, even intuitively, what makes writing *good*. Along with C. S. Lewis, I am not particularly interested in the "chronological snobbery" that prizes writing according to what is popular in a particular age. And like Lewis, I think children's books, mysteries, classics, and contemporary fiction can be excellent, but all of them should share a few basic qualities, ideas for you to consider in forming your own idea of what makes for literary quality:

- *High quality of language.* A good book wields language with skill and insight, using words that broaden your experience of the world; that help you to see in a fresh way; that bring a person, a landscape, or a history to life. Good writers also have a certain degree of particularity in the words they choose. As Mark Twain said, "The difference between the almost right word and the right word is really a large matter—'tis the difference between the lightning-bug and the lightning."[2]

- *Showing, not telling.* It's probably the first thing you'll be told to do in a beginning creative writing class, but it's vital, the thing great writers do without even thinking about it. An author who *shows* sets you as a reader in the scene, immersing you in the scents and sights, feelings and emotions of the setting. To tell is simply to relate facts; to show is to place a reader in a world.

- *Concision.* With all this praise for good words and evocative descriptions, you might think good novels have to be hundreds of pages. In fact, some of the best novels are brief. *To Kill a Mockingbird* is a fairly short story that manages to communicate the profound racial tension and moral dilemmas dividing a small Southern town, but all of it is told through the eyes and vocabulary of a child (though Scout is probably a wordier little girl than most!). Good writing is taut. It doesn't waste words; it puts them to swift, disciplined work.

- Humanity (the particular and the universal). By which I mean the capacity of a book to realistically describe the human experience on the level of the individual—whether Potok's depiction of a Hasidic Jewish boy or Eliot's depiction of a lonely English woman in the Victorian era who is caught in a difficult marriage—and through that depiction to say something universally true about what it means to be human, to suffer, to hope, to love, to work. A good book should ring true to human experience, regardless of character or setting.

Or, in C. S. Lewis's loving description: "Literary experience heals the wound, without undermining the privilege, of individuality. . . . In reading great literature I become a thousand men and yet remain myself. Like the night sky in the Greek poem, I see with a myriad eyes, but it is still I who see. Here, as in worship, in love, in moral action, and in knowing, I transcend myself; and am never more myself than when I do."[3]

Worldview

The first real doctrine essay I wrote at Oxford was on the Incarnation. I was asked to outline why Christ's human life was as important as his death. Intuitively, I understood that it was pretty radical that God took flesh at a certain point in space and time, but I struggled to get the abstract theological points straight in my head until I remembered a particular character from a Wendell Berry novel. It all came clear when I revisited Berry's tale of Nathan Coulter, a Kentucky farmer and war veteran. His experiences left him horrified at the way people and land became nameless, depersonalized, and lost in the face of violence, good only for destruction. Berry's novel recounts the way Nathan came home determined to live a life rooted in love, one opposite to war, in which he would care for the named and known people in his place on earth, tending his farm, committed to his marriage and community, faithful in the smallest, local particulars of everyday existence. As his wife, Hannah, puts it, "It is by the place we've got, and our love for it and our keeping of it, that this world is joined to Heaven."[4]

In Nathan's story I recognized an incarnational, Christ-shaped love. He helped me to understand that the Incarnation means that God himself came into a particular corner of the war-torn universe to embody a life that is the opposite of war and death; to name, know, and love each human being into redemption. The Word who spoke everything into being became flesh in the squirming, little baby Jesus, asleep in the musty hay of a Bethlehem manger. Before Jesus died, he lived, and in doing so, he started the story of humanity afresh as his perfect, faithful, loving life became the ground of renewal for the whole world.

I wrote the rest of that paper in a blaze of inspiration, delighted by the way a story I loved made theology clearer to me. But that was only the first of many such instances. The more I studied doctrine, the more I realized that the great books I'd been reading all my life had already been teaching me to think about the ultimate questions at the heart of theological study. In The Lord of the Rings, I had already learned to consider what it means to be an agent responsible for my actions. *Middlemarch* taught me about what real compassion might mean. *A Wrinkle in Time* challenged me to consider what love really is . . . and isn't.

The great stories I have read have impacted my spiritual and moral development more than almost anything else. Next to Scripture and the influence of my parents, great books have formed my worldview, developed my moral imagination, and shaped my idea of virtue. But I think this is true of most human lives, whether we get our stories from great books, from other people, or from TV sitcoms. Stories shape our existence because we recognize in a deep part of ourselves that life itself is a story. The tale of the world opens with a sort of divine "once upon a time," or "in the beginning." Much of Scripture is narrative, and the Gospels are crammed full of the parables Jesus told to announce and explain the coming of his Kingdom. The gospel itself comes to us in narrative form, and one of its great tenets is that we have the chance to join the story of the Kingdom come in this world, to be agents in the ongoing story of redemption, what Rowan Williams calls the "freedom of a sort of *authorship*."[5]

To read a story is to be shaped in the very depths of one's soul. Because of this power, this grace given by great books, I've often had to ask the question "What makes a book acceptable for a Christian reader?" Because stories engage my imagination and heart on a deep level, I am aware of the fact that what I encounter on their pages will teach me how to see the world, and this is why I've had to learn to practice discernment. As you explore the vast realm of books available today, you might have to ask, as I have, where we draw the line on the inclusion of sex or violence or "bad language" in a story. How deeply should we delve into worldviews that run contrary to what we believe? What does it mean to read faithfully?

First, let's briefly consider the cultivation of discernment, the means by which we nourish our inner capacity to love what is good and hate what is evil, to know when evil is presented to us in whatever form. The temptation here would be to create a list of rules by which each piece of reading could be evaluated, but I think this is both unhelpful and, in the long term, destructive. Discernment has far less to do with creating an outward legalism than it does with cultivating our innermost hearts. Real discernment, I believe, springs from a heart so nourished by the true, the good, and the beautiful that what is evil simply cannot find room to root.

In my earlier book on children's literature, *Caught Up in a Story*, I explore the difficult question concerning the age at which children can safely be exposed to evil, suffering, or darkness in the world of literature. While I agree with Chesterton that "fairy tales do not give the child the idea of the evil or the ugly; that is in the child already, because it is in the world already,"[6] I think the question we really should be asking is not so much "When do I expose my children to darkness?" as "Have I exposed them to light?" My contention is that in order for children to cope with evil, they need a bone-deep knowledge of what is good. Like the heroes and heroines in fairy tales, they need stories that begin in a powerful picture of joy. They need minds stocked with the imagery of love, beauty, laughter, and song before they can have the necessary hope to shield them in their battle against sin and evil.

I think the same idea applies to us as adults as we evaluate the content of the books we read. Read what is good, cram your imagination with nuanced characters and truth-telling authors, and you will know how to handle books that have questionable content. If you read Goudge and Tolkien and Chaim Potok and Chesterton, you will be equipped to evaluate a just-released novel that deals with more common modern discussions of sex or an ambiguous worldview. Because the soil of your imagination is rich in what is good, you will know how to deal with what isn't.

Now let us briefly turn to the books themselves.

As a Christian who seeks to live out my faith in every area of my life and who sees reading as a formative force to that faith, I have often asked myself, *What makes a book acceptable for me as a Christian reader?* What I have found in my own process of discernment is that I need to ask what a book communicates as a whole rather than if it explains or mentions the Christian message. What does the book seek to have me believe through the development of its characters, in their choices, in the consequences that follow, and in the way it frames belief? Does it portray the human capacity for choice? Does it deal with the reality of sin? Does it affirm what is beautiful and kind? Does it value human life?

The quality of a book's worldview cannot be measured by the

number of times the name Jesus is mentioned or Scripture is quoted. We get confused at times, I think, in contemporary Christianity and particularly in evangelical culture about the difference between Christian form and Christian vocabulary. A novel can be crammed with "Christianese," using recognizably Christian phrases but communicating in form and plot what amounts to a secular story.

Consider: *Anna Karenina* is a book about an adulterous affair, while your local bookstore may have a half dozen Christian romance novels with couples who get married and perhaps share nary a kiss until their wedding day. The dialogue of the latter may well include verses straight out of the Bible, while the former revolves round the decadence of Russian high society and its many gossipy intrigues. But many "Christian" romance novels have stories based far more on a secular model of romance and self-fulfillment, where emotion is valued as truth, where trouble miraculously disappears and the ultimate goals of ease and happiness are reached by the novel's close. *Anna Karenina*, on the other hand, wrestles with the desires of the heart and the obligations of integrity; it shows us what it really looks like to "listen to your heart" and the consequences of putting self-fulfillment above other people, above morality, even above God. *Anna Karenina* tells us the truth about the world and confronts us with the realities both of desire and of choice in our own lives, and for this reason, I consider it a novel that has much truth to impart to every Christian.

This is not to say that all Christian romantic stories are lacking in content—far from it! (I cut my teeth on Janette Oke.) But it is to say that our standard for what makes something an acceptable book for a Christian reader must be one that looks to the truth the book is telling about the human condition, the possibility of redemption, and the reality of grace, whether that book is a romance novel, a murder mystery, a picture book, or a tragedy. This applies to the author as well. George Eliot is one of my favorite writers, an author I turn to for wisdom and moral courage and for her portrayal of profound, active compassion. She is well known for her impassioned rejection of the Christian faith, but her novels reflect a call to Christ-shaped mercy, a value for human life and dignity, and an awareness of mystery that I have rarely found equaled in an explicitly Christian novel. The capacity to see and portray what is true is part of what it means to be made in the image of God, something as true for those authors who struggle with faith as those who embrace it.

However, this is also not to say that anything goes when it comes to moral or graphic content as long as the book speaks spiritual truth. I take seriously the Philippians exhortation to dwell on what is excellent, lovely, of good repute. I don't think this limits me to kittens and flowers, but I do think it means that I have to discipline my imagination and keep myself from temptation to paths that would lead me away from holiness. Here again we return to the theme of discernment—an inward standard rather than an outward rule. I have a vivid imagination and learned very early that I cannot expose myself to graphic written descriptions of violence or sex, so I just don't read books with that kind of content. (To be frank, I think there are few who can do so without a sense of unease.) But some of my favorite contemporary novels do contain moderate scenes of both as integral elements to their plots. My evaluation usually runs somewhat toward the model of the biblical narrative—an epic crammed with all sorts of human depravity, sexual desire, and wanton violence—in which the discussion and account of evil is frank but there is no detailed soak in the finer points of egregious sin.

If you read *The Brothers Karamazov*, well, you'll encounter a lot of sexual depravity. If you read *Island of the World*, one of the most remarkable contemporary novels I've encountered, you'll have to face the wanton brutality of concentration camps and the senseless violence that can be inflicted even on children. But neither of these books presents the evil in which they necessarily deal in a way that glorifies it or makes it a graphic memory. You may love these books as I do, or you may decide to put them away. That depends on your heart, your walk with the Holy Spirit, and the nourished soil of your own discerning imagination.

The Art of Discernment

Discernment really is an art—a skill we learn in the doing, something we gain confidence in through practice. In that sense, it's a forward journey, a habit we learn in the midst of reading, not a list we make before we start. If it still seems overwhelming at times to know how to choose the good and beautiful and best from the plethora of books out there, I find that a final question often helps me to come to a conclusion: *What is it I hope to become?*

My parents talked a lot about appetites and reading when I was a little girl. At the time, I usually associated this with the fact that they wouldn't let me read straight through the fifty-eight available Nancy Drew girl detective titles. I was forced (I write this tongue in cheek) to read a good children's novel, a piece of science or poetry, a book of history, and usually a biography before I could return to the next Nancy Drew. What my parents understood was that my mind and desires would be powerfully formed by what I read. They wanted me to have a hunger for good literature, for deep ideas and crafted words and the nuance and adventure of history. They wanted me to encounter characters who rang true to real life and challenged my decisions, who helped me to imagine what I might create or attempt or love. Of course, fun and relaxation were part of it (and oh, I did indeed make it through all fifty-eight Nancy Drews), but they weren't the first or most formative force in my reading.

As an adult, I'm profoundly grateful for the way my reading desires were set as a child; I'm also keenly aware that I'm now the one in charge of my own development. I know that the books I read deeply shape the person I am becoming day by day. When I come to a dilemma of discernment, I often find that if I examine what the book produces in me—in my emotions, my imagination, my desires, my sense of what is real or true—I can quickly identify whether the book is one I want to continue. In his fascinating sermon "The Weight of Glory," C. S. Lewis writes that we are all helping each other to grow, day by day, into either the divine beauty that reflects the fullness for which we were created or a corrupted self that would shock us if we could see the end result. I try to choose the books that help me toward glory.[7]

CHAPTER 2

Begin at the BEGINNING

Creating Habits, Rhythms, and Space for the Reading Life

*How many a man has dated a new era
in his life from the reading of a book!*
HENRY DAVID THOREAU

THIRTY OF US were crammed into the worn corners of an English sitting room that summer afternoon. Thirty shy, awkward, idealistic, opinionated student types who had trekked with our suitcases down the dusty path from the village (after a much longer trek via train or plane for many) to this echoing old house, the home of a Christian community formed for spiritual seekers. We'd come for various reasons: my two-week stay was in preparation for an internship with a theological ministry in Cambridge, but many others had come simply to stay the summer and wrestle with their questions about their faith in a daily, communal setting. Regardless, we'd all bunk in dorm rooms, work three hours a day, study three, eat our meals in common, and ask every question we could muster about faith. But this was our first day. And oh, the awkwardness of earnest amateur philosophers is an ice that only, well, Winnie the Pooh could break.

We had a wise hostess, you see. When every one of us was distracted by the complicated task of balancing a cup of tea and a biscuit (British for cookie), she handed round worn copies of A. A. Milne's *Winnie-the-Pooh*. Then she pointed randomly.

"You read Tigger," she said to a tanned and spindle-legged philosopher who rolled his own cigarettes.

"You read Rabbit," she said to a bright-eyed theologian whose

Liz Hoare

When I showed up at my assigned fellowship group my first week at Wycliffe, I had no idea that the tutor assigned to lead the group and shepherd me through the next few years would become so dear a friend and mentor. Liz is a fellow lover of good books and beauty, author of *Using the Bible in Spiritual Direction*, and a mentor whose encouragement and insight have shaped me deeply as both a student and a woman.

The Books That Have Shaped Me

- *Jane Eyre* by Charlotte Brontë. From the opening lines to the final "Reader, I married him," this book has shaped the kind of novels I love to read. It has a wonderful setting, which for me is close to where I call home. The moors, with all their bleakness, have a grandeur and beauty beyond what the eye can see. The house where Jane meets Rochester is atmospheric—and almost a character in the book. When I first read the book, it was as a wonderful story; when I returned to it later, it was Jane's strength of character that I found so compelling. It is a book for young and old to find insight into the human condition.

- *The Go-Between God* by John V. Taylor. This book blew me away when I first read it in my early twenties. This profound study, with its references to the Holy Spirit in art and its outward-looking emphasis on mission, often forced me to stop reading to ponder the implications. This is a book that warrants reading again—and it demands a response each time. It changed the way I understand what being a Christian is about and challenged me to pray for a greater awareness of God and his action in the world.

- *Playing with Fire: A Natural Selection of Religious Poetry*, edited by Susan Dwyer. There were lots of poetry books in my childhood home, but this was the first themed poetry book I owned. A gift from a close friend who also loved poetry, it introduced me to a wonderful range of English-speaking poets through the ages. It helped me to recognize the importance of poetry in expressing the things we know but can't find words for ourselves. The poems don't offer easy answers to questions of faith and life but instead offer that truth told "slant," which draws us further into life's big questions.

dark hair swished back and forth as she passionately informed her neighbor about her research on Barth.

"You read Piglet." The hostess smiled at the neighbor, whose eyes were beginning to glaze.

When the books were open and the cups of tea rebalanced, she cleared her throat, her eyes commanding silence. Taking the part of the narrator, she began to read:

Here is Edward Bear, coming downstairs now, bump, bump, bump . . .

Ten minutes later, the awkward quiet and the shy defenses of our little group had been shattered in the laughter kindled by the epic adventures of Pooh, the "Bear of Very Little Brain," whose childlike philosophy ("the only reason for making honey is so as *I* can eat it") turned out to have a wisdom deeper than we thought, for it taught us, on that first day of our quest for ultimate knowledge, to laugh at ourselves.

In the years since, I have often blessed that quiet English woman for her wisdom in using a children's story to open our time in her community. She easily could have begun with some sort of invigorating talk on the search for real truth or the need for spiritual diligence. After many years of witnessing the toils and troubles of young questioners like us, though, she no doubt understood that one of the first things we needed to understand is that the search for wisdom doesn't end in having the biggest pile of knowledge and hoarding it in a corner by yourself. The capacity to laugh, to listen to your neighbor, to recognize the silliness of your own self-righteousness, to discover that however much you know, it's only a drop in an ocean you didn't even make: these are the qualities—the humbled, grateful state of vision—to which real wisdom leads.

It's easy, in our age of information, to regard reading as something you do to gather knowledge. As if each page read were a coin you could put in the bank until the pile grew high enough to make you rich. There are many books out there that list the classics you must read to become "educated" (really, what does that mean?) or the modern novels you must tuck away in order to be savvy to the world in which we live. Read five books a month, we are told, to really be wise, or is it ten? But I am convinced that neither reading nor wisdom works when it is viewed as something to acquire, a status you reach after a certain number of classics consumed.

This book certainly isn't based on the assumption that books are a commodity. Reading, rather, is a journey. Reading is the road you walk to discover yourself and your world, to see with renewed vision as you encounter the vision of another. Reading is a way of walking with the wise (Proverbs 13:20) as you trek down the road of life, offering a hand to guide you, a voice to help you look up from the dust and discover the sunset, a friend in whose words you can shelter when life sends you a storm. Reading is a way to live. It requires no particular training or special knowledge (though you can grow in skill and insight), it requires no particular curriculum, and it's something you begin right where you are, whether you want to read one or ten books in the next year.

In his poem "Singing Bowl," Malcolm Guite says exactly in lovely verse what I want to say about reading in the rest of this chapter:

> *Begin the song exactly where you are* ...
> *Start with the very breath you breathe in now,*
> *This moment's pulse, this rhythm in your blood.*

There is no formula to the reading life, no law stating how many pages we must read per day or which books will set us among the wise and which won't. The reading life begins merely with the opening of a book—a novel, a poem, a cultural epic, a theological tome, or ...

Winnie-the-Pooh. Of course, we will learn and grow. The things we read will always broaden, awaken, and deepen our knowledge and experience of the world. Yes, we must begin to make habits that lead us back to reading in an age of distraction. But this is a process of walking, of seedlike growth. As we move in this chapter into the hows and habits of the reading life, I hope you will see the ideas and suggestions that follow not as laws to be kept to the letter, but as rain-splashed, heartfelt postcards sent your way from a fellow traveler who has walked long in the company of good books and found their friendship to be a gift.

In the following sections, we'll explore mindful ways that you can begin and purposefully engage as a reader. Consider them simply the passing on of maps and guides, the waymarks and skills suggested by readers who have long walked the reading road. The point is simply to help you begin, exactly where you are, to *read*.

Read What You Love

The reading life may sound like a huge undertaking for which you need a good bit of preparation; in reality, it begins the moment you open a book. But if you are just starting out as a book girl or if you used to love reading and feel that you've lost your way, beginning can be the hardest part. This is where Guite's words come into play: "Begin the song exactly where you are." In other words, begin with the books you love.

Several years ago, Alan Jacobs, a respected professor of humanities, wrote a delightful essay arguing for reading not just what you *should*, but what you actually enjoy. As James K. A. Smith notes in his fascinating multivolume work on cultural liturgies (i.e., the habits and rituals by which our lives are formed), we habitually do what we love. Don't start with *The Brothers Karamazov* if you haven't read a good novel in years. (It took me six months to get through that one.) If you love children's stories, follow in the footsteps of the venerable

C. S. Lewis and reread your favorites. (He loved *The Wind in the Willows*.) Read what sparks your spirit to life in the very place that you are, and let that book lead to another.

Read Regularly

Reading, like so many other good, rich things, must be planned for. In the midst of the crazy pace of modern life, one of the keys to beginning (or resuming) the reading life is simply to consider *when* and *what* you will read and to create daily rhythms around the answers you give to those questions.

My mother was a bit of a genius, I think, when it came to getting her children to be regular readers. Every afternoon of my childhood, an hour of quiet descended upon the house. We were given a choice: we could nap, or we could read. And what child is going to sleep when anything else is on offer? I'm so grateful for the choice, though, because what that early habit built in me was the almost bone-deep expectation that I would read every day. The habit became my default mode so that, to this day, I build space for reading into the structure of my day.

Part of this rhythm means choice. You compose the symphony of your own days, and reading requires that you craft it in as one of your themes. Often, the choice to read means you will *not* do something else. A favorite blogger of mine (at http://soulemama.com), known for a rich, farm-based life and the beautiful handcrafts she makes and garden she cultivates, explains on her "About" page (in answer to many questions, I'm sure) that, no, she doesn't "do it all." She chooses: "There are many things that I don't do, in order to do the things that I love."

This piece of advice has helped me immensely. I think choice and prioritization are valuable skills to hone in an age of hurried distraction and vital to the cultivation of the reading life. As you plan and prioritize, then, it can help to consider these two questions: *When will you read each day?* and *What will you read each day?*

When Will You Read?

Here are a few ideas to consider as you make space in your schedule for reading:

- *In the morning, before the busyness of your day sets in, read something for spiritual nourishment.* My parents each kept a book of theology or devotions next to their Bibles, and this is a habit I have taken up as well. Their morning routine of Scripture and prayer included a short space of theological reading that allowed them to progress over the years through a number of formative books that shaped their spiritual practice and theological identity. Each morning I try to include at least a few paragraphs of spiritual writing or meditation as part of my devotions. When I'm short on time, I fall back on the daily readings assigned as part of my trusty *Celtic Daily Prayer*. When I have more margin, I'm usually working through a longer book of devotion or spirituality like Eugene Peterson's *Run with the Horses* or Thomas Merton's *New Seeds of Contemplation*. In Lent or Advent, I often read a themed daily devotional like the wondrous *Watch for the Light*.
- *As part of your daily routine, read a single poem before you walk out the door.* In different phases of my life I have greatly enjoyed this habit, whether reading a classic poem before beginning writing work or reading a seasonal (Advent or Lenten) poem before leaving for work in the morning. It takes five minutes or less, but you will be investing in words every morning.
- *In the afternoon, read a book for rest or relaxation.* In my current phase of life, this is a luxury I'm making the most of while I still have the margin. I try to read a novel for half

an hour with a cup of tea, if I can manage the time. This provides a space of quiet and imagination in the midst of the day's work. And now I have scientific approval for this affinity: studies suggest that even six minutes of reading a novel can cut stress levels by two thirds![1] I'm sure this rhythm will change drastically when my own little book girl arrives to fill all my time with her presence. But that just means I'll be in a new phase of the reading life, renegotiating my time and capacity as a reader, snatching five minutes here or ten minutes in the evening or counting the picture books I perused with my little one as the reading I managed for one day.

- *In the evening, turn to a riveting novel or an engrossing book of essays, current commentary, or biography.* Perhaps you could carve out time when you might otherwise be doing something else like watching TV or spending time online.
- *Consider when you can read aloud—with family, children, friends, or a spouse.* Before we got married, Thomas and I began reading aloud the Harry Potter series after we both finished work, purely for fun. We've continued this tradition now that we're married; we're still working through Harry Potter (Thomas got me the fully illustrated copy of the second book for our first anniversary), but we also read aloud from books of theology or devotion, stopping to savor and discuss the passages we love or those that instigate debate.

What Will You Read?

Planning for what books you want to read, which you'll start with, and which are most important to you will help you put your reading time to good use. It empowers you to continue your own education, and it will make the reading life manageable. Instead of planning vaguely to read "the classics" (which I have planned and failed to do many times), you can identify a single classic to begin with or which three you want to read over the course of a year. Individual books and doable goals make the reading life realistic, while writing down your own personal book list makes the reading life tangible, a goal and project by which you can shape your days. Consider these ideas for planning:

- *Make a yearly reading list.* Take time (preferably with a cup of something warm and a slice of something delicious) to list the books you want to read over the course of the year. Be sure to plan for delight as well as growth or exploration. Be realistic but bold. Try something new as well as something beloved.

- *Make a book basket stocked with the books you plan to read in the coming months.* My mom was a good book fairy, with her habit of keeping a basket for each of us children as we grew up that had a rotation of books for us to read: a novel, something historical, a biography, a spiritual book, and a volume of poetry or science, depending on our current interests. I follow that practice to this day, keeping a small stack of "current reading" on my desk that includes books I can pick up for sheer relaxation as well as mental growth.

- *Keep a record of what you've read.* Since I was a young teen, I've jotted down the titles of the books I read in the back of my current journal. I put stars by those I especially liked. I love seeing the record of what I have actually read. As an adult, I try to jot down the big ideas I loved in most of the books I read, along with a few quotes and a brief word sketch of my impressions when I finish a book. The concreteness of this exercise allows me to mark and continue my own progress and growth on the reading journey.

What Will You Do When You Get Stuck?

I'm always a little shocked at how easy it is to get out of the rhythm of reading. Book girl I may be, but in times of travel or stress, in seasons (ironically) of intensive writing, or when my schedule becomes particularly frenetic, I often find myself surprised at how difficult it can become to manage or even desire fifteen minutes a day of sustained reading. Part of this is sheer exhaustion; a tired mind just can't quite cling to a written page. Part of this is distraction; I wish it weren't so, but the wearier my mind grows, the harder it is for me to disconnect from the click and scroll of my online feeds. But all of it is seasonal, part of the ebb and flow of the reading life, the different phases of book-girlish experience.

The first thing I've found helpful is simply not to fret and to realize that my yen to read will return as mind and body restore some balance. Part of that restoration, though, might mean creating some mental space. Here are a few of the ways I have learned to ease myself back into a reading rhythm:

- *I start with art or picture books.* Books like *Miss Rumphius* aren't just for children! The practice of savoring the illustrations in a children's classic or paging through a collection of art is strangely restorative for me, especially in helping me to focus. I think it has something to do with refreshing my imagination, feeding it with beauty so that it comes back to a strengthened interest in life and words.
- *I make the choice to step back from social media.* It's a small discipline, but I find that the buzz of a busy brain, overloaded with bits of information, is a real detriment to reading. Mental space is one of the first things I need in order to be

a reader, something I find I have to choose again and again as I make reading one of the defining rhythms of my life. It's not about legalism or never checking Facebook—it's about knowing what I value and creating the space for it to flourish anew.

- *I read what I love.* I go back to the beginning. If one more Cadfael murder mystery [2] is the only thing I can manage, or yet one more immersion in *Anne of Green Gables*, then that is where I begin.

- *I read magazines.* Whether an essay about walking in the lovely *Taproot* magazine (http://taprootmag.com) or an article about travel or writing in an old issue of *Victoria* (I collect the older ones for their excellent articles) or a poem in *Ruminate* (http://ruminatemagazine.com), a literary magazine of faith and art, the shorter content accompanied often by photos or art offers a bite-size way for me to ease back into reading.

Read Mindfully

Never tell a book girl that her books are worthless. It seems a fairly obvious point, but to the young editor invading my mom's library one summer morning, the only thing that was obvious to him was the assumption that physical books were outdated, useless, old fashioned. "All of this," he claimed, gesturing to the old oak shelves groaning with the countless picture books and novels that formed my childhood, "will be gone in another few years. We can read so much more quickly now on a screen." My mother was rendered speechless. I'm afraid I wouldn't have been.

My problem with the overconfident and ultramodern assessment of this editor is not with the idea of e-readers as a viable form of reading or with the expanding world of alternate ways of reading, whether by audiobook, e-reader, or some new technology of which

I have not dreamed. I just love my books—the creased paper my fingers have touched since childhood, the musty smell, the memory of a quote on a certain side of the page. I don't think physical books will go out of style, because we are embodied beings who need to touch and feel, smell and see reality in tangible ways. Books are more than ideas bound to black type; they are also gifts, companions, physical presences that walk with us through certain seasons of our lives. I'm not too worried about their continued existence.

That said, I heartily endorse the use of an e-reader if it makes reading accessible and doable. I know that my sister, a doctoral student, has found hers invaluable since the mound of reading she would have to lug around would be impossible without it. I have learned to enjoy my e-reader on the rare occasion I don't want to pile my suitcase with books. And when it comes to audiobooks, I am a long-term lover; I grew up listening to book-on-tape classics during back-road drives through the Texas Hill Country and the Rocky Mountains. I love the fact that I can walk to the grocery store in Oxford and catch fifteen minutes of a story on my headphones.

My only concern with the use of technology for reading is simply that the fragmentary nature of online reading—the skim from headline to blog to article to Instagram—not *replace* the habit of quiet, sustained reading, the kind that immerses you in the mind and ideas of another, giving you space to consider, ponder, and discern.

Read with Attention

When I was seventeen, I was introduced to the remarkable Dr. Joe Wheeler, a writer, anthologist, and professor of literature who mentored me through a course of literary reading that lasted over a year and established a certain way of reading that has shaped me all the way to my studies in Oxford. In one of the first letters he sent (a handwritten wonder) outlining our course and instructing me in certain habits of attention, he directed me to do something I'd simply never done before: mark up my books with abandon. Have a conversation with them, he said. Underline, argue, notate. I was hesitant at first; I'd always kept my books clean and tight. But as I began to follow his directions, I realized that as I interacted with those books, jotting my objections or my praise and underlining passages I loved, the content became much more my own, the ideas vivid in my mind long after I closed them.

Reading retention—the capacity to remember, recall, and articulate what we have read—is something that is often a focus in childhood education. But I think it is equally vital for adults. The capacity to remember the words and ideas we read equals our capacity to be shaped, instructed, and guided by them. Studies suggest that the brain retains very little of what is simply read but is instantly able to recall more of what has been underlined, notated, or interacted with in any way. It's why Scripture is crammed with directives for believers to repeat, memorize, and meditate upon God's Word. Eugene Peterson says we must "metabolize" Scripture, partaking of it daily in such a way that it becomes assimilated into bone, soul, blood, and spirit.[3] It's the same with anything we read. If we want to retain the beauty of J. R. R. Tolkien, the wry wisdom of Wendell Berry, or the wonder of Gerard Manley Hopkins, we have to read so that our reading is a conversation, an interaction, the reception of a gift. Consider these ideas for reading with attention:

- *Mark it up!* I'm with Dr. Wheeler now. Get a pencil (if you feel a bit squeamish about marking those clean white pages) or go whole hog with a pen, but get yourself in the habit of conversing with the books you want to remember. Underline favorite quotes; jot objections or praise.
- *Keep a quote book or box.* On my first trip to Europe as a teen, I spent a bit of my long-hoarded savings on an intricately carved wooden box bought in a historic market in Poland.

From the moment I bought it, I knew what it would be: my quote box. I began to copy down favorite quotes from books, snippets of poems, and theological reflections on scraps of paper. I have hundreds now, and that box is a treasure chest of the wisdom or whimsy I want most to remember.

- *Keep a reading journal.* One of my mother's requirements of me when I was a child was that I narrate to her what I had read each day. I had to retell, in my own words, the plot of a novel or the pith of a historical event. That practice enabled me to make the information my own. It's exactly what I now do in keeping notes on the books I read—summing up their content in my own words, listing the points I want to remember, the sections to which I want to return.

- *Memorize the bits you particularly love.* The words you memorize become part of you, giving shape and direction to your thoughts. They become integral to your view of the world. I've memorized Scripture, poetry, and passages from my favorite books, and I only wish I could manage more. I've recited psalms to myself in the small hours of a dark night, jotted a novelish quote for a friend, and had poetry at my fingertips when the beauty of a landscape demanded more than normal expression.

- *Read* How to Read a Book: The Classic Guide to Intelligent Reading *by Mortimer J. Adler and Charles Van Doren.* This classic, inspirational, and highly detailed guide to careful, attentive reading offers insight into what it means not just to read but to become an insightful reader, marked by "a mind made free by discipline."

Read in Fellowship

We call it STS, our Surprise Theology Society, which simply means that every week, in our little Oxford home, a group of friends and comrades gathers to discuss one person's favorite bit of current reading. The person who chooses the "surprise" brings copies for all, and we take turns reading aloud. It has become one of our favorite events of the week. The discussions, the insights, the exposure to ideas we might never have come across otherwise have become both a challenge and a delight. The sharing of what excites or troubles each of us in our reading has doubled the impact of the chosen words as we see them through the eyes of our friends, through the lenses of different histories and backgrounds. To read in company has broadened us as individuals and bound us together in friendship.

There is nothing like companionship in the reading journey, people with whom to share the delight or puzzlement or challenge of new bookish horizons. As you walk the reading adventure, consider these possibilities as ways to weave fellowship into the rhythm of your reading:

- *Start a book group.* Choose a novel, invite a few friends (and if you're me, brew some tea too), and set a regular time to meet and discuss what you are discovering. One way to do this is to meet once a month to discuss a whole novel (read in the previous month by all group members). This is a delightful way to immerse yourself in a story as a whole, and it allows you to evaluate plot, character development, and themes from a big-picture point of view. I've been part of a film and novel group in Oxford that meets every eight weeks to do just this, and I'm amazed by the ground we cover in a couple of hours. You could also meet weekly to discuss one or two chapters in a book—a rhythm I have loved, as it allows for more time to savor and mine each section of the book for its meaning and imagery. In the group I was part of, we assigned a different person to lead the discussion each week, a practice that enabled us to not only share the responsibility but also to get to know each other better. When it comes to selecting a novel, I find that it helps to choose two or three options for a group vote, lest the plethora of choices delay the actual reading.

- *Start a read-aloud poetry group.* I've taken part in one of these groups for the past three years at my theological college in Oxford, and I have been astonished at how quickly it has created friendships and how nourishing it has been to my studies and my heart. Assign one person each week to bring two to three poems to read, with a few prepared questions ready to spark discussion. No other prep is needed.
- *Start a book blog.* It doesn't have to be fancy—just set up an online platform where you can invite close friends to join in discussing or commenting on what you are reading. My first foray into the blogging world was as a teenager, when I was prompted by my brothers and a few friends to start posting about what I read and loved. I continue to do this on my own blog, and many of the reflections you'll find in this book began with a few paragraphs online as I sought to metabolize what I'd read. It was in crafting the short reviews, book lists, and reflections on what I'd read for my blog that I began to imagine a longer book—the one you now hold in your hands.
- *Consider a local or online course in literature.* If you want to delve deeper into an aspect of literature with some expert or classroom help, do a little research into college or university courses in your area. Or take a look at online resources like The Great Courses (http://thegreatcourses.com), audio and visual lectures recorded by active college professors, or iTunes U, which offers a collection of recorded, and usually free, university lectures on various subjects.

Years ago, during a browse through a secondhand bookshop, I stumbled across a memoir by the famed author of Western adventures, Louis L'Amour. I must admit that I still haven't read one of his novels (they're on my "someday" list), but I did sit straight down in that shop to explore L'Amour's fascinating account of the way regular, disciplined reading made him the writer and adventurer for which he is now famous. He put it this way, and I've thought of this quote countless times since: "I have read my books by many lights, hoarding their beauty, their wit or wisdom against the dark days when I would have no book, nor a place to read. I have known hunger of the belly kind many times over, but I have known a worse hunger: the need to know and to learn."[4] In all those afternoons of my childhood when my mom told me it was time, yet again, for an hour of reading, or when I was cuddled into bed to read one last story at night, I had little idea of how I was being equipped to sate that elemental, holy hunger to learn. I know it now, and I hope that in my passing along the tips and rhythms in this chapter you, too, will find yourself equipped to discover and live by the "hoarded beauty" of great books. May the reading life become a feast for your mind and soul.

CHAPTER 3

Books Can Broaden YOUR WORLD

Expanding Your Mind, One Title at a Time

A book, too, can be a star, . . .
a living fire to lighten the darkness, leading
out into the expanding universe.
MADELEINE L'ENGLE

I WAS TWO, maybe three, and the world around me looked like a vast impressionist painting—vivid strokes of fascinating color and unexplored shadow, all of it waiting for my exploration. For the moment, I was curled in the crook of my mother's arm as she held a book open before me, reading for the hundredth time the tale of two bears and their alphabetic escapades through an old, mysterious house. I reached out, touching the pages, losing myself in her narration, my imagination stretching toward the images and the secret nooks of that house.

I loved that book because of the world it created in my imagination, one of hidden doors and cupboards hiding surprise pots of jam or storybooks or secret passageways that led to glimpses of starlight. The book was a world unto itself, one I inhabited every time my mother opened the pages again. When she stopped for a breath and the turn of a page, I glanced up at the nearby bookshelf and stared at the toppled stacks of children's books. As I did, I had a toddler epiphany in the simple realization that every book there contained a world as distinct and dear as that of my bears. Though I could not yet put it into words, I was suddenly quick and curious with the knowledge that each of those little books was a doorway into a new realm of imaginative possibility. And all were waiting for my exploration.

In that moment, I understood a truth that would shape the whole of my life: a girl who reads is a girl who learns.

A woman who reads is a woman who taps into the fundamental reality that she was created to learn, made to question, primed to grow by her interaction with words. A book girl is one who has grasped the wondrous fact that she has a mind of her own, a gift from her Creator, meant to be filled and stretched, challenged and satisfied by learning for all the days of her life. A woman who reads is one who takes ownership of herself, aware that words give her the holy power to seek, to grow, to question, and to discern. She knows that to read is to begin an adventure of self-formation in partnership with the Holy Spirit that will shape the choices she makes, the dreams she bears, the legacy she leaves in the great tale of the world.

This was the bone-deep sense of self that came to me through a childhood crammed with good books, but it's one that has been restored to me time and again by the books that have broadened and shaped me as an adult, kindling me back to life in seasons of deep self-doubt or confusion. I am often startled to realize how easy it was to lose that confidence in myself as a learner as I grew into adulthood. A lot of it had to do with the fact that I was a restless, sensitive idealist who took most of my twenties to figure out where I belonged in the world (a work that's undoubtedly still ongoing). Part of it had to do with what I think is a modern idea that influences us in the contemporary world—of learning as something specialized, of education as something relegated to college courses or official groups, a practice that separates the ordinary person from the student or the professional. Since for many years I was neither of these and couldn't figure out where I fit in the scheme of things, I often felt inadequate, unrecognized, and ill equipped to take my own story in my hands. But the identity of a book girl, the vocation to be a learner, isn't something that's earned.

To be a book girl is a gift, the birthright of every woman, and this is something I remembered at a particularly difficult point in my twenties, something set in my hands afresh through a biography I listened to. I was twenty-eight, unsure of what to do with my life, with a book project fallen through, a college application denied, and the words of a recent rejection letter from an editor ringing in my ears. I wondered if I should give up my writing goals and my studies and just take a desk job. Since all my plans for the autumn had imploded, I decided to take a road trip. In retrospect, I think I needed some space for catharsis. I packed the tiny blue hatchback I'd named Gypsy and set off early on a frosty morning. I had no real aim other than a couple of weeks of escape, the quiet of the car, and a few visits with old friends.

But being me, I made sure I had an audiobook for entertainment—a random biography I'd plucked from the public library shelves about four writers whose work I'd enjoyed in bits and pieces. As I drove the long miles through the hills of Virginia and North Carolina, all crimson and dappled with autumn fire, I listened to the story of how Thomas Merton, Flannery O'Connor, Walker Percy, and Dorothy Day became the writers we know so well today. And as I listened, my own heart came awake.

I recently looked back at my journals from that time and was amused to realize that only two days into my listening and driving, I wrote passionately that my spirit (in the words of Robert Louis Stevenson) had been stabbed "broad awake"[1] by listening to the author's insightful account of the young Thomas Merton and Flannery O'Connor.

Their lives looked vastly different—Merton became a monk in a Kentucky monastery, and O'Connor was a young writer struck with lupus, forced to abandon her career to live with her mother in rural Georgia—but both existed within the small sphere of the ordinary, unnoticed (at first) by the larger world, hungering for meaning. The book chronicles the way they both struggled to accept the limitations of their circumstances. They were both restless, prone to depression. But they both wrote. They both read. They never ceased to see themselves as empowered in their limited spheres by the presence of the written word. And from those enclosed, faithful, engaged lives, they crafted the books that have spiritually shaped the generations that followed.

I remember staying up late after that driving day, with fresh insight in my heart like a burning star. I sat on my rickety hotel bed furiously journaling out the conviction that had come to me as I listened. "I must not be afraid anymore," I wrote. "I must not doubt whether

Gwen Todd

Gwen, as you will know from the stories in this book, has been my kindred spirit, beloved mentor, and fellow lover of novels for as long as I can remember. Her taste is superb, her savoring of a sentence a wonder to behold, and her book recommendations treasures.

My Ten Favorite Books

- *Jane Eyre* by Charlotte Brontë

- *Anna Karenina* by Leo Tolstoy

- *Pride and Prejudice* by Jane Austen

- *Hannah Coulter* by Wendell Berry

- *Kristin Lavransdatter trilogy* by Sigrid Undset

- *The Remains of the Day* by Kazuo Ishiguro

- *The Song of the Lark* by Willa Cather

- *Adam Bede* by George Eliot

- *The Good Earth* by Pearl S. Buck

- *The No. 1 Ladies' Detective Agency series* by Alexander McCall Smith my thoughts are worthwhile or wonder if I'm not up to it. I just need to read and learn and try from my own small corner of the world."

Tiny as that moment of epiphany may seem, it was a turning point for me. The next year brought two refused book proposals and three denied college applications, but each of those efforts stemmed from a heart renewed to learn and risk. It was five more years before I arrived at Oxford and seven before I began to write this book, but in that moment of epiphany, I regained the zest and joy, the confidence in my birthright as a reader and a learner that eventually led me to the joy of studying at Oxford and the words I write on these pages.

If there is one thing I would want you to know as we open this exploration of reading, it is simply that you were made to be a learner, and that identity is constantly available to you through the written word. You have the capacity for wisdom, discernment, and understanding, the power to engage in a rich and lifelong journey of education, conducted from whatever reading corner you're in at this very moment. If you've ever known the same kind of self-doubt that came to me or if you've ever listened to those whispers that learning is something mysterious that happens away from ordinary life, my goal in this book is to lead you back to the curiosity and wonder, the capacity to discover that has been your inheritance, your gift, since childhood. I think this gift is holy, set in us all by a God who made us to respond, grow, and discover through the power of language. He is, after all, the living Word who spoke the world into being. His first gift to Adam was to assign him the joyous work of discovering the world by naming it, to explore the dazzling new creation word by word, entering into its splendor as he learned to describe it.

The startling thing is that we are created from infancy to do exactly the same. One of the most fascinating things I have discovered in my research about reading is the way the human brain develops in response to the language around it, growing, discovering, expanding as it encounters new ways to describe reality. We understand our worlds through the words we are given. Parents are narrators, introducing children to the "pretty flower" or the "nice lady," using words to teach them how to view and treat people, how to experience the beauty and diversity of the world. That is exactly what books do for us as adult learners and discoverers.

Few things can change my view of someone more quickly than a novel. I remember having a fight with one of my brothers as a teenager and then reading a description by Chaim Potok of the difficult grapple of two boys to find their footing in the adult world. Suddenly I saw my brother afresh as someone in the midst of a pretty tough journey. Words revealed him to me in a new light, one that helped me to respond in the formative language of love rather than resentment.

Words are also one of the marvelous ways by which God gives us the gift of ourselves, enabling us to connect with other people and shape the world around us. I've seen this firsthand in the way that Gwen, a friend of my mother's and now as close as family, cared for her elderly mother, Larla, when she was struck with Alzheimer's. When Larla could no longer remember the people around her, Gwen became her narrator. Every time I came to visit, Gwen would use words to bring me into her mother's story. "This is our Sarah girl. We love her; we're happy she's here." As Larla eased and became happy in my presence, I realized Gwen was teaching me about the power of words to connect us, to revive or broaden our experience. What Gwen helped me to recognize was how deeply we are formed by the narrative of our conversations, the books we read, our spoken affection or disgust, our love when it spills into speech. In this light, the power of a word like "welcome" is as good as "once upon a time"; both open the possibility of friendship, of laughter, of a new way of looking at the world. Every book we read does the same thing Gwen did for her mom; it broadens our view of existence and connects us to other people. Words give us the capacity to articulate our dreams, to express our feelings, to speak of the truth that forms us most deeply.

And when those words are written and offered to the world, they become our window into a whole different view of what it means to exist, love, desire, believe.

We take hold of that power by reading.

Why should we read, and what should we read? These are the questions that drive and shape the reading journey of a book girl on her way to holy discovery. They are questions I didn't begin to ask until I was well grown, because reading was introduced to me as a way of life. My parents decided that one of the lifelong gifts they would give me and my siblings was the love of books. I am the first of four, with two brothers next in line and a sister whose later and long-desired arrival was the delight of my eleventh birthday (and created the sibling arrangement that we now call the "boy sandwich"). We are about as diverse in personality as can be: two introverts, two extroverts; a hearty mix of broody dreamers, driven writers, actors, and musicians ready to take the world by storm. We all share a penchant for strong opinions and vocations to arts or study (we can write you a novel or a thesis, sing you a song, or make you a film—just don't ask us to balance a checkbook). We are, in short, a family culture shaped by story.

We come by our ideals and artistry honestly, born to parents whose strong dreams led them into a life of ministry and writing, and the determination to raise children who loved to read. Our parents wanted us to love learning, to be curious about the world, and they understood that one of the best ways they could give us this gift was to introduce us to riveting stories written by passionate and creative authors. We learned early on that to read is to delight—in endless worlds of imagination, in relationships woven by words, in the possibility that expands on and on from the open pages of a great book.

But reading is one more choice among countless distracting options in the modern world, and we need not only the vision to make it worth pursuing but the will to make it a formative activity in our daily lives. The identity of a book girl is something that must be chosen, singled out, and claimed amid many other choices as a defining way of life. Most of the recent research on reading agrees that it's a skill and a pleasure that we in the Western world are quickly forgetting. In a world that draws us into the instant pace of the internet, with information literally at the tip of our fingers, with countless activities drawing our attention, new distractions, blogs to scan, things to buy, places to go, why should we sit down for a solid half an hour (or more) to read a mere book, with no extra links or clickable side notes? What I am coming to understand is that the reading life is a chosen gift, one we have to give ourselves and our children and our culture again and again. We can be strengthened in that choice when we understand exactly what comes to us through reading: the real, measurable growth that takes place on the level of mind, education, and childhood development.

Another way to answer that first and fundamental question—Why should we read?—is to look at the gift of reading from the point of research, something I discovered quite unexpectedly on a sunny morning on my very first visit to England.

I was twenty-one years old, sitting amid the honey-toned stone and weathered pews of an old church, on my first visit to the land of Lewis and Tolkien, Austen and Eliot, taking part in a conference based on the work of C. S. Lewis himself. With tea and biscuit in hand, and a rainbow spatter of stained-glass light over my face, I was pretty sure that whatever anyone said that first day would strike me as brilliant. What I didn't expect was a talk by a quiet, gracious poet who happened also to be the current chairman of the National Endowment for the Arts and whose message that day would shift the direction of my life and work for a decade to come.

The poet was Dana Gioia, and the subject was, very simply, reading. Or really, the death of reading. What I heard about that day was a recently completed report on one of the most comprehensive surveys of American reading habits ever conducted. The survey was commissioned to look at the amount of time Americans spent reading "literary books," such as good novels, essays, or poetry, and even further, to see if reading had any influence on how people spent their free time or invested in the kinds of things that deeply form cultural identity (e.g., the arts, charity work, sports, and civic life).

The report was called *Reading at Risk*, because all the research pointed to the startling fact that Americans across the board were reading less and less. Age, education, location, finances—these made no difference. Americans as a whole just weren't reading (though they *were* spending a huge amount of time on various screens instead, a fact I will address in chapter 9 from the dizzying height of my soapbox). What was startling as well was that the survey made a clear connection between the fact that people who read less were also far less likely to go to a concert or volunteer for charity or even take part in as traditional and common a thing as a baseball game.

That talk set an urgent sense of curiosity right into my bones. Why? Why were readers more likely to be involved in the arts or charity? How do words actually form us? And if reading was this important, this vital to forming strong minds and creative selves, what could be done if it was in decline? I left the conference and began a season of research into reading, imagination, and language that catapulted me into years of writing and speaking on the power of reading that, well, still hasn't ended. Since those early days of study, I pretty much want to hand out books to children on the street. I want to press novels into the hands of my friends. For reading, I discovered, really does change a reader's reality. An open book opens possibilities to its reader that are startling in their power, and my deep belief in that fact drives my work to this day and my conviction that you, book girl, were made for the glory and growth of reading.

Consider this: at just the level of measurable brain activity, reading kicks the brain into acrobatic motion. After hearing Gioia's talk,

I discovered an article by researcher Sebastian Wren describing the many tiny wonders taking place as you read even one line of printed words.[2] Even as you read this sentence, your brain is decoding the little black marks, turning them into words that are then translated into sound (you are actually "hearing" these words inside your head as you read). At the same time, your brain is already figuring out what those words mean, comparing the message with all the other ideas you have stored in your memory about brains and reading—the articles you've read about books, the headline you saw recently about literacy—and you're already beginning to decide if you think what I've written here is true.

To read is to waken and engage multiple aspects of mind and eye, a process that makes you active in the process of learning, an actor in your own drama who is able to discern, decide, accept, reject, and grow.* Reading has long been seen as "the golden key" to educational success. One report, responding to *Reading at Risk*, boldly claimed that the research seemed to "suggest that the key to unlocking the door to higher education regardless of the student goal, whether work, transfer, graduate degree, personal development or engaged citizenship, is reading."[3] This is a massive claim to make, because it links reading to pretty much every area of adulthood and growth. But it's one educators across the board recognize as true. Reading, whether you are four or twenty-four, provides you with the words and comprehension to encounter a new idea and understand it; to walk forward into new subjects, new facts, new possibilities, and thus a constantly expanding self.

Words make worlds, and the more words we encounter, the richer our concept of the world becomes, the more we are able to see what

---

* This becomes even more intriguing when you compare the activity of the brain when reading to watching TV. Half an hour of TV consumption actually shuts down the left side of your brain, the side that helps you to reason and discern, to accept something as false or true. See Wes Moore, "Television: Opiate of the Masses," *Journal of Cognitive Liberties* 2, no. 2 (2001), http://www.cognitiveliberty.org/5jcl/5JCL59.htm. The right side, which deals in image, emotion, and memory, remains active, receiving the images and ideas presented on screen *without* the filtering power of the left hemisphere.

is possible. This exact phenomenon was described decades earlier by the bookish C. S. Lewis, who rejoiced that good books allow us "an expansion of being," so that when we set a book down, we "become what [we] were not."[4] It's the power described by Madeleine L'Engle, author of the beloved *A Wrinkle in Time*, when she said that we are a "vocabulary-deprived culture," in need of imaginative expansion so we can have a vocabulary large enough to "recognize injustice and to speak out loudly about it."[5] What these delightful authors recognized was that reading gives us the capacity not just to experience reality but to name it, shape it, and do something to change it.

It's a fact echoed throughout Scripture. The Bible is rich in its descriptions of the way we are formed by the words we read and remember. It's why God commanded the Israelites again and again to "impress these words of mine on your heart and on your soul" (Deuteronomy 11:18, NASB), to "meditate . . . day and night" on the Book of the Law (Joshua 1:8). It's why Paul begins his letters with the story of the gospel, reminding his readers through his stirring words and heavenly narrative exactly who they are. It's why the "word of Christ" must "richly dwell within you," and why believers are supposed to speak to one another with "psalms and hymns and spiritual songs" (Colossians 3:16, NASB). It's all because the words we speak and read make the world around us. They open our eyes to the reality of God; they liven us to what is possible; they draw us onward into maturity, wisdom, and love.

To be a book girl is to own the identity of holy learner to the full.

The Beloved Dozen:
The Novels That Taught Me
How to Live
(OR, IF YOU READ NOTHING ELSE, READ THESE)

AUTUMN LIGHT sifted thin and golden through the curtains at the window of Gwen's study, casting a late-day sheen over the bookshelves. I was on my annual autumn visit to Kentucky, but I had forgotten what is usually the first item on my packing list: a novel. Gwen's bookshelves, however, in whatever place I have visited her, are a treasure mine for a book lover.

Gwen was the roommate, fellow missionary, and beloved friend of my mother when she lived in Vienna before she got married. My mom and Gwen were committed to the kind of lifelong friendship that meant Gwen came to visit my family at least once a year. From tiny girlhood, I grew up delighting in the exotic gifts and loving presence of my *tante* (the German word for "auntie"). When I reached my teens, I had the gift of inheriting my mom's friendship as I began to visit Gwen regularly on my own.

Gwen and I have always shared a love for books; she is a wide and discerning reader, so on this visit, I felt I was in safe hands as she led me to her collection of favorite novels. A slim yellow book sat halfway down the shelf, with the name of an author I knew Gwen loved.

"How about this one by Wendell Berry?" I asked. "You've told me for ages that I should read him."

Gwen took the book into her gentle hands and gave the cover a thoughtful dusting. For a moment she was silent. Then she smiled, still holding the book to herself. "I don't know," she said. "You should only read this one when you have enough quiet in your heart to give it full focus. You have to savor it. It's precious."

I've thought often of that afternoon scene as I composed this list. Having now read *Hannah Coulter* (the slim yellow book), I understand that Gwen wanted me to encounter that book in its full power, because it's the kind of story that summons me to a new understanding of the world. I think Gwen knew my heart was hungry for the kind of wisdom that Wendell Berry offers in his themes of rootedness, faithfulness, and place, and she knew that *Hannah Coulter* was one of those quietly powerful books that might just shape the course of my future. The novels I discuss in this chapter are the ones that have formed and gripped me with the same kind of power, and I recommend them to you with the same tenderness and sense of possibility with which Gwen recommended *Hannah Coulter* (at the right time) to me.

How in the world can I possibly choose just a dozen stories as core to my heart? It's close to impossible, but these novel essentials are the ones whose narratives shaped my idea of who I am, of what is possible, of what should be fought for, delighted in, created afresh. These are the books that broadened my world, drove my discovery, shaped my idea of self. They inspire the same sense of transformation in my mind as Gwen observed in *Hannah Coulter*. I won't tell you to wait for quiet though; I want you to dive in, to just begin, to pick even one of these stories and know that I have set it here because it has in some way been essential in forming my heart and directing my life.

If you read nothing else, read these. They're treasures, all.

Persuasion by Jane Austen

"The person, be it gentleman or lady, who has not pleasure in a good novel, must be intolerably stupid"; with this slightly tongue-in-cheek comment by one of the world's sanest novelists, I offer you the matchless Jane Austen. Wisdom, wit, and a calm but excellent humor are the terms that come to my mind when I think of Jane Austen's classic works. Her stories are all "romances" that end, of course, with a wedding, but there is nothing of the agony and ecstasy or the wild, indulgent emotion of a romance novel. There is, rather, the gentle and expert probing of a woman who observed human nature with sympathy, wisdom, and kindness, demonstrating the way that love in ordinary time must often travel the rocky ground of pride, silence, and inherited prejudice. She is patient with her characters, allowing them to confront their own obstinacy, selfishness, or regret, but she is also plain funny.

Austen's famed classic *Pride and Prejudice* opens with the matchless line "It is a truth universally acknowledged, that a single man in possession of a good fortune, must be in want of a wife," thus beginning a story of five sisters in want of just such a husband. While *Pride and Prejudice* is one of those books that everyone should read, it is also one of those BBC miniseries that everyone has watched (with the unforgettable Colin Firth as Mr. Darcy). Because of this, I'll assume you will read *Pride and Prejudice* and take this chance to list one of Austen's lesser-known novels as my first and favorite, the one not often read but the one I wouldn't want to miss. *Persuasion* is a bit more rueful, more mature in its portrayal of Anne Elliot, a self-giving, gentle woman past her prime who lives with the knowledge that she passed up the opportunity to truly love and be loved by the good and manly Captain Wentworth. She rejected his proposal on the worldly advice of an older friend worried about fortune.

The book opens eight years after the fact, when Anne and the captain (both still unmarried) are thrown back into each other's company, forced to face the frustrated hope, the bitterness, the yearning of their old love amid the small dramas of their mutual friends and local society. I said above that there is little of the wild, intense emotion of the romance, but Austen was no cynic. When passion breaks through, it is something that has grown up from the depths, rooted in patience, suffering, and self-revelation; Austen so wields her pen in this book that Captain Wentworth's single line "You pierce my soul" is enough to make a grown reader go breathless.

Also by Austen:
- *Pride and Prejudice*
- *Sense and Sensibility*
- *Emma*

Hannah Coulter by Wendell Berry

This was the book put in my hands with the caution that I was only to read it "when my heart had space to be quiet." Love, as the divine life in which all things living have their being, and also as the action by which we humans join that reality, is the theme of this quiet story. It is the simple narrative of a Kentucky housewife—Hannah Coulter's recollections from her childhood on a hardscrabble farm and her marriage to Virgil Feltner and the farming "membership" she subsequently joined in the small town of Port William. From her early days as a young bride to her widowhood in World War II and her remarriage to a man whose desire for a rooted life of farm and family is formed "by going through everything that was opposed to it," Hannah narrates the quiet drama of rural farm life, a story illuminated by her understanding that her daily work could be "one of the acts of the greater love that holds and cherishes all the world."

Berry never whisks his readers away to exotic realms; he settles them down, roots them into the workaday loves and ordinary heartbreaks and miniature miracles of normal life in Port William. In doing so, he also roots his reader in the present, challenging his readers to look up from his novels onto their own lives with a rekindled sense of the way that grace can invade our smallest actions, the way the Kingdom comes in *this* moment, *this* choice, *this* claimed bit of earth. Berry is one of those authors whose stories directly shape the way I live; the rhythms of outreach, of homemaking, of work. He helps me to a vision of *why* I am faithful to love, relate, cook, and create order when those actions at times seem meaningless. I may live in a cottage on a backstreet of Oxford, but Berry's Kentucky life walks alongside me, modeling what love looks like enacted on the scale of the everyday.

Also by Berry:
- *Remembering*
- *The Memory of Old Jack*
- *Jayber Crow*
- *A Place on Earth*

David Copperfield by Charles Dickens

There is no one quite like Dickens, and for me there's nothing quite like *David Copperfield*, in which the young and innocent protagonist, David—fatherless and oppressed by the intractable Mr. Murdstone— sets out to discover if he will "turn out to be the hero of [his] own life." This was the first Dickens novel I read, my introduction to his skill as an intricate weaver of plot, a prophet of social ills in the Victorian era, and the creator of characters as memorable as they are idiosyncratic. I can still recall, almost verbatim, the passages describing the "shadowless red eyes" of the villain Uriah Heep; the bluster of the generous-hearted Betsey Trotwood, who tells David to "never be mean in anything" and speaks of her past romances in the third person; and the quiet good humor of the loyal Peggotty, whose own courtship is sealed by the famed words "Barkis is willin'." In his grasp of human nature in its foibles and beauty, his care for the forgotten of society, and the sheer knotted brilliance of his plot, Dickens is an author who ranks among my most beloved.

Also by Dickens:
- *A Christmas Carol*
- *Our Mutual Friend*
- *Bleak House*
- *Hard Times*
- *Little Dorrit*

Middlemarch by George Eliot

George Eliot (the pen name of the Victorian author Mary Ann Evans) is one of those authors whose every work I want to read before I die. I am fascinated by her stories and her passionate belief in mystery, in a Christ-shaped compassion, and in the sacred beauty to be glimpsed amid the ordinary. When I studied theology at Oxford, I wrote one of my papers on her as an example of someone who embraced and later rejected evangelical Christian faith. What is curious and compelling about Eliot is that her rejection was based on her strong conviction that the Christianity she saw lacked what she believed was the real depth of Jesus' compassion for the suffering. She left formal religion (if only she could have had a chat with Dietrich Bonhoeffer or Thomas Merton, I wonder if she might have remained) but continued to live in awed awareness of the "roar which lies on the other side of silence" and to create characters who embodied her belief that "the immediate object and the proper sphere of all our highest emotions are our struggling fellow-men and this earthly existence."[6] I encountered her first in her novel *Middlemarch,* which ranks in my top ten of all time.

I read this book when I was in my late teens, and when someone asked me what I thought of it, I blurted, entirely without previous thought, "It reminds me of the Bible." It still does. What I meant is that Eliot has a profoundly realistic but deeply compassionate grasp of human nature. Of her novels she said that "if art does not enlarge men's sympathies, it does nothing morally."[7]

The whole of this thick novel is set in the town of Middlemarch, centered on the private dramas of its various inhabitants: their marriages, their money troubles, their faith or hypocrisy, their discontent or joy. It opens with the tale of Dorothea (a would-be Teresa of Avila), who, as a well-off young idealist, yearns for a life of meaning, service, and noble action. Her marriage to the much older Casaubon begins her journey to an actual grasp of what love in action may be, formed far more by suffering than by triumph. Her story is one of several woven through the book, each driven by the deep desires, reluctant compromises, and consequences of choice lived out by each character.

I wish that everyone could read this masterpiece of a book before embarking upon adult life, or even the choosing of a spouse (read this with an eye to the three romances, and watch what it tells you about marriage). The closing quote of the book is one I can only hope could be applied to me upon death; it contains what a priest friend of mine said is one of the best descriptions of Paul's "quiet life" (1 Thessalonians 4:11), as lived in real Christian devotion:

> But the effect of her being on those around her was
> incalculably diffusive: for the growing good of the world
> is partly dependent on unhistoric acts; and that things are

not so ill with you and me as they might have been, is half owing to the number who lived faithfully a hidden life, and rest in unvisited tombs.

Also by Eliot:
- *Silas Marner*
- *Scenes of Clerical Life*
- *The Mill on the Floss*
- *Daniel Deronda*

Pilgrim's Inn by Elizabeth Goudge

I love Elizabeth Goudge. She is one of those authors to whose pages I come with the same deep relief I know in arriving on the doorstep of home: here I am known, here I will be sheltered, here there is strength for the road ahead. I didn't encounter Goudge's writing until adulthood. Her novel *Gentian Hill* was the first of hers I read, placed in my hands by a mentor in literature. It was given with an injunction similar to that accompanying my first Wendell Berry book: "Oh, save this one until you can really enjoy it." I did. And then I tumbled headlong into a vivid tale of life in Devon in the eighteenth century, when the green hills and cupped valleys still brimmed with sacred presence for those who lived in them; when plowmen chanted ancient music to the oxen as they tilled the soil; and where a small, gifted, orphaned girl grew up amid the hearthside magic of Weekaborough Farm.

As a writer, Goudge combines a Dickensian talent for character description and plot twist, with a Montgomeryish delight in the created world and the sacramental vision of a poet like Gerard Manley Hopkins. Her books are a juxtaposition of wry, amused, and very English evocations of human folly and desire, with an almost mystical vision that recognizes in the beauty of the earth, in the making of home, and in the rhythms of worship the real presence of God, charging the earth with his grandeur, as Hopkins would say.

To be honest, I'd list every Goudge book as one of my favorites. But if I had to pick one, I'd go with *Pilgrim's Inn*, a novel that more than almost any other I have read evokes the power of home as "a brick in the great wall of decent living that men erected over and over again as a bulwark against the perpetual flooding in of evil," as a tangible space in which we may "taste and see" the goodness of the Lord (Psalm 34:8). The story is of the Eliots, a large family shattered by the brutality of World War II, who make the somewhat crazy gamble to buy a rambling old house in the English countryside. Headed by the cool and elegant Nadine (and her divided heart) and the irresistibly idealistic matriarch Lucilla, the Eliots claim the old house as their own, discovering along the way that it used to be a pilgrim's inn, one of the religious hostels run by monks for pilgrims on their way to one of the great English cathedrals in medieval times. The house seems to take them to itself, drawing them one by one out of their bitterness, grief, and regret into a health that allows them, in their turn, to take part in the sacred hospitality for which the house was built. A novel exploring both beauty and home, and their power to restore, this is a book I read just about every year.

Also by Goudge:
- *Gentian Hill*
- *A City of Bells*
- *The Little White Horse*
- *The Scent of Water*
- *The Bird in the Tree*
- *The Dean's Watch*
- *The Rosemary Tree*
- *Green Dolphin Street*

To Kill a Mockingbird by Harper Lee

I first read this when I was sixteen; I remember finishing it in the front seat of a car, feet propped on the dashboard in the Colorado sun as I waited for my mom and siblings to emerge from some lesson or event. I can still recall the silence that enveloped me when I finished the book and tried to narrate to myself the deep sense of sympathy—of insightful understanding, even of compassion—that tale summoned in a self-centric and teenaged me. The story, narrated by the tomboy Scout, introduces us to the small Southern town of Maycomb in the 1930s and the drama that descends upon it when Tom Robinson, a black man, is falsely accused of raping a white woman. Atticus Finch, Scout's father and a respected white lawyer, steps in for the defense.

The novel is a masterpiece of indirect communication: a story exploring prejudice, hypocrisy, and violence through the matter-of-fact eyes of a little girl who is far more concerned about the escapades she shares with her brother and the neighbor boy Dill in their shared goal to lure the reclusive and supposedly mad Boo Radley out of his house at the end of the street. Both Scout and the town of Maycomb are challenged in their unquestioned prejudice by Atticus Finch, who insists that his children and fellow citizens see Tom Robinson, Boo Radley, and even the crotchety old widow up the street (mocked and hated by Scout) as people as valid and valuable as themselves. "The one thing that doesn't abide by majority rule is a person's conscience," says Atticus.

This novel offers a picture of a man willing to live and willing to risk much for the dictates of faith and conscience. The book called me as a reader to an honest evaluation of my own unquestioned reactions, judgments, and tendency to discount people I find difficult or different from me, and to a renewed understanding of what integrity and courage might look like. Scout says, "It was times like these when I thought my father, who hated guns and had never been to any wars, was the bravest man who ever lived." In finishing Lee's story, I began to yearn for that bravery in myself.

The Anne of Green Gables Series by L. M. Montgomery

You will soon gather from the chapters that follow that I love the Anne books with a bright and abiding love. The series follows the radiant-eyed Anne, an orphan, from her girlhood days at Green Gables, where she has been adopted by dour, faithful Marilla and quiet Matthew. The books trace her life as she grows to young womanhood as an ambitious student and teacher (dogged by humorous and accidental escapades) and to her life as a new wife and mother (still with imagination and writerly ambition intact). These books are touchstones for me; they consistently help me to center my own life, to return to joy and creativity when I am discouraged. Their realistic view of small-town life and family relationships is so hysterically, cathartically true. Their delight in the natural world and the crafted comfort of home reminds me of the daily possibility of beauty in my own sphere. And their honor of loyal love and kindred-hearted friends kindles me afresh to cultivate relationships with the people I have been given in my own little world. The Anne books are funny because they are realistic— about gossip and household disasters and the work it takes to get anywhere in the world. They're radiant, like Anne herself, because they root themselves in the possibility of joy—lurking in a firelit evening with a book, in a meadow starred by spring, in the sometimes mute but deep affection of the people who make up our own small worlds. Every woman should get to know Anne, and that's all there is to it.

Island of the World by Michael O'Brien

Imagine that a medieval mystic poet wrote a modern novel with Communist Yugoslavia as his setting and a little boy as his hero.

Throw in a hearty dose of down-to-earth humor and word craft of the sort that sets scenes of both beauty and terror vividly in your imagination for years to come, and you will begin to get the feel of this tale. The story follows the almost Homeric journey of Josip Lasta, a Croatian boy raised in the joyous and remote mountain village of Rajska Polja (translation: "the fields of heaven") as he travels from the mountains of his innocence into a turbulent adulthood as a mathematician, a professor, and a "cultural rebel" under Tito's regime. From the book's opening paragraphs, tragedy looms on the horizon. But the novel begins in an evocation of beauty so simple and profound—in the love of Josip's parents, the homey delights of their home and farm, the deep faith in which they are led by the faithful Fra Anto—that you forget to be afraid. As the reader, you watch as love and light form a land at the center of Josip's soul, creating a refuge right in his heart.

When Josip's life is shattered and he is exiled, not just from his home but from that place of joy in his deepest heart, the journey begins. I warn you, this is a book that might cause embarrassment if read in public places. I laughed out loud in a quiet restaurant at the novel's merry debate between a Croatian Catholic and a Pentecostal from Harlem. But I have also cried over this book, and the tears weren't the surface kind; whatever hurt or struggle you bear, this story will touch it. This book will not spare you as a reader (and if you are squeamish about violence, be warned that it is squirm-worthy—not gratuitously graphic, but definitely matter of fact). Josip's life—the brutality that comes upon him unawares, his fight to escape not only evil men but the "heart of Cain" in himself—describes the battle in which I think we all are daily locked. But it also offers the affirmation that through pain and despair, we are all truly walking toward a world remade by love, a world beyond this one, and yet one growing up and present even now in the innermost regions of our souls. For as one of Josip's fellow prisoners explains,

With his one good foot he nudges Josip, pushing him gently, making him turn to face the opposite wall. The bar of light is climbing higher now.

"Do you see?"

Josip shakes his head.

"Surely you see," says the man.

"I see the light, but the walls imprison it."

"The light has entered the prison. Nothing can keep it out."

"If there is no window, the light cannot enter."

"If there is no window, the light enters within you."

Lila by Marilynne Robinson

Robinson's *Gilead* was the favorite book of my most-respected bookish friends for several years in a row. I tried to read it three times and failed. But when Robinson herself arrived for an evening reading in Oxford with a new novel called *Lila* just out, I decided to give that one a try. The end result was that both *Lila* and *Gilead* now list among the books I pretty much consider necessary for life.

Gilead, Robinson's first novel published, is a book of letters written by an elderly pastor in small-town Iowa to the young son whose adulthood he knows he will not live to see. Lila, mother of that son, glimmers in the background of the book, her presence a grace that still startles the old man to wonder. We know, from the old man's words, that his marriage was surprising, if not scandalous, to the small town and the flock in his keeping. We know that Lila was a drifter, a woman with an unknown past.

In *Lila* the novel, we are taken into Lila's mind, seeing the story, the marriage, and the coming child through her own eyes. Through a masterful stream of narrative, in which Lila's thoughts leap between memory and present, past events and current meaning, we encounter not just a story but the shape of a mind that has been molded by loneliness, suspicion, and a long, hard life on the road. Lila's inner voice is inclined to distrust everyone, and yet . . . she has married this "old man" purely on trust, a decision that surprises her as much as it does him. Her journey toward a heart that can live by that trust is the pith of the novel, a story so masterfully written that I often forgot that I was not Lila, thinking her thoughts along with her. *Lila* is in many ways the story of two inner voices wrestling for primacy in Lila's heart. First of loneliness, the one that says "That's one good thing about the way life is, that no one can know you if you don't let them." Then of love, as the child grows, as she begins to think she may just stick around:

> She thought, If we stay here, soon enough it will be
> you sitting at the table, and me, I don't know, cooking
> something, and the snow flying, and the old man so glad
> we're here he'll be off in his study praying about it. And
> geraniums in the window. Red ones.

Also by Robinson:
- *Gilead*
- *Home*

The Lord of the Rings Trilogy by J. R. R. Tolkien

What can I say about this beloved story? The realm of Middle-earth has etched itself into my imagination and formed the way I think about my own story in the world. This epic tale, forged in Tolkien's imagination in the trenches of World War I and written in part to reestablish "sanity, cleanliness, and the love of real and true beauty in everyone's breast"[8] has been one of the defining novels of the twentieth century. I assume you know the general outline of the plot after the blockbuster success of the movies and the bestselling status of the books (and *of course* the books are better than the movies). I will simply add two reasons why you should read them. First is the sheer intricacy of Tolkien's creativity. I don't think the world has yet seen his equal in the creation of an imagined universe: in the elvish languages; in the rich and historic cultures of Rohan and Gondor, Hobbiton, and Lothlorien; in the crafting of the refuge city of Rivendell, "the last homely house"; and in races as distinct as they are delightful, hobbits and dwarves, elves and men.

The second reason I think every person should read this epic trilogy is because it stands, I believe, as a great and profoundly Christian defense of hope in an age of despair. The Lord of the Rings is based on the belief every person alive has the choice to be an agent of goodness, love, and courage in the face of evil. The heroes and heroines in Tolkien's tale are those who give their lives for the preservation of beauty, the choice of compassion, and the will to resist evil. Tolkien was remarkable as a writer in his age, partly because he was a member of the "lost generation," with authors like Hemingway, Owens, and Fitzgerald, whose writing reflects their turn to existentialism and despair in the face of World War I. In stark contrast, Tolkien wrote a story in which the humble hobbit Sam could look up out of Mordor's filth to see

a white star twinkle for a while. The beauty of it smote his heart, as he looked up out of the forsaken land, and hope returned to him. For like a shaft, clear and cold, the thought pierced him that in the end the Shadow was only a small and passing thing: there was light and high beauty for ever beyond its reach.

To read The Lord of the Rings is to taste that beauty and know that it is eternal.

Also by Tolkien:
- *The Silmarillion*
- *The Hobbit*

Anna Karenina by Leo Tolstoy

If you know anything about this Russian classic, it is probably the basic fact that it chronicles an affair, that of Anna Karenina, young and passionate, married to a man stunted in his capacity to love, unable to show her affection. Anna's choice is the core theme of this novel—her hunger for love, for peace, and the process of thought and decision by which she chooses to defy society and tradition in order to follow her heart's desire in an affair with the dashing Count Vronsky. Anna's reasoning tugs powerfully at the heart; we yearn with her for her happiness. But can the road she has chosen lead to peace?

That is the question spun out in the plot of the novel. But Anna's story is not the only one in this sprawling book, considered by many to be the greatest novel of all time; the counter theme to Anna's affair is the dutiful life of Konstantin Dmitrievich Levin, also faced with the choice of whom he will love and how he will live as he, too, searches for peace and happiness. His quieter tale parallels the drama of Anna, presenting the reader with different ways of living, two roads by which the self may be expressed and fulfilled. "You have a choice," my mother often said to my siblings and me in childhood, and her words echoed in my mind as I encountered this remarkable novel of choices and the paths on which they set us: those of life and those of death.

Till We Have Faces by C. S. Lewis

One of the fundamental Lewisian stories, to me, is one of his last full pieces of work, a tale that reimagines the Greek myth of Cupid and

Psyche. (Before becoming a medievalist, Lewis studied the Greek and Roman classics.) The tone of this strange and compelling "myth" is different from anything Lewis wrote before; narrated in the stark and accusing voice of Orual, the ugly sister of beautiful Psyche, it is Orual's complaint, her accusation of the gods for what she feels is the utter unfairness of her fate. It took me three tries to get into this book. It isn't comfortable reading; Orual isn't a woman whose company you'd readily seek; and the bloody, bawdy reality of ancient pagan culture shapes the atmosphere. But ah, this is a story of excavation—Lewis's exploration of fate and suffering, choice and culpability in which the veiled and belligerent Orual (and with her, the reader) is forced, by her own outraged narrative, to this fundamental question: "Are the gods not just?" And a startling answer: "Oh no, child. What would become of us if they were?"

Also by Lewis:
- *Out of the Silent Planet*
- *Perelandra*
- *That Hideous Strength*

Books That Talk Back:
My Favorite Books about Books
(OR, WHY READING IS IRREPLACEABLE)

HAVING BEEN A DAILY and voracious reader for most of my life, I had never thought deeply about *how* I read until my seventeenth year, when I began a mentorship with a wise and generous professor of literature who agreed to guide me through a course of reading. Entirely through handwritten correspondence, this kind lover of literature taught me how to read all over again and, in the process, began my conscious passion for the formative power of great books, one that drives my writing to this day. He opened our course by challenging me to examine my habits of reading. Did I interact with the ideas on the page? Did I "talk" with them in notes and underlining? Did I write out or memorize portions I loved? How did I make sure that I would remember the life-changing things I read, the moments when the world opened to me in a fresh or convicting way?

What came alive to me in those months of study, deeply confirmed later on by the research I discovered through Dana Gioia and other authors, was the formative power of reading and the great need to teach people to read well. Reading had first come to me as a gift through my parents and a childhood home filled with books. It came to me now as a responsibility, a power I needed to cultivate and yield. Dr. Wheeler summoned me to read with attention, not a thoughtless consumption of story but a dance and conversation with it that allowed its full power to shape my thoughts and change my ideas. The following books bear the same kind of wisdom, the same challenge to read thoughtfully, to recognize the power present in the books we read and their capacity to change the very way we live.

How to Read a Book: The Classic Guide to Intelligent Reading by Mortimer J. Adler and Charles Van Doren

In this classic and eminently practical guide to reading well, Mortimer Adler explains that "a good book deserves an active reading. . . . *It must be completed by the work of criticism, the work of judging.* The undemanding reader fails to satisfy this requirement. . . . He also dismisses a book simply by putting it aside and forgetting it. Worse than faintly praising it, he damns it by giving it no critical consideration whatever." Adler is determined to make demanding readers of us all, and this is the primary resource I'd recommend as a guide to reading with attention, intelligence, and discipline.

A Jane Austen Education: How Six Novels Taught Me about Love, Friendship, and the Things That Really Matter by William Deresiewicz

This is a humorous and lively memoir, written by a young graduate student who thought the old-fashioned Jane Austen had nothing to teach him . . . until he read *Emma* and confronted his own arrogance.

A book that vividly explores the formation of character and affection that comes to an Austen reader and the way classic stories can bring us to helpful (and sometimes painful) self-knowledge, this is a delightful tribute to the matchless Jane from a very unexpected reader.

Tending the Heart of Virtue: How Classic Stories Awaken a Child's Moral Imagination by Vigen Guroian

In this nuanced look into the classic fairy tales and fables we associate with childhood, Guroian argues for the power of classic stories to shape children from infancy. These stories, he contends, have the power to teach children a love of what is good by presenting them with characters that embody virtues like goodness, kindness, and honesty. This warmhearted work is a celebration of the power of story to form virtuous imagination.

The Pleasures of Reading in an Age of Distraction by Alan Jacobs

This is a "playfully irreverent guide for aspiring readers," written by a professor who encourages modern readers to reject the idea of reading as the equivalent of eating brussels sprouts and instead read for delight. Read what you love, urges Jacobs, in a more positive exploration of reading in the modern era, one crammed both with insight and practicality.

An Experiment in Criticism by C. S. Lewis

This is Lewis's slightly dense but highly worthwhile crack at what makes some books "good" and others "bad." With his usual capacity to get to the heart of things, he turns the question of literary quality on its head by asking what kind of *readers* are made by the reading of certain books. A fascinating perspective, with a helpful exploration of genre and a marvelous definition of what makes myth.

Reading Lolita in Tehran by Azar Nafisi

I list this fascinating memoir here because I think it speaks to the power of books to keep a strong sense of selfhood, hope, and possibility alive in almost impossible circumstances. Based on Nafisi's experience of living and teaching in Iran during the revolution, it follows the story of the secret book club she formed with seven young women, their reading of Western classics, and the way those books kept their determination alive.

Booked: Literature in the Soul of Me by Karen Swallow Prior

In this story of a soul formed by books, Prior explores the way that a series of great stories—from *Charlotte's Web* to *Madame Bovary*—shaped the tale of her own faith. A thoughtful exploration of literature from the pen of a literature professor who also revels in the insight and wisdom that good books bring to the souls who read them.

Also by Prior:
- *Fierce Convictions: The Extraordinary Life of Hannah More: Poet, Reformer, Abolitionist*

CHAPTER 4

Books Can Shape YOUR STORY

What If You Were the Sum of the Characters You've Read?

Stories are light. Light is precious in a world so dark. Begin at the beginning. Tell . . . a story. Make some light.

KATE DICAMILLO, *THE TALE OF DESPEREAUX*

ONCE, in a blaze of book love, I sent a copy of *Anne of Green Gables* to an eleven-year-old girl I had never met. This happened because of a conversation I had when I was twenty-three, sitting knee-to-knee with an extroverted flight attendant on a plane so small it was termed a "puddle jumper." The jumpy engines and rattling sides of our rickety old aircraft made conversation and peace of mind seem impossible. But not for my seatmate, who cheerily shout-chatted away about life and the flight and her young daughter, and who suddenly stared me down with a good dose of curiosity. "What takes you to such an out-of-the-way little place as Prince Edward Island?"

"Why," I said, gripping my seat a little tighter, and introvertedly shouting back, "Anne of Green Gables, of course. I love the books, and I've always dreamed of visiting."

"Anne of Green who?"

I fumbled. I stuttered. I was aghast. My bookish brain felt as shaken as my bones as I tried to explain why everyone should read the Anne books. Especially eleven-year-old girls. I was almost embarrassed at my own enthusiasm over this one old tale of a sprite of a girl coming of age in a remote Canadian village. But I rose to the fray, attempting to shout a description of Anne's wonders to my new friend. As I did, scene after scene came into my mind—images of Anne's spunk and imagination, her determined curiosity, her tender heart. I thought of the woman's young daughter, hating that any girl should grow up without Anne as an imagined companion, and in a tumbled, startling moment, I looked the flight attendant in her bright eyes and said, "Give me your address, and I'll send your daughter a copy."

She did. And so did I.

In that half-startled act, I came to a full understanding of something I already knew in the depths of my heart after years of reading, a fact fundamental to what it means to be a wise woman reader. A book girl is *storyformed*, shaped in her very concept of self by the characters she has encountered on the written page, by the narratives that teach her what it means to be a woman. A book girl is one who has looked through imagined eyes vastly different from her own so that her view of the world is broad and bright with countless varied perspectives. But a savvy book girl also knows that she who walks with the wise becomes wise (Proverbs 13:20), and the viewpoints she inhabits in imagination will shape the woman she becomes.

I am, I must confess, of the immovable opinion that every young girl (and woman) should read the Anne books, not just for their beauty and charm, but because they offer a particularly hearty and healthful view of womanhood. I was confirmed in this conviction by a conversation with two other women a couple of years back, strangers until the moment we discovered that all of us had read the Anne books in our formative girlhood years. We met at a conference: all three writers, all feeling a bit shy, but the mention of Anne pulled us out of our awkwardness and into a swift conversation that profoundly shaped my ideas about the power and development of self that comes to women who read, and read well.

For what we discovered was that each of us felt that the Anne books had helped to alert us to our vocation and creative capacity, challenging us to growth, grit, and wisdom. We listed the ways Anne had convinced us that we, too, were capable, creative, made for friendship, able to dream, created to learn. The Anne books, we realized, set a surprisingly powerful and attractive picture of womanhood before us in the years when we were beginning to wrestle with those fundamental questions of budding maturity: Who am I? Who should I be? What does it mean to live, love, work? What does it mean to be a woman?

I'm still struck by the way Anne came alongside me in my imagination during my teenage years. She challenged me specifically to friendship, something I was struggling to find after a cross-country move in my fifteenth year, as my shier, more introverted self emerged amid the fomentation of hormones and teenage emotion. My impulse in that season was to withdraw, to brood, but Anne's cheerful openness to friendship—in unlikely people, in new places—her quickness to encourage and affirm and delight helped me to look around and start a conversation, a lunch group, a little book club of my own. After all, how could I expect Anne to find *me* a kindred spirit if I wasn't willing to be one myself?

When it came to larger questions of vocation and identity, Anne was still my mentor, a model of intellectual curiosity who loved books and big words and helped me to add those attributes to my idea of healthy womanhood. Anne answered my big, budding questions about self and purpose via narrative, in the image of a curious, imaginative, resourceful young woman whose stubborn optimism could not be defeated.

Consider these quotes, characteristic of certain virtues embodied by Anne and encouraged through her story:

- *Anne is curious, engaged, and full of wonder:* "Isn't it splendid to think of all the things there are to find out about? It just makes me feel glad to be alive—it's such an interesting world. It wouldn't be half so interesting if we knew all about everything, would it?"
- *She is plucky and ambitious:* "I've done my best and I begin to understand what is meant by the 'joy of the strife.' Next to trying and winning, the best thing is trying and failing."
- *She values friendship:* "Kindred spirits are not so scarce as I used to think. It's splendid to find out there are so many of them in the world."
- *She loves to learn and isn't embarrassed to say so:* "People laugh at me because I use big words. But if you have big ideas you have to use big words to express them, haven't you?"
- *And she's downright determined:* "It's been my experience that you can nearly always enjoy things if you make up your mind firmly that you will."

Apparently my friends and I were not alone in our enthusiasm. A simple Google search will quickly reveal how many women from vastly different backgrounds share a sense that Montgomery's story was a powerful gift of discovery for them as young women. I found articles in major publications both in the United States and abroad with titles such as "Ten Things Anne of Green Gables Taught Me"[1] in publications from the *Atlantic* to *Vanity Fair*. When Netflix released a contemporary update on the beloved 1985 TV miniseries version of the books, literally dozens of articles sprouted up across the internet in praise of the red-haired dreamer whose vim, tenderness, tenacity, and intelligence were a model of womanhood to a generation of young women.

And this was the reason I sent *Anne of Green Gables* to a little girl I'd never met. I knew that in a confusing, turbulent world where she will receive countless contradictory and often negative messages about what she, as a budding young woman, ought to be, Anne would come alongside her with health, possibility, innocence, and joy.

This is the ongoing and wondrous gift of all good literature. I have long argued that children cannot think in abstract terms, but I'm increasingly convinced that adults cannot either. What does it mean to be good, brave, and resourceful? We struggle to define those vague, existential ideas, but we know exactly what they look like when we see them embodied in Lucy from the Narnia books or Dorothea in *Middlemarch*, or described in the sparkle and wit that is the spiritual writing of G. K. Chesterton. A great book meets you in the narrative motion of your own life, showing you in vividly imagined ways exactly what it looks like to be evil or good, brave or cowardly, each of those choices shaping the happy (or tragic) ending of the stories in which they're made. Books teach us to take hold of ourselves—to be, in philosophical terms, agents, with the capacity to learn, dream, think, and shape the world around us.

Stories, to my book-girlish mind, are the lifeblood of existence. They come to us first in the epic of Scripture, the one real story of the world, told by God, peopled by the imperfect, brave, striving, loving characters of the Bible who show us what it means to be fallen and yet to desire redemption. They come to us afresh in each generation through the works of great writing that echo Scripture's challenge to choice and action, to creativity, to endurance, to joy. Word by word, the narratives we read equip our hands and broaden our imaginations for the real and daily narratives of our lives. It's not that we read the tales of perfect people or unerring heroines. We read all kinds: comedies, tragedies, stories that show us the depth of our sin, stories that teach us the beauty of which we are capable.

Regardless of the genre, stories form us. Each narrative shapes the tale we are weaving in the real and daily world, and I remember this especially because of the solemn note on which my kindred-spirited conversation about Anne ended that long ago day. One of my new friends from the conference was a teacher, and her wistful words toward the end of our discussion echo as a challenge to me both as a reader and as one who recommends books for others to read.

"I worry about the girls I teach," she said. "Anne certainly isn't on their book lists. Their generation is far more defined by *Twilight* and teen magazines. I cringe when I realize that every word they're reading is teaching them what it means to be a woman. I wish they had Anne or Narnia or Elizabeth Goudge in their heads instead."

I think all young women should read Anne. But that's just the beginning. I think pretty much every woman should go on to read Jane Austen and George Eliot, Marilynne Robinson and Wendell Berry, Thomas Merton and C. S. Lewis, because these authors really do help us to understand what it means to be a woman of life and grace. Those authors work in the great tradition of writing that reveals what it means to be an agent in the real and urgent drama of our actual lives, and to do it with grace, love, and hope.

For as a book girl knows, great stories shape us to live great *life* stories.

Girlhood Classics:
The Books That Began It All for Me

(OR, WHAT TO READ ON YOUR WAY TO BECOMING A FULL-SOULED WOMAN)

For MANY YEARS (eleven, to be exact), I was the only girl in our sibling lineup. This certainly toughened my muscles, of both mind and body, but it also meant I was sometimes in special (and occasionally desperate) need of some girl-only time. My mother, delightful woman, filled this need by instigating tea and reading dates for just the two of us on Monday evenings. We'd brew cups of tea (cambric for me, which meant it was mostly milk and sugar) in special bone china cups and find a corner somewhere in the house where the boys were sternly told (by me, though I'm sure the actual obedience had more to do with the lifted eyebrow on my mother's face) *not* to intrude.

Thus girded and sustained, tucked into a space just ours for the moment, we ventured forth together into a series of classic stories of girlhood, books chosen by my mom for the spunky heroines and girlish adventures she knew would tickle me and shape me for health, good sense, and curiosity. In compiling the lists for this book, I realized they wouldn't feel complete without a list of the classics that began my love for novels, my sense of characters as friends, my deep awareness of suddenly having companions who dwelled in my very imagination and showed me the kind of girl I wanted to keep becoming.

Let no one despise children's books. I am entirely with C. S. Lewis when it comes to children's classics: "No book is really worth reading at the age of ten which is not equally—and often far more—worth reading at the age of fifty and beyond." Before I started writing about books for adults, I spent ten years studying and writing about children's literature (in *Read for the Heart* and *Caught Up in a Story*), and I am convinced that great children's books, in their clarity of language, in the disciplined simplicity of their themes, bear as much insight into the workings of the human heart and its desires as the great adult classics. But they manage to do all that while being accessible to a child's wonder and innocence.

In the epilogue of this book, you'll find a few lists of my very favorite picture books and childhood readers. But this list specifically speaks to the girlhood tales I love as a book girl, the stories that helped me rejoice in the possibilities of my developing womanhood, my own capacity for insight and adventure. If you missed these classic tales in childhood, I might suggest you begin with this list. To me, they are of equal stature with every other "grown-up" book in the lists that follow. These are the stories that continue to inform the way I think about womanhood, to shape my experience of the world as something wondrous. There is a value to innocence, to remembering the clarity with which we saw the world as children—something that is richly evoked in the following books. I find that the quality of these books, along with their emotional depth, actually equips me to evaluate the ideas of the novels I read now. I'm often struck when reading literary interviews by how many childhood classics shaped the novelists writing today. You could also explore these books in the company of a daughter or other young girl in your life, as my mom did with me. She says that one of the best parts of having kids was the chance to read all the books she'd missed, and our shared delight in them just doubled the joy.

The Wolves of Willoughby Chase by Joan Aiken

I wanted to be as brave as Bonnie, the doughty little heroine of this adventure tale, set in an imagined (alternative) history of England when it is invaded by wild and dangerous wolves. When Bonnie's parents seem to be lost, it falls to her to resist the evil Miss Slighcarp and to protect her fragile cousin Sylvia and the honor of the family home at Willoughby Hall.

Little Women by Louisa May Alcott

I love the sisterly dramas in this novel—the entangled dreams and dramatic creativity of the March girls and their wise Marmee, as loyal to each other as they are humorously different and creatively bent. (Reading about their attic dramas and in-house post might have inspired me to a few such escapades myself.) But it was Jo, the burgeoning writer in her tension between ideals and home, her need for adventure, her love for family, whom I most identified with. A classic of exploring the bonds between sisters, the difficulty and wonder of growing up, and the capacity of family to survive both trouble and grief.

A Little Princess by Frances Hodgson Burnett

A Little Princess was one of the first books my mother and I read aloud together. It follows the story of Sara Crewe, once the wealthy star student of Miss Minchin's Select Seminary for Young Ladies, then orphaned and cast on the none-too-gentle mercy of the school. But she is undaunted: "Whatever comes," she said, "cannot alter one thing. If I am a princess in rags and tatters, I can be a princess inside. It would be easy to be a princess if I were dressed in cloth of gold, but it is a great deal more of a triumph to be one all the time when no one knows it."

Also by Burnett:
- *The Secret Garden*
- *Little Lord Fauntleroy*

The Little White Horse by Elizabeth Goudge

Maria Merryweather may be orphaned, slightly afraid, and uncertain of what awaits her in the ancient home of the uncle she is traveling to meet in the hills of Devon, but courage is a trait of the "moon Merryweathers," as is a love for elegance. Girded by lovely new boots and the comforting presence of Miss Heliotrope (her loyal governess), Maria rises to meet the occasion and soon finds she will need both her courage and a strong character to defend Moonacre Manor, the home she comes to love, from the old feuds brooding on its borders. A magical tale blending fantastical elements with real-life detail in a captivating weave.

The Story Girl by L. M. Montgomery

You'll encounter my love for the Anne books in other lists, so here I'll mention one of Montgomery's lesser known but oh-so-vivid characters in a story of siblings and childhood fancy. Sara Stanley is a girl with the gift of story whose powerful imagination seems able to draw those who listen right into her tales, including the cousins whose many foibles, adventures, and squabbles she shares. Montgomery demonstrates her usual skill in capturing the pettiness and affection of family, the tempest in a teacup of a small-town world, and the way beauty haunts and brightens the ordinary.

The Railway Children by E. Nesbit

When disaster strikes a Victorian family in London, forcing Mother and the siblings Bobbie (Roberta), Phyllis, and Peter to leave their townhome for a country house of questionable upkeep and a much more frugal existence, they find themselves in a new world of responsibility and unimagined adventure, at the heart of which are the daily trains they watch like friends. As an older sister, I felt such sympathy with Bobbie in her quest to help her mother and be a good example to her siblings amid their many explorations.

Pollyanna by Eleanor Porter

Pollyanna is an orphan, sent to live with her stern and wealthy aunt after the death of her beloved father. But she is a girl of determined joy, playing the "glad game" to survive her sorrow. She teaches those around her to look for something glad in every situation, as her father first taught her. A pert, warming story about a little girl's optimism as it confronts and shatters the cynicism of those around her.

Heidi by Johanna Spyri

Perhaps my abiding memory of *Heidi* is of how good melted, toasted cheese on crusty bread sounded as described in this tale of a little girl sent to live with her grumpy and solitary grandfather in the Swiss Alps. This is a story of alpine meadows and friendship, of old grudges, and of the triumph of love.

Treasures of the Snow by Patricia St. John

A story of guilt and grace and the power of forgiveness, set in the cold beauty of the Swiss Alps. The story centers on the thoughtless act of the boy Lucien; its consequences for little Dani, a boy of good heart and cheer; and the bitter anger of Annette, Dani's big sister, as she comes to terms with her own capacity for hate and her own need for forgiveness.

Charlotte's Web by E. B. White

Charlotte, the wise and gracious spider, is one of my imaginative types for Lady Wisdom as portrayed in the marvelous Proverbs passages. She has just the right word for the moment, and by her wisdom the life of the young pig Wilbur is saved and Fern, his owner, brought to greater maturity. A clever, sparkling tale.

Biographies:
The Real-Life Epics That
Shaped My Dreams
(OR, HOW REAL-LIFE HEROES INVITE US
TO REAL-TIME HEROISM)

WHEN I WAS GROWING UP, my parents were always pushing biographies into my hands. They seemed intent on cramming my brain with real-to-life tales of heroes—historical and biblical, spiritual and artistic. I read them as quickly as I could and then turned to what was usually my reward: a novel of some fantastical or imaginative bent. Tending as I did (and still do) toward the world of imagination, with the open horizons of the possible, I was never as interested in the more defined horizons of the actual—at least until I reached the cusp of adulthood. It was only then that I began to understand what those countless biographies had built within my heart: an expectation that I was meant to do something worthwhile with the life I had waiting before me and evidence, actual evidence, that all sorts of worthy options awaited me.

There is particular power in well-crafted biographies. Such works do not obscure the flaws or frailties of their human subjects, but they manage to reflect the vision burning at the heart of the artist or preacher, the driving love or force that led them to exceptional acts of compassion, artistry, sacrifice, or courage. To glimpse such vision is to desire that fire in yourself.

My parents knew exactly what they were doing. Following their example, I set the following list before you. It's mixed: missionary tales and nature-centered memoirs, stories about the lives of musicians and the ruminations of old writers, but they are the true-life epics that glimmered for me with that contagious, inspiring fire.

God's Smuggler by Brother Andrew

My siblings and I sat riveted as we listened to my mom read aloud this real story of a mischievous Dutch boy who grew up to become a famed and fascinating smuggler of Bibles behind the Iron Curtain. A memoir that thrums with the adventure of radical trust in God and the divine intrigue of mission work under communism.

The Life You Save May Be Your Own by Paul Elie

I listened to this one on a road trip in an autumn of vocational confusion, and at the end of the book (and the journey), I knew I wanted to be a writer because I hungered for what I saw in the lives examined here. A fascinating exploration of four Catholic authors—Thomas Merton, Dorothy Day, Walker Percy, and Flannery O'Connor—Elie's book traces the way in which each person was formed to both a strong faith and an articulate faith and then expressed that belief in words. A fascinating look at the way each wrestled with the issues of their day and wrote uniquely to the hunger and doubt of the turbulent 1960s.

A Chance to Die by Elisabeth Elliot

This was one of those landmark biographies I read as a teen that startled me into a consideration of my own looming adulthood. Elliot's insightful biography follows the life of Amy Carmichael, the intrepid and determined Irish missionary and writer who spent a lifetime serving the orphaned and poor in India. I still clearly recall Elliot noting that the surname of Amy's mother was Dalziel, literally, "I Dare," a name and characteristic that defined Amy Carmichael's fierce and creative faith. Elliot's account of Carmichael's sacrificial life gave me a vivid model of womanhood and godliness as my own daring dreams began to form.

Also by Elliot:
- *Through Gates of Splendor* (Elliot's moving memoir about five missionaries martyred in Ecuador, including her husband, Jim Elliot)

The Diary of a Young Girl by Anne Frank

This well-beloved, poignant record of a young Jewish girl in hiding during the Nazi occupation makes the heart ache with the sheer normalcy of a teenage girl's thoughts and hopes, her curiosity about the world, and her brush with romance, all of it undiminished by the tragedy of the outer world or the limits of her own daily experience. This book made me deeply grateful for the ordinary I so easily took for granted as a teenager.

Tolkien and the Great War by John Garth

I loved this book for the way it got to the roots of Tolkien as a writer—a career forged by his remarkable friendships, his love of beauty, and the devastation he witnessed in the trenches of World

War I. This is the story of Tolkien's youth: the school friends who formed his ideals and urged him to write, the love of language that began to blossom into a myth of his own creation, the terror of the trenches, his early marriage, and the faith that burned in him despite a culture steeped in despair. A book I loved partly because I loved The Lord of the Rings but also because it examines the way in which idealism, when tempered by suffering, can be forged into a redemptive, hopeful vision.

No Compromise: The Life Story of Keith Green by Melody Green

This is the story of Christian musician Keith Green, whose music touched thousands with the love of Christ and whose tragic death grieved the Christian world. Something about this loving biography, written by his widow, has stirred and encouraged every person I know who has read it to a quickened sense of God's love and of the gospel's power to transform. My siblings and I all read it with the same sense of wonder. There is an immediacy to this work; you feel immersed in the same joy that drove Green and his wife in the early days of their faith.

Christy by Catherine Marshall

Part novel, part memoir, this engrossing story is based on the experience of the author's mother and follows the idealistic Christy Huddleston, a young teacher inspired to volunteer for an Appalachian mission program, as she moves into the mountains to become a teacher to the needy youngsters of the fictional Cutter Gap. Her resolve is challenged within the first hours of her arrival as she witnesses the filth and poverty, the violence and revenge of the mountain world even as she comes to respect the beauty and resilience of its people. A story of spiritual endurance, of conversion, even of romance (will Christy favor the sarcastic doctor or the earnest preacher?), *Christy* put courage in my bones when I was a teenager in a season of physical illness.

A Man Called Peter by Catherine Marshall

Also unforgettable is Marshall's memoir about her husband, Peter, who started life as a poor Scottish immigrant and became a beloved minister and the well-respected chaplain of the United States Senate. The book has excerpts of Peter's sermons, and I still recall the sweeping life and vision in his words. Marshall's story is tender, an account of Peter's deep faith and her own loving marriage.

The Seven Storey Mountain by Thomas Merton

A memoir that speaks with urgent truth to Merton's wide readership, this is the autobiographical story of his conversion, his search for truth and hunger for meaning, and his ultimate choice to leave behind a literary career for the confines of Gethsemani, a monastery in the hills of Kentucky. Rich with Merton's luminous prose, the book (according to *Time* magazine) "redefined the image of monasticism and made the concept of saintliness accessible to moderns."[2] Through his books, Merton is a mentor and friend, with his humorous, insightful grasp of human nature; his yearning for transcendence; and his choice to submit himself to the religious life in all its beauty and demands.

A Passion for the Impossible: The Life of Lilias Trotter by Miriam Huffman Rockness

Told by the famed Victorian art critic John Ruskin that she could be "the greatest living painter and do things that would be Immortal," Lilias Trotter easily could have chosen a life of privilege, uninterrupted creativity, and social approval. Instead, she chose the life of a missionary to Algeria, taking both her talent and her prospects into the desert, where they were spent bringing the gospel to the Muslim world. But she never stopped drawing, and this excellent biography of her life includes samples of the paintings and sketches she made of the desert world she served with every ounce of her remarkable creativity.

L'Abri by Edith Schaeffer

In the years just after World War II, Francis and Edith Schaeffer moved into a chalet amid the rugged peaks of the Swiss Alps. Their goal was to open their home to seekers and searchers, those whose faith had foundered in the confusion of the postwar world. Any question could be asked, no spiritual topic was out of bounds for discussion with Francis, and no one was excluded from the warmth and beauty of Edith's wide table and home. This is a memoir of adventurous faith, of God's provision, and of the power of hospitality and fearless spiritual search in opening the way to faith. Edith's account of the power of home and table to communicate spiritual reality deeply influenced the rhythms of my own childhood home and continues to shape my philosophy in the home and ministry I share with my husband.

Rich Mullins: An Arrow Pointing to Heaven by James Bryan Smith

This is the story of Rich Mullins, beloved Christian songwriter and musician, whose lyrical skill and spiritual insight drove his creation of songs that echo with timeless awe of God's grace in the face of human frailty. (These songs also accompanied all the road trips of my childhood, I might add.) From his boyhood in Indiana to his tragic early death in a car accident, this book traces Rich's unconventional life—his discomfort with affluence, his desire to serve the poor, his love for Saint Francis, and his embrace of a gospel for ragamuffins.

Reading this biography helped me understand the power and love I sensed behind the music that shaped my childhood, while leading me deeper into an encounter with that love myself.

The Hiding Place by Corrie ten Boom

It was only upon marrying my Dutch husband that I discovered I had pronounced Corrie's name incorrectly all my life. (*Corrie* is pronounced by trilling the *r*'s at the back of the throat—not easy for a native English speaker. And *Ten Boom* sounds more like "tin bome"—*o* as in "boat" rather than "room.") That didn't diminish my love for this remarkable story of a Dutch family whose deep, obedient faith drove them to risk their lives to protect their Jewish neighbors during the Nazi occupation. Both riveting narrative and heartrending memoir, this story is rich in its exploration of conviction, forgiveness, and the power of God's love.

A Severe Mercy by Sheldon Vanauken

I'll admit, I both love and hate this book. I love it for its idealism; for the total affection of the young couple at its heart; for the painful, inexorable journey they traveled toward faith during their sojourn in Oxford. I just can't stand the gushiness at times. (Do everything together and share everything? We'd go crazy, said my husband—and I had to agree.) But that objection is small beans and does not temper my appreciation for this story of conversion driven by loss; its account of C. S. Lewis's kindness and insight; and the deep, severe mercy that came to its author in his acceptance of faith.

The Nightstand List:
Classics You Should Eventually Read
(OR, BOOKS TO EXPLORE, SHOULD YOU EVER HAVE THE TIME)

THIS IS A VERY SHORT list that could be much longer. You could find far more comprehensive lists of Western classics with a quick Google search. But these are the essential titles I have encountered in my reading that stood as pillars, both marking eras and helping me understand the way Western thought and literature have developed. Some of the books on this list I've labored to finish; some I've read in part; a few I have yet to read. But these are the classics mentioned again and again by the writers I most respect, books that have shaped not only my favorite thinkers but Western culture as a whole.

Some of these titles will be more demanding for a modern reader. Their language may be difficult or arcane. Not all are happy; many reflect the struggle of past cultures, sorrows through which we may identify our own. Their plots may require some research (I was greatly helped in reading *The Divine Comedy* by getting an annotated version that explained the significance of the figures Dante meets on his journey). These books take work, but they will richly repay you for the time you invest in them by helping you to gain a larger understanding of your own world: why we think or see in certain ways; where we get our ideas of culture, virtue, or love. These stories were hugely influential in their eras, and their themes continue to echo in the writings of today.

Where do we get the idea of life as a voyage or a journey, our romanticized image of a soul on a quest? One of the major sources is from Homer's *Odyssey*. Many scholars trace our widely shared images of hell and heaven to Dante's influential and vivid descriptions, while quite a few of our modern words, not to mention our stock characters for sitcoms, romantic comedies, and contemporary dramas, come from Shakespeare. The authors in this list are the ones whose ideas have shaped the way we think together, and you'll begin to recognize their words and ideas in the world around you.

I certainly wouldn't begin with this list. These are the sorts of titles (apart from, maybe, *The Great Gatsby*) that I read slowly, a chapter or a few pages at a time, giving myself space to digest and understand them (possibly with dictionary in hand). But having slogged my way through these and a good few more, I can honestly say that they have been some of the books that made me most passionate about reading and writing because I began to recognize their profound power to shape not just my view of the world and of myself but the worldviews of entire cultures. When we recognize the power of these books and their ideas, we begin to more consciously form our own ways of looking at the world.

The Canterbury Tales by Geoffrey Chaucer

A bawdy and entertaining medieval series of tales recounted one after the other by a group of pilgrims on their way to Canterbury, this collection of stories was one of the first to be written in vernacular

Middle English (instead of Latin or French), thus paving the way for the flowering of literature in English.

The Divine Comedy by Dante Alighieri

This is the medieval and allegorical tale of Dante's divine journey into the depths of hell, through the vales of purgatory, and into the bliss of paradise, guided by the Roman poet Virgil. Considered one of the greatest books ever written, it is a spiritual masterpiece. (As a companion to this classic, you might enjoy C. S. Lewis's *The Discarded Image*, his evaluation of the medieval view of reality suffusing Dante's work. Also of interest might be Rod Dreher's *How Dante Can Save Your Life*.)

The Brothers Karamazov by Fyodor Dostoevsky

Dostoevsky looked the worst of human nature straight in the face and wove it into what could be called the tragedy of *The Brothers Karamazov*, the story of three brothers—the sensual and irresponsible Dmitri, the calm skeptic Ivan, and the gentle-hearted Alyosha intent upon the religious life—in their relationship to their debauched and greedy father and the tragedy that surrounds him. In each of these men, we encounter the grapple of the soul, the intellect, and the heart with the claims and reality of faith as worked out amid their need, their fallenness, and their deep desires. It took me six months to finish this book, and I still get confused by the plethora of Russian names. But the slow reading work is worth every word because Dostoevsky manages to excavate the darkness of the human condition to discover the startling reality of what Philip Yancey termed "the safety net of absolute grace."[3]

For a great deal more insight into the story (though it takes as much work as the novel itself), you could also read Rowan Williams's excellent exploration of the religious themes within Dostoevsky's novels in *Dostoevsky: Language, Faith, and Fiction*.

Also by Dostoevsky:
- *Crime and Punishment*
- *The Dream of a Ridiculous Man*

The Great Gatsby by F. Scott Fitzgerald

Steeped in the haunted decadence of the "lost generation," which largely turned to nihilism after the shattering of World War I, this is the exquisitely written account of a man's meteoric rise to wealth and notoriety, and the yearning, the aching desire, and the faulty love that destroyed him. The word craft and character descriptions are unforgettable.

Beowulf by Seamus Heaney (Translator)

This epic Anglo-Saxon account of Beowulf, hero of the Geats, who defends the Danes against the monster Grendel, is the longest epic poem in Old English and one of the oldest surviving pieces of English literature. Focusing on themes such as the triumph of good over evil and the doomed courage necessary to heroes, it is a story fundamental to the development of English literature and myth. I love the translation by Heaney—be sure to read his introduction on the intricacy of the language—as he masterfully captures the immediacy and the dark, courageous energy of this ancient story. (You might also enjoy taking a look at J. R. R. Tolkien's lecture "Beowulf: The Monsters and the Critics.")

The Odyssey by Homer

This ancient Greek poem recounts the arduous journey of Odysseus, determined to reach home after the war of Troy. Tempted by goddesses, beset by storm and raging sea, and forced to battle monsters, the epic journey of *The Odyssey* formed Western imagination and informs the way we think about identity and home to this day. I've encountered this poem in the works of countless favorite authors, whether used by Wendell Berry in an essay on the need to be rooted in place or retold in Tennyson's stirring "Ulysses," the account of Odysseus in old age, still determined . . .

> To sail beyond the sunset, and the baths
> Of all the western stars, until I die.

Les Misérables by Victor Hugo

"There is one spectacle grander than the sky, that is the interior of the soul," writes Victor Hugo, and this novel is a spectacle of the grandest order. It traces the interior journey of Jean Valjean, convict and breaker of parole, toward grace, even as his outward journey leads him to the streets of Paris, hot with the fervor of revolution.

Paradise Lost by John Milton

The epic poem exploring the fall of Adam and Eve in the Garden, in which Milton seeks to "assert eternal providence, / And justify the ways of God to men." A poem that still informs the way we understand the Fall and stands as one of the great standards of English literature.

King Lear and Much Ado about Nothing by William Shakespeare

Everyone should read a bit of Shakespeare. Yes, the language is intricate and sometimes difficult for modern ears, but ah, the word craft, the psychological insight, the spiritual depths, and the sheer wordy glory of Shakespeare is vital, I think, to a well-rounded education. But here's a tip: read him aloud. Get a few friends, assign parts, and watch as the words (which were intended to be spoken aloud) glitter with life, as this marvelous playwright's humor and pathos strike right at the heart of your own existence.

I don't really care which play you read, but I love *King Lear* as a representative tragedy—the exploration of human hubris and the depths to which we must sometimes be brought in order to discover the truth about ourselves. And there's nothing quite like *Much Ado about Nothing*, the comedy of mistaken identities, misplaced outrages, and flirtation by verbal combat.

CHAPTER 5

Books Can Stir You to ACTION

Becoming a Heroine in Your Own Story

I used to think that [adventures] were things the wonderful folk of the stories went out and looked for, because they wanted them. . . . But that's not the way of it with the tales that really mattered, or the ones that stay in the mind. Folk seem to have been just landed in them, usually—their paths were laid that way, as you put it. But I expect they had lots of chances, like us, of turning back, only they didn't.

J. R. R. TOLKIEN, *THE TWO TOWERS*

I WAS SEVENTEEN, and it was actually, in the words of so many mystery novels, "a dark and stormy night." Oh, I felt the drama of it with all my teenage intensity. I was wrestling for the first time with real pain, with the reality of circumstances I hated and could not change. In many ways, the world I knew was coming to pieces around me. After a terrifying two months of anxiety, I had been diagnosed with obsessive-compulsive disorder. I felt that my mind was broken; I could not control the images or thoughts that intruded upon my consciousness. In the same time period, I watched our church experience a painful and bitter split that made me question the whole concept of Christian integrity. And my family decided to move across the country and away from the starlight and mountains we all so deeply loved. I felt a sense of bitter vulnerability as the things I considered immovable—a controllable mind, a beloved home, my lifelong faith—revealed themselves as frail and faulty. I had the comeuppance we all must face, the smack of my heart against the fallenness of the world as I discovered that what I best loved could be harmed, broken, lost.

My reaction was outrage—a grieved sense of betrayal, compounded by the drama and shifting identity of my teenage years. I was hopeless on that stormy night, and my faith felt very frail as I reached for my current book, *The Fellowship of the Ring*. It was distraction I was after, but ah, it was a challenge I found as I was swept into a story about dark lords; evil powers intent on destruction; and the good elves, the wise wizards, the small but courageous hobbits who give the whole of themselves to fight for beauty and health and kindness. I stumbled across Frodo's grieved wish that such things "need not have happened in my time" and nearly wept in agreement. But I was also gripped and almost mercilessly challenged by Gandalf's gentle rebuke that such wishes are not in our gift; rather, "all we have to decide is what to do with the time that is given us."

The words seemed to be aimed directly at me, confronting my undisciplined bitterness so that I felt myself begin to wonder, *What must I do with the time given to me?* In that moment, with Gandalf's challenge ringing in my imagination, I encountered the reality that a girl who reads is a girl who understands that she has a part to play in the drama of the world. A woman who reads is a woman who knows she must act: in courage, in creativity, in kindness, and often in defiance of the darkness around her. She understands that life itself is a story and that she has the power to shape her corner of the drama. She has learned, with Frodo, that reluctant but faithful hero, that the heroes in the best stories are simply the ones who "had lots of chances . . . of turning back" but didn't. To know yourself as an agent in the story of the world, one able to bring light and goodness in the midst of suffering, is a profoundly empowering knowledge, one that I believe comes to every woman who reads.

My teenage encounter with The Lord of the Rings was a turning point in my idea of myself and my faith because that story helped me to perceive the epic narrative of Scripture, the real divine drama by which my own life was defined. It helped me to contextualize my suffering within a larger story, to realize that bitterness was something I must fight, that hopelessness was something I had to resist. I remember wishing one day that real life were more like The Lord of the Rings, that I had a clear part to play. But even as the thought crossed my mind, I began to realize that if Tolkien created Middle-earth and God created Tolkien, then God's story must be far better, far more epic even than the great and beautiful dramas of Middle-earth. That fantasy novel paradoxically helped me to reengage with Scripture, to see it for the divine drama it is, one with a beauty beyond even the elves' imagining, and a call to the brave beyond even Aragorn's echoing challenge. Tolkien's story helped me to recognize Scripture as *my* story, the one in whose decisive battles I was caught, the narrative that drew me into the conflict, requiring me to decide what part I would play: heroine, coward, lover, or villain.

I count my adult embrace of faith from the day I finished The Lord of the Rings on a humid summer morning, in the drafty garage-apartment that was now my room after the dreaded cross-country move. I sat with Tolkien's book open on one side, my Bible on the other, and on the pages of both, words that brought me to a crisis of decision. In *The Fellowship of the Ring*, I had read about Frodo's choice to accept a great burden and enter the battle:

> A great dread fell on him, as if he was awaiting the
> pronouncement of some doom that he had long foreseen
> and vainly hoped might after all never be spoken. An
> overwhelming longing to rest and remain at peace by Bilbo's
> side in Rivendell filled all his heart. At last with an effort he

spoke, and wondered to hear his own words, as if some other will was using his small voice.

"I will take the Ring," he said, "though I do not know the way."

And in my Bible, I read this:

This day I call the heavens and the earth as witnesses against you that I have set before you life and death, blessings and curses. Now choose life, so that you and your children may live and that you may love the LORD your God, listen to his voice, and hold fast to him.

DEUTERONOMY 30:19-20

The choice was clear. I simply said yes—to believing in God's goodness despite pain, to acting creatively and lovingly even in discouragement, to fighting for light in the midst of whatever darkness I found myself. Of course, I felt instantly opposed by the forces of darkness when, the moment my stumbling prayer was complete, a roach (an orc-like thing, if ever I saw one) dropped from the ceiling onto my shoulder so that I began my part in the great story with a wild dance and a hearty dose of humor, quite the regular feature in God's storytelling, I have discovered. And yet, from that moment, however hysterical, I knew that I was all in, that I would work and suffer and act in courage in my imperfect but heartfelt way. In that choice, I also realized that heroism begins with a challenge and a choice—to fight the dragon, to pay the debt, to tell the truth, to act rightly when the cost is high. Will I act in accordance with what I know to be true, regardless of the cost? When a character, when a girl with a book in her hand and a burning in her heart, answers yes, a heroine comes into being.

But what does it mean to be a heroine in the modern world? This is one of the questions that great books have helped me to answer, particularly because we live in a culture that is a little suspicious of heroism. After a century of war and cynicism, as faith falls away and relativism grows, we are increasingly shaped by the postmodern idea that our lives and personal choices have little meaning beyond what

Dillon Naylor

Years ago I embarked on a crazy, literary-themed road trip, and along the way Dillon bravely hosted me in her lovely home, having never met me before. Thus began a kindred-spirit exchange of ideas and friendship, along with very long letters, that have enriched my heart immensely.

My Favorite Books

- *Gaudy Night* by Dorothy L. Sayers. One of my friends, an academic librarian, called this the most romantic book she had ever read. It took me a while to take her recommendation, but when I finally did, I started reading this book once a year. There is no book quite like it: 1930s detective story, Oxford atmosphere, literary epigraphs, witty banter, and plot twists. And at its center, it's a love story about uniting the mind and the heart, and the process of saying yes to love.

- *The Mill on the Floss* by George Eliot. George Eliot's second (and most autobiographical) novel is the story of Maggie Tulliver in rural 1820s England. It is heavily weighted in the first half: it took me about a year to get through those first two hundred pages. Then Maggie's family falls apart, she has a religious conversion, and she falls in love . . . and I ended up reading the second half of the book in one night. I have never read such a strong account of a woman choosing not to give in—to a society that undervalued her intellect, to the wrong guy (even though she was crazy about him), or to despair.

- *The Brothers Karamazov* by Fyodor Dostoevsky. My experience with *The Brothers Karamazov* is unique in my reading life—I read it faster than any other book of the same length. I am not generally a fast reader and tend to get bogged down in books, which is why I'm glad I somehow read this one in ten days. That experience has stayed with me—I remember how immersed I was in the action and how after I'd finished it, I took walks through my city and felt like I was seeing things through the eyes of the central character, Alyosha.

- *Dombey and Son* and *Martin Chuzzlewit* by Charles Dickens. When I was just married, had moved to a new city, and didn't have a job yet, I had time to read. I had always loved Dickens, so I decided to start from the beginning and work my way through all his novels (I'm still at it). I would absolutely recommend doing this with any favorite author—you get to know them so much better, like getting to know a friend through committing to spend time with them regularly. If I hadn't, I don't think I would have discovered gems like *Dombey and Son* and *Martin Chuzzlewit*.

brings us ease or happiness. Even if we believe in the larger story of Scripture, we're still a little afraid of the idea of heroes because the ones we have trusted have so often failed. And of course, we don't want to be extreme. We don't want to place impossibly idealistic burdens on the shoulders of frail, sinful human beings, which is precisely what all of us are. We are often caught between the desire to become something more than we are when we glimpse a heroic life and the knowledge that we are flawed and confused about what this means for our own lives.

Heroes and saints: surely these are the exceptional (or fictional) few who somehow stumbled into extraordinary acts of love or sacrifice.

But I think this is a misunderstanding of heroism, one corrected by the reading of great stories. You can't read Tolkien or C. S. Lewis or George Eliot or Chaim Potok and come to the conclusion that heroism is something like a rare gift or special talent, something rooted in the extreme effort of a single human being. When you read those authors, you quickly come to see that heroes and heroines are formed by the narratives they believe. Frodo didn't become a hero by gritting his hobbit teeth and pumping his small muscles; rather, he glimpsed the greater story of which his small, faithful actions were part. He understood that his life was caught up in a narrative much larger than his cozy one in the Shire, one in which real goodness and evil battled for domination of the world he loved.

Heroism isn't about taking your own life in your hands; it's about being taken hold of by something much bigger and more beautiful than yourself, by a story that draws you into its larger drama and empowers you to act in hope.

I think it's fascinating to realize how many of the characters in Tolkien's drama begin by listening to a story. Aragorn is told that he is a king meant to restore his people from the time he was a small child. Gandalf tells Frodo the whole history of the evil ring before he ever asks him to take it, and Sam hears the whole thing while he is eavesdropping. Éowyn is driven by her love and her longing for the nobility of her ancestors whose stories she has heard from childhood. And even Merry and Pippin, those comical hobbits, make good on their vow to follow Frodo in all his danger by first telling him that "we know most of what Gandalf has told you. We know a good deal about the Ring. We are horribly afraid—but we are coming with you."

Heroic action begins with an identity rooted in story, the understanding that our small choices are part of the battle for light or darkness, goodness or evil. I think this is exactly the kind of identity Paul is calling new believers to take on when he calls them saints and "holy ones," when he tells them the story of redemption and reminds them that in the new heavens and the new earth, when the end of the battle has come and every tear has been wiped away, they are destined to be kings and queens in God's renewed cosmos.

And this is the same identity that comes to a woman who is immersed in the great stories of literature and Scripture. In those dramas she begins to understand that she has been given what Rowan Williams calls "the burden and the freedom of a sort of *authorship*,"[1] the understanding that life is a story, and that she, bookish girl that she is, has the power to act, and act for the good. When she comes to that knowledge, the page turns and a marvelous new chapter begins.

Girl Power:
My Favorite Novels about Brave and Faithful Women

(OR, BOOKS TO GIRD YOU WITH THE GRACE TO ENDURE)

I DISCOVERED my dear friend Esther on a day when I felt ready to quit in just about every area of my life. With a book deadline looming and three chapters still to be written, the imminent arrival of holiday guests, taxes to be done, and a house to be cleaned, I greatly wanted to abandon ship. What I would do or where I would go I did not know, but remain in my life as it was, I certainly would not. My angst was compounded by the fact that I had spent the last six months in transition, unable to determine the right job, location, or future for my life. Worn in body from work and travel, weary in mind from the uncertain days, I had come to the end of myself. Then the phone rang with news of a missing tax document (there is nothing that makes me feel existentially useless more quickly than doing my taxes). I finished the call, closed my computer, and retired to my room to plan my resignation from the responsible life.

Esther, blessed girl, halted me in my steps. She met me as I sank into my chair, hot faced and nervous. In need of mental focus,

I reached for the worn and dusty book from the top of a stack I had recently found at Goodwill. My interest at that time ran toward Dickens, and the book I opened was *Bleak House*. The first chapters had been a bit difficult; my reading until then had been distracted and languid, and I expected no better of the story than a few moments of calm. But Esther entered the room of my mind that day—the calm, kind woman who is, I think, the unlikely heroine of Dickens's tale. So potent was her presence on the pages of that old book that half an hour had passed before I glanced up again.

When I did, it was with a sigh of resignation; apparently I couldn't in all honor quit the responsible life after all. My imagination was filled and my heart challenged by the story of this girl who determined to bring order and love into every place she dwelled, despite her own past as an unwanted child. Born in disgrace, raised by a mad and resentful aunt, cast on the charity of strangers, Esther still managed to become the heart of warmth and practicality at the center of Dickens's mad and beautiful story. Her response after a devastating illness struck me to the core:

> I found every breath of air, and every scent, and every flower and leaf and blade of grass, and every passing cloud, and everything in nature, more beautiful and wonderful to me than I had ever found it yet. This was my first gain from my illness. How little I had lost, when the wide world was so full of delight for me.

I finished the chapter and looked up amid a great quiet. I suddenly felt that the abandonment of my own tasks, or even great complaint, was not as necessary as I had imagined. Perhaps these responses were even cowardly. Throughout the next month, I mentally dwelled in Esther's story. She was my comrade in arms in the difficult endeavor of life. Her presence punctuated my difficult days with an image of grace in the midst of weariness. I felt we were companions in a sister-hood of faithful women who brought order to the whirlwind of life. Esther helped me to see the constant round of dishes and ordinary work as the realm in which beauty is recaptured and love made tangible. She helped me, in the middle of a pile of tax documents, to look out my window, to take joy in the wonder of mountain sunlight and the calming steam of my morning cup of tea. She helped me to choose strength and to receive the fact of existence as a gift; to resist the modern idea that my frustrated feelings should rule my choices or even my outlook. In her quiet way, she empowered me to see myself as blessed; to recognize grace in the love of the family that so often irritated me in that season; to experience normal, responsible life as a story in which my own laughter, my own peace of heart could create the same joy that Esther so richly brought to hers.

But Esther is just one of a bevy of fictional women whose faith-fulness, courage, and strong spirits have shaped my character and challenged me to act in a redemptive way. The list below is composed of the novels whose female protagonists stand beside me to this day with words and lives that challenge me to follow their example. Their courage is of countless kinds: of determined love amid the ordinary, of moral bravery in wartime, of artistic daring, or of spiritual endur-ance, but each models the power of a woman whose choices reflect her loving and creative heart. I still hope to be counted among their number when my own life's story is someday told.

Sense and Sensibility by Jane Austen

Elinor is the character I love in this book—a woman of deep feeling challenged by the death of her father, the care of her mother and sisters, and a prolonged (and seemingly permanent) separation from the man she loves, who yet resolves, "I *will* be calm; I *will* be mistress of myself." This book is a fascinating exploration, through Austen's gentle, incisive narrative, of the nature of true love. Is love to "burn," as the passionate young Marianne claims? Is it a deep and abiding friendship, as Elinor, the older sister, knows? And how ought true love to affect the lives of those connected to it? A novel that explores self-giving, sorrow, and the nature of passion and of patience, it tells the story of two sisters who are some of my favorites in literature as they come to terms with society, each other, their difficult suitors, and their own understanding of love in its truest sense.

Jane Eyre by Charlotte Brontë

This is a strange novel, both dark and soaring in its depiction of a young woman with an indomitable spirit, raised without love and left to her fate as a belittled governess, but certain of love's power and the strength of her own conscience and desiring soul. Considered scandalous to its Victorian audience at the time of its publication in 1847, this novel depicts Jane's sojourn as a governess in a mysterious country house; her unconventional love for its master, Mr. Rochester; and her even more unconventional boldness in describing the strength, capacity, and freedom of a woman's inner mind. I love Jane's passionate response to Rochester, her insistence that he treat her as an intellectual and moral equal: "I am not talking to you now through the medium of custom, conventionalities, nor even of mortal flesh: it is my spirit that addresses your spirit; just as if both had passed through the grave, and we stood at God's feet, equal—as we are!" A haunting love story, slightly gothic in touch, but masterful in its insistence upon truth, frankness, and integrity.

The Song of the Lark by Willa Cather

A novel of artistry and vocation, this is the story of Thea Kronborg, who has a soul as big as the skies of her Western American world in the early days of the twentieth century. This is a woman who "only want[s] impossible things," a woman in whom music grows and burgeons, longing for release. Often considered autobiographical, this is a story of an artist coming into her powers, wrestling with ambition and desire almost beyond her grasp, and facing the discouragement that dogs the heels of the creative life. I love the fierceness of Thea's spirit, her defiance of discouragement. As one who creates, I appreciate the realistic portrayal of the hard work vital to artistic success and the way one great vision always inspires another.

Also by Cather:
- *My Antonia*
- *Death Comes for the Archbishop*

Bleak House by Charles Dickens

The story that so challenged me to faithfulness, this is Dickens's dark, vivid, intertwined tale of the case of Jarndyce and Jarndyce, a lawsuit regarding a disputed inheritance whose complications entwine the lives of the orphaned Esther Summerson with the cousins Ada and Richard as they are all taken in by the kindhearted Mr. Jarndyce. A story of mystery and murder, a critique of a corrupt justice system, and an exploration of the forces that shape lives toward generosity or greed, this Dickensian novel is a marvel. And Esther, with her compassion, calm, and daily good sense, is one of my favorite characters in literature.

Middlemarch by George Eliot

This book is so good I'll risk including it in two lists. This is one of my dozen best-beloveds, but it is also a marvelous novel of womanhood, so I couldn't keep from mentioning it here. As I said in my earlier review (found on page 49), there are several marriages at the heart of the story. The women in each of these—Dorothea, Rosamond, and Mary Garth—are studies in the ways a woman's choices and her responses to difficulty, challenge, and love both form her own powerful character and have infinite and continuing influence on the lives of each person she touches. I have rarely encountered such a profound and insightful exploration of feminine character and influence.

The Scent of Water by Elizabeth Goudge

You have already encountered Goudge as one of my great favorites, but this story is one I return to for spiritual sustenance again and again. This is the tale of Mary, a competent and accomplished woman in London who inherits a country home and abruptly decides to leave the whirl of modern life behind. Her startling choice leads her to a radically altered life shaped by the deep thoughtfulness of the countryside and the journey she begins in reading the journals of the brave mentally ill woman who lived there before her. For me, Goudge's story is almost devotional, a riveting narrative that traces the making of one woman's soul in the wild solitude of mental illness and follows another woman on a journey of quiet revelation. At the moment I have a quote from the book as the background of my laptop screen: "There are three necessary prayers and they have three words each. They are these, 'Lord have mercy. Thee I adore. Into Thy hands.' . . . If in times of distress you hold to these you will do well."

Two from Galilee: The Story of Mary and Joseph by Marjorie Holmes

I first encountered this fictional retelling of the events surrounding the Christmas story when I was a teenager. I was riveted by Mary and by the rich, girlish humanity with which the author describes her love for Joseph, her loyalty to her sometimes-difficult family, and her personal engagement with the Yahweh of her people. This book was one of the first to liven me to Mary's intelligence, strength, and what Denise Levertov, in her beautiful poem "Annunciation," termed her courage, as the author imaginatively portrays the rare qualities necessary for one young girl to partner with God in revealing the love behind creation anew.

The Emily Series by L. M. Montgomery

The Emily books present a character in some ways similar to Anne of Green Gables—an imaginative orphan girl sent to live with two maiden aunts—but Emily's character wrestles with loneliness and discouragement, with the burning sense of a vocation to write that made this series instrumental in helping me come to terms with my own teenage identity. The Emily books get to the heart of what I felt as a young writer, trying to capture the wonder I saw in the beauty of the world (what Emily calls her "flash") even as I began to wrestle with the reality of suffering, of loneliness, and of my own capacity for darkness.

Two of the things I value about the Emily books are their honesty and their kindness. Their honesty lies in their portrayal of the frustration Emily feels at being misunderstood; her scorn for some of the sillier social constrictions of her age; her difficulty in disciplining herself to write, to work, to hope. Their kindness lies in Emily's insight into the people around her—her refusal to simply resent the aunt who most frustrates her, her gratefulness for friendship when it comes, her capacity to find humor and interest in the most ordinary of souls. In her stubborn, hopeful, amused walk through her teenage years, Emily was my companion on the road to adulthood and the writing life.

Parnassus on Wheels by Christopher Morley

Imagine if you were a middle-aged woman on a farm altogether fed up with caring for an old house and an ungrateful brother, when a charming little wagon with a bookshop on wheels rolled into your yard. Imagine, further, that you bought this movable wonder on the spot and set off posthaste for a new life both gypsy and literary in nature. Good. Now go finish the tale in this endearing novel.

A Girl of the Limberlost by Gene Stratton-Porter

This is a book whose delight is heightened for me by the fact that it was one of the novels my mother and I read aloud together in our special "girls only" times when we stole away from the clamor of the boys. I returned to it in adulthood to discover its power afresh, to rejoice in its portrayal of the strong-hearted Elnora, and to delight in a greater knowledge of its author. *A Girl of the Limberlost* follows Elnora Comstock, impoverished and neglected, whose home lies in the many-splendored Limberlost swamp of northern Indiana. Determined to gain an education, she turns for help to the swamp world she knows like the inside of her own heart, collecting the fascinating moths of the Limberlost to sell as specimens to collectors. Aided by the inimitable and generous Bird Woman—part scientist, part poet, and part ecologist—Elnora grows into a woman with "a compound of self-reliance, hard knocks, heart hunger, unceasing work, and generosity. There was no form of suffering with which the girl could not sympathize, no work she was afraid to attempt, no subject she had investigated she did not understand. These things combined to produce a breadth and depth of character altogether unusual."

This book was one of those, like the Anne books, that met me in the formative years of girlhood and modeled what determination, spunk, gentleness, and a holy hunger for life could look like in a young woman. There is a reveling in the beauty of the world in this book, such a hearty faith in what may be accomplished by determination. A bit more research introduced me to the marvel of the author herself, a real-life bird woman, who, like Elnora, begged God to "help me to unshackle and expand my soul to the fullest realization of Your wonders." Porter's work as a self-trained naturalist and conservationist meant the preservation of the riches of the actual Limberlost, along with novels that led her readers to the wonders of nature.

Also by Stratton-Porter:
- *Freckles*
- *The Keeper of the Bees* (reviewed on page 191)

Kristin Lavransdatter Trilogy by Sigrid Undset

Undset's story of Kristin, a medieval woman of deep religious faith and long endurance, won the Nobel Prize in Literature in 1928. Riveting from a historic point of view, as Undset draws deeply on Nordic myth and culture and crafts a novel of both gritty reality and beauty, it is even more compelling for the depth of its religious insight, as it examines the complexities of Kristin's difficult life as daughter, wife, and mother. She is an image of womanhood in its power, its frailty, and its capacity for strength and beauty.

"Courage, Dear Heart": The Spiritual Classics That Made My Heart Strong

(OR, BOOKS TO NOURISH AND STRETCH THE SOUL)

When I first arrived in Oxford amid a golden and crimson October, I intended to stay only a single year. I had just turned thirty, and I was ready for a change of scene. It seemed a perfect season in which to study the history of my faith a bit more in depth. Then, too, it was Oxford, city of my many teenaged hopes and literary dreams. I thought a year of theological immersion would deepen my faith and stretch my mental muscles, but I never intended theology to become the full-time fascination of my life, the subject whose irresistible depths would end my twelve-year spate of "gap years" as I finally signed up to finish a bachelor's degree.

What captivated me, within the very first weeks, was the depth and breadth of Christian doctrine and the intricate way it influenced not just my general belief in God but the way that faith works itself out in the smallest details of my life. How do I regard my body? What value do I place on creation? What does forgiveness look like in a violent culture? What does it mean to be ethical when it comes to medical technology? Within the first weeks, I recognized that even though I was a long-time believer, I had been unconsciously operating by tiny heresies. As I moved more deeply into the realm of theology and more clearly grasped the core doctrines of my faith, I felt as if floodgates had been opened in my heart. Understanding rushed in to free me from fear and guilt and to widen my view of God's goodness.

This is the sense that has come to me through the reading of spiritual and theological classics throughout my life, books that widened my view of God, helped me to understand myself in light of his love, and empowered me to act from that redeemed identity. Some of these I read in high school, books that became the foundation of my young Christian faith. Some I encountered in hours of intensive study in my lonely twenties; some I have discovered in Oxford, books that in some way revolutionized my understanding of God. Some are contemporary, some ancient. All of them are classics that specifically shaped both my identity as a Christian and my capacity to act, love, create, and give out of that core understanding. I hope you will find freshened hope and brightened vision as you encounter their depths.

On the Incarnation by Athanasius

We're off with a bang with this church father! This book was assigned for one of the first essays I wrote in Oxford. I considered it basic (if ancient) Christian stuff, as in "God became human." But what took me entirely by surprise was the way every aspect of my Christian identity is affected by this doctrine: my view of the body, my concept of the material world, my idea of what Jesus' death accomplished, and how relevant this ancient text is to the dilemmas of my age. Don't be put off by an old name; Athanasius was the bishop of Alexandria in the fourth century, and his whole point in writing this classic work was to help the common Christian understand the fullness of what Christ accomplished by taking on human flesh. We often think of Christ in terms of the Cross, our understanding dominated by his sacrificial death. But redemption began the moment "the Word became flesh, and dwelt among us" (John 1:14, NASB), for as Athanasius says, Jesus "became what we are so that he might make us what he is."

Also by Athanasius:
- *The Life of Antony*

Telling the Truth: The Gospel as Tragedy, Comedy, and Fairy Tale
by Frederick Buechner

The title alone could hook the eyes of fairy-tale loving me, but Buechner's poetic account of the gospel, his narrative view of Scripture, and his capacity to get past the sometimes primness of theology into the depths where we wrestle like Jacob and dream like Joseph have made this book a touchstone in my Christian walk. In an account that is part story and part sermon, in words that glimmer and sing, Buechner tells us the truth of the world and of ourselves:

> The tragic truth of the Gospel, which is that the world
> where God is absent is a dark and echoing emptiness; and
> the comic truth of the Gospel, which is that it is into the
> depths of his absence that God makes himself present in
> such unlikely ways . . . the tale that is too good not to be
> true because to dismiss it as untrue is to dismiss along with
> it that catch of the breath, that beat and lifting of the heart
> near to or even accompanied by tears, which I believe is the
> deepest intuition of truth that we have.

Prayer: Finding the Heart's True Home by Richard Foster

I first encountered the writing of Foster as a teen, and his words worked powerfully in my heart in those early days when the shape of my faith was molded by what I read. Foster is a theologian and writer in the Quaker tradition, best known for his *Celebration of Discipline*, the 1978 book that introduced a more evangelical audience to the power of spiritual disciplines such as prayer, fasting, solitude, and simplicity. His quiet, clear, heartfelt tone captivated me in three specific books, which I will briefly mention here. First, his *Streams of Living Water* helped me grasp the width and breadth of the church throughout the world. Foster examines six major church traditions, evaluating their particular strengths, acknowledging their gaps, and demonstrating the grace possible in recognizing the way that each reveals and prizes different aspects of God's character and action in the world.

His *Freedom of Simplicity* continues to inform the way I think about work, worship, and the cadence of rest. In the midst of a culture increasingly shaped by materialism and a consumeristic mindset, Foster urges us to "still every motion that is not rooted in the Kingdom, become quiet, hushed, motionless until you are finally centered," to live in attention to Christ, basing our use of time, our material gain, and our activities on a profound trust in God's provision and attention to his movement in the world.

Finally, when I read his clear and deeply moving primer on prayer, *Prayer: Finding the Heart's True Home*, it felt like having a guide take me by the hand and lead me safely through the gorgeous wilderness that is prayer, showing me the hidden caves of contemplation and the clean, clear road of liturgical prayer and the windy mountaintop of waiting for the Spirit. John Wesley described his conversion as having a "heart strangely warmed," and my heart felt kindled, quickened, and companioned throughout the reading of this book.

Also by Foster:
- *Celebration of Discipline*
- *Streams of Living Water*
- *Freedom of Simplicity*

Against Heresies by Irenaeus

When Gnosticism (the belief that matter is evil and only spirit is good) threatened the early church, Irenaeus went to war with his pen, not only composing a refutation of Gnostic belief, which is profoundly relevant in our own materialistic culture, but articulating the redemptive power of the Incarnation in a way that rings with victory to this day. One of the best things I read in my studies. (For an excellent and beautiful commentary, read Hans Urs von Balthasar's *The Scandal of the Incarnation: Irenaeus against the Heresies*.)

Revelations of Divine Love by Julian of Norwich

Part of me has to love this one simply because it was the first surviving English book that was written by a woman. Composed in the fourteenth century by the remarkable Julian, an anchoress (someone who withdrew from the secular world for the purpose of solitude and prayer) who was known as a counselor and consoler to many in an age marked by plague, death, and poverty, it deals with sixteen visions or "showings" that came to Julian, revealing God's love and presence. This book is considered a classic Christian mystical work (see my review of Evelyn Underhill's *Mysticism* on page 118 for a definition of Christian mysticism). I read it over a spring holiday in Oxford, when I was mostly alone in the deserted college, wrestling with loneliness in the days leading up to Easter. Julian's awed love of Jesus, her grasp of his presence in our suffering, and her radiant affirmation that "all shall be well, and all shall be well, and all manner of things shall be well" has helped me to imagine, to trust, and to live more deeply in the worship Julian describes this way: "The greatest honor we can give Almighty God is to live gladly because of the knowledge of his love."

The Prodigal God by Timothy Keller

A teacher and theologian who preaches the gospel and teaches the Word in a way uniquely relevant to twenty-first-century believers, Timothy Keller has a grasp of Scripture, and a way of making it practical and plain, that offers constant encouragement. My husband and I regularly listen to his sermons and find ourselves girded up for the daily walk of obedience in the midst of a confusing culture and secular society. The first book by Keller that I read (also one of his shortest) is still my favorite, *The Prodigal God*, an exploration of the inexorable Father-love of God as it pursues not only the desperate younger sons but also the angry older children who keep themselves outside the feast of love.

Also by Keller:
- *The Reason for God*
- *Counterfeit Gods*
- *Prayer*
- *Generous Justice*

The Genesis Trilogy by Madeleine L'Engle

When I was seventeen, I went through a year of profound doubt and, let's be honest, outright anger at God. It had to do with my first real experience of suffering, and my small rebellion (which I have to chuckle at now) was to stop having quiet times and reading my Bible. At all. Which was really something for a child of ministry parents raised with all the ideals of evangelical Christian devotion. What I did read (for oh, God knew how to get to me) was this luminous trilogy by Madeleine L'Engle. The books in that series saved my faith, for what I encountered in these personal, narrative explorations of the stories in Genesis was what I most needed at that point: a reaffirmation of God's goodness dancing in the beauty of creation, his love at work to redeem us, his powerful presence available to us as we battle and hope, work and love in this broken place.

(Caveat: L'Engle strays at times from the bounds of orthodoxy, especially in her earlier work, including The Genesis Trilogy. Some find her difficult to read because of her open exploration or questioning of the doctrines surrounding topics like penal substitution or God's sovereignty, as well as her imaginative—some would say too liberal—interaction with Scripture. Her honesty, her capacity to both doubt and trust, and her affirmation of God's love make her, for me, a worthy and encouraging author, but this is something to be aware of as you begin.)

The Great Divorce by C. S. Lewis

Lewis said that George MacDonald was his "master," and when Lewis wrote this remarkable book—a mix of spiritual fantasy, allegory, and devotion—recounting a supernatural bus ride from hell to heaven in which each passenger is invited to remain in paradise, he cast MacDonald as the guide sent to meet him. In MacDonald's wise company, both narrator and reader listen in to the conversations of each passenger, witnessing the resentment, wounded pride, or outrage by which each chooses to return to hell even with the glory of heaven stretching out before them. By leading us through an incisive exploration of the self-deception and pettiness by which humans refuse heaven, Lewis also leads us to a fuller realization that "all loneliness, angers, hatreds, envies and itchings that [Hell] contains, if rolled into one single experience and put into the scale against the least moment of the joy that is felt by the least in Heaven, would have no weight that could be registered at all."

While *The Great Divorce* ranks as one of my favorites, I would honestly recommend all of Lewis's spiritual books. *The Screwtape Letters* has guided me to more practical spiritual maturity than almost any other book, and *The Four Loves* has become my reference point in describing both divine and human ways of loving. Lewis has a remarkable capacity to articulate the doubts and distractions, the yearnings and ordinary frustrations of the workaday Christian. He is also a writer of vivid imagination; his concepts are never abstract but illustrated by images that remain in the mind for years to come. Consider each of the works below on equal footing with the one described in more detail above:

- *The Screwtape Letters*
- *Mere Christianity*
- *The Weight of Glory*
- *Letters to Malcolm, Chiefly on Prayer*
- *The Four Loves*

Café Theology: Exploring Love, the Universe and Everything by Michael Lloyd

If there is one book I would recommend as both a beginner's overview and a sensitive and nuanced exploration of the core topics of Christian doctrine, this would be it. My husband and I have both been deeply fortunate to sit under Lloyd's teaching at our college in Oxford, and we have given this book to more siblings and friends than I can count. In this volume, which covers roughly the same topics I covered in my first year of theological study, Lloyd explores ten basic doctrines such as Creation, the Fall, the Incarnation, the Atonement, and Providence. In a conversational tone, with more than occasional humor (he is famous at Oxford for his jokes), Lloyd guides readers into a theologically rich understanding of the beliefs that lie at the core of the Christian faith. I kept returning to this book for clarity as I worked on my papers, and it never failed me once.

Unspoken Sermons by George MacDonald

In my view, the glorious theme that runs through MacDonald's work like a gleaming golden thread, weaving his fiction, sermons, poems, and essays into a magnificent whole, is his absolute trust in the Father-hearted love of God. With deep spiritual passion formed by his intimate knowledge of grief, MacDonald preached to his small congregations on what it means to be truly converted, on the call to absolute obedience to God's will, and on the profound mercy of the Father, who never leaves us in our sin but draws us onward into a life and identity we are only beginning to imagine. For "it is to the man who is trying to live, to the man who is obedient to the word of the Master, that the word of the Master unfolds itself."

(A note: MacDonald is a Victorian writer, which means his sermons have all the flourish and floridity of high Victorian thought. Stick with him. The gems at the heart of the occasional fluff are the kind to change one's life.)

The Sign of Jonas by Thomas Merton

I find it difficult to choose a single Merton title, as I have come to know him mostly by skimming and dipping into the borrowed or secondhand copies of friends. But whenever I read him, I find a voice that can articulate the struggles I feel as a believer in the modern world—of distraction, of fear, of identity, of self-absorption—while still calling me into a space of silence and contemplation where I can meet God afresh. Merton was a Trappist monk, a poet, a spiritual writer, and a social activist whose spiritual autobiography *The Seven Storey Mountain* reached thousands hungering for faith in the aftermath of World War II. My favorite, though, is probably his journals in *The Sign of Jonas*, his musings in the early days of his religious life. His small delights in a cloudscape or a note of music, his frustration with the brothers, his boredom with details, his hunger for something beyond the horizon match the ruminations of my own restless soul and help me to see that whether in the cloister or the world, the possibility of wonder, the presence of joy, and the need to love with grit and grace are ever the same.

Humility: The Journey toward Holiness by Andrew Murray

I read this Victorian spiritual classic at the height of teenage self-righteousness, and its gentle challenge has sweetly dogged me ever since. The total commitment to Christ present in older spiritual literature offers a constant challenge to the self-centric atmosphere of the modern world and of my natural self. In Murray's words, "Humility is nothing but the disappearance of self in the vision that God is all," a statement I need as a corrective more often than I like to admit.

Knowing God by J. I. Packer

"Oh, I love that book," said my husband when I mentioned it would make its way onto this list. My mom said the same, and aside from the intriguing way this book has impacted the lives of believers from the US to the UK to the Netherlands, I have been often struck by the way it so impacted two people in very different phases of life whose spiritual lives I so respect. I see this as a foundational book of discipleship written by someone who has walked far in the company of Jesus. It's the gospel explored, the attributes of God made clear, the way to a real and living relationship outlined and offered to the believer. It's the kind of book that makes a perennial child of every believer as we confront the incredible gift of knowing and being known by God. As Packer says, "I need not torment myself with the fear that my faith may fail; as grace led me to faith in the first place, so grace will keep me believing to the end."

Christ Plays in Ten Thousand Places by Eugene Peterson

This is the foundational book in a five-volume series that Peterson, a lifelong pastor, wrote after decades spent in ministry and in daily conversation with Scripture. Weaving together the discipline of theology with the more practical, daily aspects of Christian spirituality he developed with his congregations, Peterson masterfully presents a livable theology based on his conviction that "God's great love and purposes for us are all worked out in messes in our kitchens and backyards, in storms and sins, blue skies, the daily work and dreams of our common lives." Divided into three sections—Christ plays in creation, history, and community—this was another book I encountered in my teens that helped me to grasp the way the life of Christ is meant to invade every corner of my existence. I cannot recommend Peterson's spiritual writing highly enough. His insight into the difficulties of discipleship in the modern age, his rich grasp of Scripture, and his conversational, creative tone have made him a mentor to many of my friends in pastoral ministry.

Also by Peterson:
- *Run with the Horses*
- *A Long Obedience in the Same Direction*
- *Tell It Slant*
- *The Contemplative Pastor*

For the Life of the World by Alexander Schmemann

This is a splendor of a book, one joyfully written in order "to remind its readers that in Christ, life—life in all its totality—was returned to man, given again as sacrament and communion." Written by an Orthodox priest concerned both by the rise of secularism (which sees nothing divine in creation) and by the rise of a Christianity that could only "equate the world with evil," Schmemann wrote a book that helped me to grasp the comprehensive nature of Christ's redemption, one that reaches into every corner of the physical cosmos as well as the spiritual. "Man is what he eats," Schmemann reminds us in the opening line of this exuberant book, and "the world of which he must partake in order to live, is given to him by God, and it is given as *communion with God*." That we have received this gift afresh in Christ's incarnate and risen life means that a believer's life should be the sort in which the world can literally taste and see the goodness of God (Psalm 34:8) as the Kingdom comes in our homes, our feasts, and our fellowship.

Incarnation: The Person and Life of Christ by Thomas F. Torrance

This book is a systematic and riveting (two adjectives that don't usually go together) examination of the doctrine of the Incarnation. Torrance was a famed professor of theology in Scotland, and this book is a transcription of the lectures he gave with such loving verve that whole classrooms were held in fascination by what he taught. He looks at the Incarnation throughout Scripture, exploring the Old Testament as pre-Incarnation history, making clear what was accomplished not only by Christ's death but by his human life, as it embodied the active, loving obedience that humanity was meant, from its inception, to live out to God. Torrance's knowledge is staggering, but there is a current of excitement thrumming through his work that is downright contagious. I clearly remember sitting in the hushed and sophisticated Bodleian Library with tears in my eyes as the scope of God's redemption became clear to me in this book.

Mysticism by Evelyn Underhill

The title alone can make some nervous. In a modern world where mysticism is often associated with "vague or ill-defined religious or spiritual belief, especially as associated with a belief in the occult" (definition courtesy of Oxford Dictionaries), mysticism can seem anything but orthodox. But to medieval Christians, and to countless devout believers throughout the ages, Christian mysticism is simply the practice of intentional, contemplative, disciplined prayer, or as Underhill puts it, "the determined fixing of our will upon God, and pressing toward him steadily and without deflection."[2] In this comprehensive exploration of Christian mysticism, the saints who are its heroes, the prayers of worship, the practices of silence by which they "fixed their will" upon love, Underhill invites every believer to journey more deeply into the reality and life of God. Now, I'll admit, this is quite a tome. I include it here because for me it was a turning point in my prayer life, a book that demonstrated the focus, depth, and devotion that is possible for every Christian who yearns to become increasingly suffused with the life and reality of Christ. If you're looking for an easier place to begin, you might want to try *Concerning the Inner Life* or even the chatty and practical *The Letters of Evelyn Underhill*.

Jesus and the Victory of God by N. T. Wright

N. T. Wright is one of the most influential theologians in the Christian church today, and one of his driving messages is that Jesus is King—not just over the church, but over the whole world. Wright's gift lies in his capacity to see the full story and power of what Jesus has accomplished in his death and resurrection, and the goal of this book is to draw readers into a fresh confrontation with the Gospels— the aspects we know and the ones we haven't noticed nearly enough in their implications for a world reclaimed by God.

I also have greatly benefited from Wright's everyman commentary in *Paul for Everyone*. I have found him indispensable in getting to the pith of Paul's letters or tracing the theological themes in Romans. A serious but readable commentary accessible to the average reader.

Also by Wright:
- *Surprised by Hope*
- *After You Believe: Why Christian Character Matters*
- *Simply Christian*

What's So Amazing about Grace? by Philip Yancey

The core of this book boils down to the single assertion that "God loves people because of who God is, not because of who we are." Grace is central to the gospel: it's what makes us believers, but it is also the thing we struggle to internalize on the level of our everyday actions and emotions. Using startling stories and Scripture, literature and personal history, Yancey weaves a book that follows the old writing maxim of showing us grace instead of just telling us about it. It's why I love him as an author: his books are honest explorations of the topics he tackles, starred by great stories and his own history as a Christian. He asks the hard questions and finds a way to answer them in a way that makes what could be abstract—grace, doubt, faith—near and real for his readers.

Also by Yancey:
- *The Jesus I Never Knew*
- *Soul Survivor*
- *Reaching for the Invisible God*

"What to Do with the Time We've Been Given": Books That Helped Me Navigate Contemporary Culture

(OR, HOW TO LIVE WITH GANDALF-LIKE WISDOM)

I AM AN UNABASHEDLY old-fashioned soul who sympathizes with Frodo's wish that he had not been born in such a difficult or complicated age. There is much to treasure in the contemporary world, but also—oh my goodness—much to wrestle with amid a host of contending voices. What is culture? How does one think about creation care and racial reconciliation? In the midst of those questions, I have often wished I could ask my grandparents what in the world they think about iPhones or the travel age. I have deeply craved a wisdom larger and longer than my own.

Most of my grandparents passed away before I was old enough to really know them or even reach the first pangs of existential angst. But I've often felt that the authors of the cultural commentaries I have read who offer that broader, more nuanced view of the world have served as honorary grandparents, helping me to make sense of the world I have inherited. For example, there's Charles Taylor, who has helped me handle my doubt by his explanation that nobody gets to just stumble into faith in the modern age because we are aware of so many choices, and Wendell Berry, who has shaped the way I think about community with his grumpy (but spot-on) assertion that the problem of the modern world is that everyone thinks they would be better people if they could only go somewhere else. And then there's Gandalf, saying to me as much as to Frodo that bemoaning the age of my birth isn't really a faithful reaction. To look about, take stock, and set to creative work—that's what's faithful, and that's what the books in the list below have helped me to do.

Whether helping me to think wisely about technology or the tension between online interaction and actual connection, or helping me to make sense of the yearning I feel for home or the recent movement toward the local and small, these authors explain the hunger, frustrations, and needs of my own generation with a calm wisdom I could not muster alone. They teach me how to see and work for the health of the world in which I stand.

The Art of the Commonplace by Wendell Berry

Reading *The Art of the Commonplace* was an epiphany for me. For the first time in my twentysomething life, I felt I could finally articulate my vague unease with big business, consumer culture, and the impersonal nature of the online world. I've developed a reputation with my tutors and fellow students in Oxford as being slightly obsessed with Berry because I recommend his essays to every person who is willing to talk books with me and because I can usually draw some connection between one of his novels and a given theological point. I do this because his voice comes to me in the clear, sane, ringing tones of a mentor who stands a little outside my age, able to explain it to me and call me back to my senses. Berry is known as an agrarian author, one whose wisdom as a farmer drives his contention that the health of a culture begins with fidelity—to marriage, to our "place on earth," and in our membership to the community that grows up around us. This is my favorite collection, and "Health Is Membership" is an essay I try to read once a year. But then, I'm trying to read all of Wendell Berry before I die.

Life Is a Miracle: An Essay against Modern Superstition by Wendell Berry

How can you resist a title like that? This was one of the first Berry books I read, having discovered it on a low and dusty shelf in the crammed apologetics library at English L'Abri. I read it in various garden corners, engrossed by Berry's spirited skewering of the reductionist or materialistic view of life, which reduces humans to physical parts and denies the living mystery of divine, creative love so richly evident in the beauty and complexity of creation. The world might soon be divided, he thinks, between "people who wish to live as creatures and people who wish to live as machines," but Berry will be with those who see life as a miracle and live in its wonder.

Also by Berry:
- *Sex, Economy, Freedom and Community*
- *Standing by Words*
- *The Unsettling of America*

The Discoverers: A History of Man's Search to Know His World and Himself by Daniel J. Boorstin

This is my bit of history with this title. First, this book was recommended to me by a professor who had just given a riveting talk on history at a C. S. Lewis conference I attended. Then I happened upon a copy at a library sale. When I looked inside the cover, I found the previous owner's name next to this intriguing inscription: "The best book I have read." Of course I bought it. And I reveled in a lively, learned, and fascinating adventure through the history of humanity's yen to *know*. A book both philosophical and historical, tracing the great discoveries and explorations of history. A mesmerizing historian, Boorstin has also written the following titles:

- *The Seekers: The Story of Man's Continuing Quest to Understand His World*
- *The Creators: A History of Heroes of the Imagination*

The Shallows: What the Internet Is Doing to Our Brains by Nicholas Carr

If you were to read one book on the impact of media and information technologies, let it be this one. "Is Google Making Us Stupid?" was the question Carr posed for a cover story in the *Atlantic*, the answering of which led to this convicting book. Information technologies all carry an "intellectual ethic," Carr contends, tracing the history of humanity's intellectual tools and the impact they have on the way we think. While the printed book shaped us to patterns of contemplation, attention, and creativity, the internet bears an industrialist ethic of efficiency, speed, and consumption. Google may not make us stupid—we are trained to scan and skim at ever quickening speeds—but it certainly makes us shallow, less inclined to reach depths of insight, wisdom, and creative reflection. I have found this book helpful and convicting as I consider my own use of media technologies.

Culture Making by Andy Crouch

What is culture? Until reading this exhilarating book, I tended to perceive culture as a nebulous force that dwells in cities, drives moral decisions, and is the arbiter of the arts world. It's the thing about which

Christians are often confused, which leads to the various unhelpful postures Crouch lists in his book—critiquing, condemning, consuming, and copying. How joyous then to read this declaration that culture is simply what I as a human, in the company of other humans, make of the world: the cooking of an omelette, the stewing of chili, the crafting of a house, the jotting of a poem. This is Crouch's joyous affirmation that what we are meant to be when it comes to culture is no more and no less than creators, acting in the image of God.

Sophie's World by Jostein Gaarder

A swift and engaging history of philosophy explored in the charming form of a story, Sophie's story. Every day fourteen-year-old Sophie receives a letter with various questions, then a package from a mysterious mentor who sends her bits of philosophy to help her explore and answer the questions in the letter. Part mystery, part history, part delightful novel, this is an excellent introduction to the world of Western philosophy that helps a reader (along with Sophie) to recognize how we come by our assumptions, our identities, and our patterns of understanding.

After Virtue by Alasdair MacIntyre

I've heard this book quoted so often I feel I've actually read it. I haven't. But I know it will shape my thoughts in profound ways when I do. So I asked my sister, Joy, a PhD student in the realm of virtue ethics, to review it instead (she's brilliant). Here's what she says:

> Have you ever wondered why our culture seems incapable of engaging in meaningful conversations about moral issues without dissolving into shrill, seemingly irresolvable disagreement? In *After Virtue*, Alasdair MacIntyre contends that the culprit of this trouble is emotivism (moral

statements are meaningless), and the solution to our present confusion is the reclamation of the sturdier (and more imaginative) Aristotelian tradition of virtue ethics (in which virtuous character is a foundation for ethical judgment). The text is interspersed with compelling literary and historical examples—he finds Jane Austen's heroes and heroines particularly inspiring! This book is for anyone who wants a baptismal introduction to the history and substance of modern moral philosophy. It is a book of hefty substance that you will feel proud to have finished, but I would recommend reading and discussing it with a friend to get the most out of this meaty masterpiece.

Begotten or Made? by Oliver O'Donovan

This is one of the books I discovered as part of an ethics course at Oxford, a slim volume constructed of five lectures O'Donovan gave regarding bioethics and the formation of personhood. More than any other book I've read, this tight, keen volume has helped me to frame my understanding of modern bioethics in the profound identity that was meant to come to each child born as someone begotten by love, as Christ was the "only begotten of the Father" (John 1:14, KJV). What O'Donovan demonstrates is the dangerous way in which we are now tampering with human biology and identity through the use of medical technology. Our modern mind-set, O'Donovan explains, comes from a radical redefinition of freedom as the "abolition of limits," a modern view equating personal freedom with release from the bonds of religion, society, and nature. In reading this (and I have little scientific background), I have been equipped to comprehend and discern the spiritual issues underlying the current cultural debates on gender, sexuality, procreation, and personhood. I think this resource will be indispensable in the years to come.

Amusing Ourselves to Death by Neil Postman

Written in the early days of media technology, Postman argues that "form excludes the content," that some mediums of communication are limited in the complexity of the ideas they can communicate. Postman's concern was with TV, but consider this quote (before social media was even around) in light of our multiple technologies now: "Americans no longer talk to each other, they entertain each other. They do not exchange ideas, they exchange images. They do not argue with propositions; they argue with good looks, celebrities and commercials." Yikes. A book to help us examine our use of media technologies and to weigh their influence on the way we learn, debate, and perceive each other in modern society.

Also by Postman:
- *Technopoly*

Too Small to Ignore by Wess Stafford

In this moving memoir and plea, the president emeritus of Compassion International powerfully argues for the Christian responsibility to consider the "little ones," the hungry and lost, the deserted and lonely children of the world. Drawing on the painful circumstances in his own childhood, Stafford articulates a vision of the gospel that engages, protects, and cultivates "the least of these" in every society. I found this a profoundly helpful and compassionate book, both practical and visionary in empowering the average believer to act as an advocate for those with no voice.

A Secular Age by Charles Taylor

I haven't been in the studies of many professors or priests, but this book has been on the shelf of every one I have been in, and it seems to inform quite a few of the theologians I've read as well. A masterpiece written from a lifetime of philosophical study, this book identifies the profound implications of living in a "secular age," one in which every person alive must choose faith out of a multitude of competing options. A fascinating history of faith, doubt, and human consciousness, this book more than almost any other provides an explanation of the cultural atmosphere in which we learn, love, and believe. It's a couple of inches thick, though, so take it slowly. I certainly do.

Exclusion and Embrace by Miroslav Volf

In a world increasingly shaped by violence, with cultures emerging from the war-torn twentieth century, Volf contends for the powerful possibility of reconciliation as modeled by Jesus, who had all power and yet did not retaliate against his enemies. Rather, Christ opened his arms in the embrace of forgiveness, the divine gesture that halts the circle of retaliatory violence. Volf's writing is shaped by his first-hand knowledge of violence and forgiveness as witnessed in his home country of Croatia in its conflict with Serbia.

From Nature to Creation: A Christian Vision for Understanding and Loving Our World by Norman Wirzba

How should Christianity shape our care and use of the natural world? This is the question Wirzba sets out to answer. Confronting the difficulty of many Christians in separating creation care from nature worship or knowing how to use natural resources with integrity, Wirzba defines the world not vaguely as nature but as creation, God's wondrous gift, which requires our gratitude, responsibility, and care.

CHAPTER 6

Books Can Cultivate the IMAGINATION

Believing the Truth That Beauty Tells

Fairy land arouses a longing for [a child] knows not what. It stirs and troubles him (to his life-long enrichment) with the dim sense of something beyond his reach and, far from dulling or emptying the actual world, gives it a new dimension of depth. He does not despise real woods because he has read of enchanted woods: the reading makes all real woods a little enchanted.

C. S. LEWIS, OF OTHER WORLDS

THE YEAR AFTER THOMAS and I were married, I found myself in London very early on a frosty January morning. Thomas was in town for a conference, and I'd tagged along, in need of a change of scene. But I was tired. The day had barely begun, and I already felt bone weary, dogged by the half-finished work of my final papers, by a case of the blues brought on by reading the morning headlines on the bus, and by the anxious weariness that I was soon to learn signaled the coming of a baby. The walking day ahead looked very long, and my adventurous spirit seemed to have wandered off without me as I rambled aimlessly around the squares of Covent Garden, down-hearted, waiting for shops to open, hoping for a café.

And then, abruptly, there was music. Music so full and living and quick it was like sunlight slicing through fog. The tint of the air seemed to visibly brighten. I watched people all around me startle, stop, and search for the source of the music, something golden and swift by Mozart. I followed. We found the musicians, four of them, by leaning over a balcony, looking down into one of the warmer corners of Covent Garden. The group stood in a half moon: a cellist, a flutist, and two violinists. They were bundled in faded sweaters and battered boots, with sly flairs of color in one violinist's blue scarf and the flutist's red beret.

They danced as they played, stomping and twirling in laughing sync. They played with frost-reddened noses and fingers, but the cold seemed not to bother them at all. It was as if the music was their warmth; it sprang from deep within them, part of heart and muscle, emerging into their fingers, received by the strings of the violin or flute or mellow-throated cello. I watched with a dozen others, fascinated. People smiled. Toes tapped. Who knew why they had braved the cold and the dawn to shatter the fog with their song light. All we knew was that they laughed as they played. They caught our eyes and winked.

And in a sudden, unraveled happiness, standing at that rail, I knew a quality of joy that comes more and more rarely to me since childhood. I knew innocence. Happiness without shadow of fear. I stood there for half an hour as they played, and I left the cold and heaviness of my heart behind. The music made me childlike, because for an instant, its potent beauty allowed me a shifted, inner vision of the joy that is coming, coming, coming. The fleeting shadows of my morning trouble, my weariness, my fear were phantoms that blessedly died in the strong light of the singing around me.

And I knew afresh, in a knowledge that was grace to my heart and health to my body, that the great promise of beauty, the thrummed message that sings to us in those moments when we are struck by art or music or story, is that, as Sam Gamgee breathlessly puts it at the end of *The Return of the King*, everything sad is going to come untrue.

That moment helped me to remember something that I have known in some of the surest, happiest times in my life: that a woman who reads is a woman who has been prepared to accept the truth that beauty tells, to embrace the good news that imagination brings, the promise of joy that greets us in the happy endings or poignant insights of the novels we love. She has learned to glimpse eternity as it shimmers in story or song, to receive the satisfaction of a happy ending as a promise. She has come to recognize the voice of love speaking in the language of image and imagination and to trust what it speaks as true.

But it took me a very long time to come to that trust.

I was in my teens when I began to be aware of the tension I felt between what I experienced as deep, spiritual comfort in the novels I was reading and my sense that faith was supposed to be based on facts. I felt like half a heretic to admit that The Lord of the Rings kept me believing in redemption or that Aslan made God real to me when I was sick of church. I felt guilty when a novel made me feel closer to God than a psalm.

I don't think I'm alone in this: the suspicion of the spiritual comfort afforded by a story is a theme I've encountered countless times in my work on reading. I've had numerous conversations with concerned parents who questioned my recommendations (in books and in talks) of the Narnia books, The Lord of the Rings, or even classic fairy tales, because they were not "real" and might lead children away from the truth. I have argued with close friends who chose to give up the reading of novels in order to focus only on what is "true," and I have watched teenagers struggling with doubt feel guilty for the way a story helps them feel close to God.

The problem is that we in the modern world have been taught to largely equate truth with fact. We are shaped by an Enlightenment view of human reason and an increasingly mechanical model of science, leading us to believe that reality can be defined only by what is visible and measurable, by what we can prove and thus control. In the wider secular culture, this is expressed as materialism, the belief that there is no spiritual reality and that the observable world is all that actually exists. Secular materialism dismisses belief in spiritual reality and the use of imagination as false; it sees beauty as dispensable and subjective, emotion as chemical, imagination (and with it, religion) as mere fantasy. Ironically, this view increasingly influences the way we live out our faith and speak about God, as apologists seek to argue God's existence on materialism's own terms, using scientific proof–style reasoning and analytical debate to "prove" the reality of the spiritual world. It filters down to us in a thousand ordinary ways, shaping our models of spiritual growth on lines of productivity or casting faith as an assent to a list of doctrinal statements rather than the renewal of our whole selves and stories. It makes us doubt the "usefulness" of beauty or the spiritual purpose of imagination.

But this is a profoundly *un*-Christian view of faith and personhood. To reject image, emotion, and story as peripheral to faith is to ignore the way God created us—as beings made in his image to create in our turn, as souls capable of both reason and analysis but also equally capable of imagination, creativity, and emotion. We are living stories whose lives turn on our hope of the ultimate happy ending, and we too quickly forget the fact that faith is described as "the assurance of *things* hoped for" (or perhaps, imagined), "the conviction of things not seen" (Hebrews 11:1, NASB). We miss the reality that much of Scripture comes to us as narrative, that the Psalms are also poems, that allegory and metaphor make up much of the prophets' writings, and that the gospel appeals to us in the form of a story. If Jesus himself used parables to illustrate and announce the coming of his Kingdom, if he felt that the tale of a prodigal son was the best way to introduce the glory of grace or that the story of a lavishly merciful Samaritan was the ideal means to speak of God's compassion, then we, too, can embrace both story and imagination as realms in which we may encounter and know God's own truth.

But before I came to peace with that fact, I needed someone to explain how imagination worked, to give me permission to accept the grace I found in my books. This gift first came to me through an Oxford tutor who led me through a study of C. S. Lewis and the way he understood imagination. I can still remember my urgent sense of curiosity on the March afternoon when I sank into a green armchair in my tutor's office, glancing up at an illustration inspired by *The Great Divorce* of a godlike man instructing a small mortal. I felt this to be an appropriate image as we began our conversation and I read my essay aloud to someone who could, by memory, finish every Lewis quote I started. But in real God-like fashion, he came straight down to my level, noticing the troubled look on my face and asking what was bothering me.

The question burned on the edge of my tongue, and driven by the hunger in my heart, I blurted it out: "How can a story or a moment of beauty be as true as a doctrinal statement? Sometimes it's the only way I can believe in God. But how in the world can I defend that?"

My tutor kept his place by the window, wrapped in a woolen coat warm enough for a Narnian winter. A beam of low, wintered sunlight fell across his face, obscuring the keen eyes behind his glasses, lending an inscrutable calm to his countenance as he turned to face me and, in a voice of perfect English precision, told me that I must not, "simply must *not*," think of stories as untrue. He was almost stern.

"Remember the beam!" he commanded. Then he sat down to explain the essay I'd studied that week, one written after C. S. Lewis converted to Christianity, an event driven by Lewis's discovery that there was more than one way to "know." As a young man, Lewis was an atheist, one who totally embraced secular materialism. But like me, he was also a lover of stories—Norse myths and *The Wind in the Willows*, Arthurian legends and Dickens novels—and he felt that the books he loved communicated something holy, beautiful, and true. They filled him with a knowledge that he called joy, the sense of something eternal and good that simply didn't fit the narrow box of materialism. Lewis came to faith largely because he grew to understand that what he encountered in those stories was every bit as true as a scientific statement of fact, because there's more than one way to encounter reality.

Lewis wrote about this in an essay called "A Meditation in a Toolshed," in which he imagined himself standing in a dark little garden shed with a beam of light coming in over the closed door. He used that beam of light as a metaphor for two different ways to know. To look at the light, standing apart from it, was an image of scientific, modern knowledge, the kind of knowing we prioritize in the modern world because we can observe something, measure it, prove it is real. But there's a whole different way to know just waiting for us if we step into the beam of light and look along it into the golden day outside, into a green summer world that comes to us as color, warmth, and beauty. That, said Lewis, is the knowledge of experience, an encounter with reality that comes to us from inside the emotion we know in loving family or children, the awe we encounter in worship, the thrill of a happy ending in our favorite fairy tale.

To look at it another way, consider me, in this moment, as I write at my favorite local café on a sunny English morning. I can look at the table under my laptop and see that it is made of scuffed old pine board, that it is sturdy (if uneven), with legs painted green. I can observe the surprisingly good weather, the hum of my laptop, the word count for this chapter, and in so doing I stand apart, I analyze. But some things today I know only from experience: the hope and strength I drew from listening to Ralph Vaughn Williams's "The Lark Ascending" on my walk here; the love that suffuses my being when I glance up from my keyboard to glimpse my husband sitting across from me, conjugating Greek verbs; the joy I find in striving to get these complicated concepts down on the page. I can't stand apart from that satisfaction or love or the joy of the music, and I can't measure it; I can only know it by being within it.

And here's the key: the joy and assurance we find in reading a story is an instant when we know truth from the inside. We inhabit it. Lewis loved the myths surrounding the Norse god Balder, who died a sacrificial death, and realized later that what he loved in that tale was its echo of the true God incarnate coming to die in order to save the world. I love the epic of Middle-earth; I melt into a puddle of aching, grateful tears at the image of Aragorn entering his war-torn city not to conquer but to heal, "for the hands of a king are the hands of a healer."[1] But this is only an echo of the beauty surrounding the real victor in the world's battle, the hero who makes us like himself: Christ. When I read *Pilgrim's Inn* by Elizabeth Goudge, its story of a home whose beauty brings healing to the brokenhearted fills me with both joy and aching desire. It gives me an inward glimpse into the belonging that will come to me in the new heaven and new earth, and in that taste, I can believe that it's true.

Stories, in Alison Milbank's lovely phrase, leave us with "a feeling of homesickness for the truth,"[2] and that is why you, my reading friend, need never fear that the hope you encounter in imagined worlds is somehow separate from the faith you embrace in the real world. All of us, as we read, are like the Pevensie children in Narnia when Aslan sends them back to their own world and tells them,

> There I have another name. You must learn to know me by that name. This was the very reason why you were brought to Narnia, that by knowing me here for a little, you may know me better there.[3]

We grow to know God better as we encounter his reality in stories that richly image his splendor or his power or even his humble presence among us. Can imagination be false? Of course. We can be deceived in the language of story just as we can in the language of atheistic science. But we humans are not merely "thinking things" (as James K. A. Smith puts it) who can survive by assenting to a list of doctrinal truths. Rather, we are "defined by what [we] love," and our loves are deeply shaped by the stories we tell, the narratives we believe. Our worldview, Smith argues, is "more a matter of the imagination than the intellect," because our desires are shaped by our image of "the good life."[4] We find those images all around us; we might draw them from the narratives thrown at us in nonstop advertisements, alluring us with the promise of a thinner or more stylish self. We might draw our images from people we admire. Or we might draw them from a story: the bravery of Aragorn, the faith of Lucy Pevensie, or the tale that Paul is always telling us in his letters, calling us saints and holy ones.

The luminous truth I came to, won by hours of study and the patient words of my tutor, was the truth that a book girl imagines. She looks for God's reality in the realm of story; she finds hope in beauty, grace in a fairy tale; and she revels in the crimson truth of a sunset. A woman who reads understands that symbol and image, story and song, the heft of mountains and the arc of the heavens speak to us in a language without words. A book girl knows that imagination—that faculty by which we perceive meaning beyond the mere surface of things, by which we picture and believe in "*things hoped for . . . not seen*" (Hebrews 11:1, NASB)—is vital to faith in the God who crafted the world to tell of his presence and made us in his image as artists, storytellers, and creators.

A book girl is free to imagine the full glory of what that might mean.

Novels of Eucatastrophe:
The Fantastical Stories That
Taught Me Hope
(OR, THE QUEST FOR A GOOD KIND OF MAGIC)

LET US SPEAK BRIEFLY of magic: enchantments in old fairy tales, spells spun by Hermione, runes intoned by Gandalf. I grew up reading fantastical tales with imaginative abandon—magic, that fantastical and otherworldly resource pervading some of the most fascinating stories the world has had the pleasure to read. Precisely because of magic, however, many of those stories have long been seen as suspect by Christian readers who are uncertain of how imagined magic fits into a healthy account of the actual power of the spiritual world. Mindful of the biblical prohibition against mediums and interaction with the occult, a careful reader is entirely justified in questioning the use of what seems to be supernatural power in these classical stories. As C. S. Lewis himself said, the supernatural was, for him, an "illicit dram,"[5] a hindrance to his journey toward faith.

Yet C. S. Lewis went on to articulate his deep and profound belief in the Christian faith through a series of fantastical stories complete with enchantments, witches, and magic. His lack of concern was based at least in part on his understanding of the difference between magic based in incantation and that accomplished by invocation. Incantation involves the saying of spells, something present in many of the fantastical novels on this list. This is the presentation of magic as an element in a fantastical otherworld (not the real world). Like electricity, magic is a neutral force that can be used for good or ill. Invocational magic is very different; it is a power gained through calling on a person or spiritual power and is the kind of magic we associate with the occult.

While discernment is always needed and magical worlds should not be taken lightly, this definition may help you in identifying healthy and harmful magic in the fantastical books you read. A more in-depth exploration of this subject can be found in Michael O'Brien's wise and compelling *A Landscape with Dragons* (see review on page 148).

Jonathan Strange and Mr. Norrell by Susanna Clarke

Imagine a slightly more grown-up Harry Potter, set in an alternate history of nineteenth-century England in which magicians are respected members of British society, consulted in matters ranging from the military to medicine. Add that it is written in imitation of an actual Victorian novel (complete with annotation and learned asides) whose prim order is invaded by the ancient presence of the Raven King, and you have one of my favorite recent fantasies. I've read this twice for the sheer delight of its world-crafting splendor, its capacity to evoke mystery, and its ability to re-enchant the world of the everyday, which is as magical as anything we could imagine.

The Pendragon Cycle by Stephen R. Lawhead

My brother Joel and I listened to the first book of this series, *Taliesin*, on a three-day road trip through the wintry American West, and even after driving twelve-hour days, we could have hopped back in the car for a few more hours of this riveting story. Drawing on the legends of the Welsh *Mabinogion* and the richness of Arthurian legend, Lawhead has crafted a cycle of tales that feel historical in their evocation of ancient Britain and their imagined accounts of Taliesin, the great bard and singer, and Arthur, the fabled king. But the series is also fantastical, beginning on the lost isle of Atlantis, a world in which the Christian faith is woven in beautifully with a rich historical vision of the ancient world.

The Chronicles of Narnia by C. S. Lewis

You'll find the work of C. S. Lewis scattered throughout every genre in this book. His hearty, intelligent, imaginative voice, with its capacity to make the deepest truths of Scripture plain to my hungry heart, has been a companion and mentor to me in every phase of my life. He's one of those authors I hope to read in entirety before I die (and there's a lot to read), but if you could read only one portion of his work, I'd argue for The Chronicles of Narnia. Yes, over his many learned works, I'd choose his stories for children, because in them, he uses the language not of reason but of vivid and holy imagination to tell us afresh the story of the world. You are probably familiar with the plot: of English children drawn through wardrobes or by magic rings into a fantastical world where animals talk and a White Witch rules in wintered cruelty. You've probably heard of Aslan, the great lion who isn't safe but is good.

What you might not know until you actually read the books (and the movies do not count!) is that in Narnia, from the instant Aslan sings the stars and talking beasts to life to the moment he dies at the hand of the White Witch to free Narnia from the curse that makes it "always winter and never Christmas," you as a reader, like the Pevensies, are being drawn into the presence of the great Lion of our own world. For as Aslan himself said to Lucy, "This was the very reason why you were brought to Narnia, that by knowing me here for a little, you may know me better there."

(Read Michael Ward's *Planet Narnia*, reviewed on page 149, to discover the larger literary and spiritual scheme shaping the creation of the Narnian world. And read Rowan Williams's *The Lion's World* for an exploration of the spiritual insights so richly to be found within the Narnia books.)

> Also by Lewis:
> - *Out of the Silent Planet*
> - *Perelandra*
> - *That Hideous Strength*

Lilith by George MacDonald

In all my reading, I have rarely encountered a writer who could use symbol, image, and fantastic narrative to evoke the spiritual world as powerfully as MacDonald. Nor have I read many authors who so deeply grasp the Father-heart and love of God. It was on reading MacDonald's *Phantastes* as a convinced young atheist that C. S. Lewis first encountered holiness. In that story of a young man's sojourn in fairyland, his yearning after an ideal lady, his discovery of his own "shadow," Lewis felt that his imagination was "baptized."[6] This is the quality so radiantly haunting all of MacDonald's fantastical works, a quality that comes to its fullest power, I think, in *Lilith*, one of MacDonald's final books.

In this story, loosely considered a companion to *Phantastes*, another young man named Mr. Vane finds his way into another strange world. There he meets the enigmatic Mr. Raven, whose appearance is half that of a tall, dark bird and half of a man wearing a coat with long tails. Mr. Raven, we find, is actually the biblical Adam, forgiven and redeemed, who with his radiant wife, Eve, has been given the keeping of a house where repentant souls come to sleep and to die, in order that they may wake to life indeed. Their daughter, Mara, the veiled and tender lady of sorrow, is the figure whose presence haunts this story. This story is ultimately MacDonald's exploration of sin and repentance, of the self-love that is a living death, and of the grief that comes like a fire to heal us. This is a strange book; I'll make no bones about that. The reader, with Mr. Vane, will encounter dancing skeletons, little people, stupid giants, and an evil princess who can transform herself into a leopard. But in this tale, there is also the holiness that so gripped the young Lewis, present not only in beauty but also in the ministry of sorrow. MacDonald wrote this in fevered creativity, convinced that it was more vision than idea, a gift of grace to his readers.

Also by MacDonald:
- *Phantastes*
- *At the Back of the North Wind*
- *The Princess and the Goblin*
- *David Elginbrod*

The Harry Potter Series by J. K. Rowling

I didn't read the Harry Potter series until I was an adult, living for a summer in a Catholic boarding house in Cambridge (it's a very long story). On the day the seventh book released, I walked down the Cambridge streets to see literally half of my fellow pedestrians carrying copies of the book, and when I stumbled into my lodging that night, I found the three resident nuns on the couch, each with a copy of her own. I decided right then and there that it was time I figured out what this Harry Potter madness was about. Thus, in the ivy-walled garden the next evening, I sat in the half-light and discovered (along with a whole generation) a series of novels centered on the redemptive power of love to defy death and overpower evil. This is the intricately imagined and adventurous story of the orphaned Harry, the "boy who lived," as he discovers his place in the wizarding world, his history as the child of parents who died in their fight against the evil Voldemort, and his own doom as the hero who must lead the fight in his own time. Accompanied by the bookish Hermione and the loyal (if clumsy) Ron; and guided by the wise, sparkling, and enigmatic headmaster, Dumbledore, Harry comes into his identity as the chosen one who must prevail over Voldemort, not by might, but by love.

Some Christian readers were alarmed at the magical element in Harry Potter in the early days of its publication, fearing that the use of spells and wands would interest children in witchcraft. But many people now recognize the books' profoundly Christian themes (consider *How Harry Cast His Spell* by John Granger), and Rowling herself has been frank about the "religious parallels" and Christian imagery of her books—stories that she wrote in part to process the death of her mother. I wrote part of my final project at Oxford on the theological aspects of this series because I think that one of its defining passages powerfully describes a love that can only be rooted in the image of Christ. It comes in the first book, *Harry Potter and the Philosopher's Stone*, when Harry is known in the wizarding community as the only known person to have survived the dreadful and forbidden "killing curse" moments after his mother died to protect him. The infant Harry survived, to everyone's astonishment, and it is Dumbledore who explains to Harry that it was his mother's sacrifice of her own life for her son that instantly left its mark. "To have been loved so deeply," Dumbledore explains, "will give us some protection forever."

The Lord of the Rings Trilogy by J. R. R. Tolkien

I had to include this series here just to remind you one more time that you simply must read these books. But since there is quite a long review already on pages 57–58, you should probably turn there to find out more.

The Book of the Dun Cow by Walter Wangerin Jr.

A fierce, strange tale, an animal epic set in a time before humans roamed the earth. A rooster named Chauntecleer is its hero, tasked with defending the animals in his care from the dreaded Cockatrice, the fell and terrible Wyrm. The troubadour rooster, "blessing" the day with his canonical crows, leading the animals in brave resistance, is the riveting center of a story that immerses us in questions surrounding evil, the Fall, and the battle of God against Satan. Wangerin is both a medievalist and a pastor, identities that marvelously inform this remarkable tale.

The Once and Future King by T. H. White

Oh, the wonder and wit of this enchanting tale! It begins in King Arthur's boyhood, when he was a sprite called Wart, immersed in an eccentric education by the temperamental Merlyn, yearning for greatness and not yet imagining his destiny as Britain's most famous king. Loosely based on the famous *Le Morte d'Arthur* by Sir Thomas Malory, this retelling of Arthurian legend is quirky and human, making the characters of legend come alive with wit and affection, the series suffused with Arthur's yearning for true knighthood.

Books about Imagination: Why You're Never Too Old for Narnia

(OR, WHY IMAGINATION IS WORTH FIGHTING FOR)

I ONCE TOOK five children under twelve on a walk. We rambled a bit wildly down a country road whose maples and oaks were on fire with autumn color in air so crisp and cold we had to keep moving lest we freeze. The road was quite narrow, and I quickly realized that when the occasional car appeared, I needed a means by which I could get all five (including the two boys, always a dozen yards ahead) off the pavement in an instant. The solution was obvious: we needed a touch of imagination. I gathered them round and told them a story that ended with this: What if we were brave captains of explorers' ships on the high sea, sailing in search of treasure and adventure, and the cars were pirates, come to plunder our gold? From that moment forth, I had only to yell "Pirates!" at the sight of a car, and all five would dive instantly off the road and into the forest on either side.

However effective that use of imagination was in preserving the health of those children, what I remember most vividly is what happened afterward. Our game suffused the whole of our walk, and we began to hunt for treasure. The littlest ones scavenged the brightest leaves off the ground and put them in my hands as if they were rubies; they seized acorns like compact jewels and walnuts like nuggets of gold. Meanwhile, the bigger children came back waving curious branches that looked like the staffs of kings or yelled their discovery of the moss that clung to the trees like emerald velvet. Very quickly we forgot we were pretending. The world opened itself to us, a realm of actual treasure and real adventure that we had the chance to uncover. I remember the joy I felt in seeing afresh the autumn world in its splendor, the quickened delight of the children as the earth came into their hands as a gift. My silly little story shifted our sight, and in that moment, we experienced what C. S. Lewis calls "a dipping in myth" (or imagination). "By putting bread, gold, horse, apple, or the very roads into a myth, we do not retreat from reality: we rediscover it."[7]

That's what works of imagination do for us every day. What we rediscover in reading them is the extraordinary nature of real life. What we reclaim is a view of the world as charged with meaning, as shot through with the truth, beauty, and wisdom that we were created to find. From the disenchantment of a materialistic or simply bored viewpoint, in which things like trees and babies, music and story have lost their power to amaze or shape us by their truth, we are startled back into a wondering engagement with reality in its fullness. Sometimes this comes to us as worship, a renewed capacity to perceive that creation isn't just matter or atoms but a gift crafted of love. Sometimes it comes to us as hope, a quickened ability to glimpse beauty and wholeness beyond our current moment of doubt.

Always, it comes to us with the power to show us the world "in a new and strange light"[8] that cleans away the grime of cynicism or boredom and invites us to treasure our existence as a gift. The authors that follow include many of my favorites—C. S. Lewis, J. R. R. Tolkien, Malcolm Guite—each of whom has argued for imagination as a "truth-bearing faculty,"[9] one we desperately need to cultivate in our busy, materialistic age, one that is crucial to our capacity for faith, for joy in existence, for hope.

Poetic Diction: A Study in Meaning by Owen Barfield

Barfield, close friend and interlocutor of C. S. Lewis, wrote this classic exploration of the way imaginative language (the kind we use in poetry or story) can help a reader to experience—actually experience—the world in a different way. With Lewis, he believed that the modern world needs to have its vision reenchanted from the dulling effects of materialism. In this book, he shows us how imaginative language specifically works to kindle and quicken both mind and vision.

Following Gandalf: Epic Battles and Moral Victory in The Lord of the Rings by Matthew Dickerson

An invigorating and revelatory exploration of Tolkien's work from a philosophical perspective. Dickerson's lively book makes clear that the runaway success of The Lord of the Rings has deep roots in the redemptive philosophy it communicates.

Ten Ways to Destroy the Imagination of Your Child by Anthony Esolen

Esolen is often grumpy and frequently repetitive in this slightly sarcastic but eloquent book on the ways we increasingly stunt childhood imagination. In the role of devil's advocate, Esolen exposes the danger of such modern trends as dismissing the skill of memorization, keeping children indoors, and denying the transcendent. But he also offers a vision of the opposite kind of life—of children exposed to beauty, allowed to wonder, steeped in ancient words—a recipe for restored imagination that is always available to those who would choose it.

Faith, Hope and Poetry: Theology and the Poetic Imagination by Malcolm Guite

Reading this book was a watershed moment in my life, the point at which I finally felt I understood historically why the status of imagination as "a truth-bearing faculty" has to be defended and must be reembraced. Tracing the history by which the language of imagination, story, and even parable was forced out by scientific precision, Guite advocates for a revival of imagination, specifically through poetry, and for the importance of the imagination to our faith. In eight themed chapters, he surveys the work of poets from Shakespeare to Heaney whose works of poetic imagination bear spiritual truth to the world in a powerful way.

On Stories: And Other Essays on Literature by C. S. Lewis

This themed collection of Lewis's essays on imaginative fiction brings together some of his best ideas about the power of atmosphere in story, the qualities that make for excellent storytelling, and the transcendent beauty evoked by works of imagination. It includes classics such as "On Three Ways of Writing for Children" and "Sometimes Fairy Stories May Say Best What's to Be Said," essays that articulate his understanding of imagination and story as some of the best ways we understand the ultimate truths about ourselves and the world.

The Renaissance of Wonder: The Fantasy Worlds of C. S. Lewis, J. R. R. Tolkien, George MacDonald, E. Nesbit, and Others by Marion Lochhead

A PhD thesis that turned into an exploration of the great fantastical books of the twentieth century, this book first looks in depth at the work of writers such as E. Nesbit, Tolkien, Lewis, and MacDonald before surveying the greatest fantastical works for children at the time of publication. I'm still trying to get to all the titles so beautifully described in this celebration of fantastical children's literature.

A Landscape with Dragons: The Battle for Your Child's Mind by Michael D. O'Brien

This is a book I recommend with caveats. On the one hand, I highly value O'Brien's perspective on the way fantasy and fairy tale shape a child's inward and spiritual realities. I prize his affirmation of good fantasy to aid a healthy development of courage and virtue, the qualities needed in a real-world resistance of evil. But I disagree with his conclusions deeming the work of J. K. Rowling and Madeleine L'Engle harmful. I think they are rather the opposite. So I would advise you to take this book with a grain of salt. It's excellent in many aspects and flawed in some, but eminently worth the read.

The Christian Imagination: The Practice of Faith in Literature and Writing by Leland Ryken

A collection exploring some of the best Christian writing on the joyous relationship between faith and literature, this volume of excellent essays could be themed in the words of Francis Schaeffer (quoted by Ryken): "The Christian is the one whose imagination should fly beyond the stars."

Tree and Leaf by J. R. R. Tolkien

Herein you will encounter Tolkien's eloquent defense of fantastical stories as vital to the human condition. In his landmark work "On Fairy-Stories," he identifies a threefold process through which fairy stories (and fables, myths, and fantastical tales) allow us fresh spiritual insight and a renewed interaction with reality through recovery, escape, and consolation. Here, too, you will find his description of "eucatastrophe," the "sudden and miraculous grace" that comes to us in a happy ending and "denies (in the face of much evidence, if you will) universal final defeat and in so far is evangelium, giving a fleeting glimpse of Joy, Joy beyond the walls of the world poignant as grief." One of my favorite quotes in literature.

Planet Narnia: The Seven Heavens in the Imagination of C. S. Lewis by Michael Ward

If you love Narnia, this book will rivet you from first page to last. Ward, called the world's foremost C. S. Lewis scholar by no one less than N. T. Wright, here makes his fascinating claim that the Chronicles of Narnia are each individually themed on a single planet in the medieval model of the cosmos. It seems a wild scheme at first glance, but Ward's painstaking and detailed research, his appeal to the (wholly provable) evidence of Lewis's lifelong fascination with the medieval model, and his demonstration of his thesis in a careful exploration of each book brought me to total agreement. But the reason this book is here is because Ward's claims are based in part on his understanding of how Lewis viewed imagination and how he sought to imbue his novels with the person of Christ, and the chapters exploring those themes are as vital in their way as the rest of the book.

Dostoevsky: Language, Faith, and Fiction by Rowan Williams

This is a dense and difficult book, the kind I wouldn't usually include on a nonacademic list, but it helped me to think with rigor about the power of language, image, and character as employed by Dostoevsky to evoke and explain religious faith. If you want to delve into a contemporary evaluation of the way literature presents us with what could be considered incarnational opportunities and characters—when the divine breaks into the ordinary—or what it means for people to be iconic in their nature—gesturing to a larger grace—Williams's book is well worth the struggle.

CHAPTER 7

Books Can Foster COMMUNITY

Forming Friendships through the Pages of Good Literature

There are no faster or firmer friendships than those formed between people who love the same books.

IRVING STONE, *CLARENCE DARROW FOR THE DEFENSE*

IT WAS THE SUMMER after I'd turned twenty, and I was perched on one of the creaky white rocking chairs on my family's front porch in Colorado with my "little" (both over six feet) brothers beside me. In true Clarkson tradition, we'd decided to read a novel aloud during our summer at home. But we felt a little trepidatious, the scuffles of siblinghood and competition lurking at the edges of anything we did, all complicated by the newly adult selves we had become. We felt slightly strange to each other, our emerging maturity, our growing dreams the secrets that sat on the edge of our tongues too new and dear to articulate, too strong in us for ease. But we settled in bravely, cups of hot chocolate in hand, as I began the perilous tale of *Peace Like a River*, a book whose pastoral title belies its drama of asthmatic boys and cowboy-poet little girls, of miracles and murder.

Day after day we returned, immersed in the story, comrades in the shared space of imagination. As we voiced the vivid characters, marveled at the word craft of the author, and laughed at the fierce loves and wild creativity of the little girl, Swede, we were set in a unique camaraderie of experience that loosened our tongues, revealing us to each other. We argued over the choices of the characters, debated the bold actions of Davy, and shared the quiet of a character's death. In those spaces we saw one another anew, discovered one another afresh, as compelling as any characters a novel ever offered. We recognized each other as unique as the book drew out our individual ideas, and yet we were connected together as the story pulled us into a shared language of experience, a shared understanding of what is right and good as imaged in the beauty of the novel's end. In the hush of the final word, the closed cover, with the first autumn leaves in their turn on the aspens around us, we knew ourselves woven together anew, bound as friends and siblings by the power of a shared story.

I discovered afresh in that moment that a woman who reads is a woman who relates. A book girl knows that a shared book is a ground of mutual discovery, a space in which the soul and thoughts of another may open to her in a wondrous way. Just as a week's stay with a friend can bring you closer than any number of coffee dates or run-ins, the sharing of a story accelerates the comradeship of souls. When people inhabit a realm of imagination or theology or poetry together, their own realms of soul and spirit are revealed to the others who sojourn with them in that place. Reading, when shared, begins a conversation that breaks down the barriers of isolation and connects us, one to another, as we exclaim, in C. S. Lewis's description of friendship in his book, *The Four Loves*, "What! You too?"[1]

I sometimes wonder if the stock image of a reader is of an introvert curled up in a curtained window seat. There is definitely truth (and, I'd argue, delight) in that image, but one of the strongest impressions that comes to me when I reflect on what reading has created in my life is the image of fellowship and the widened horizon of relationship. This was a reality I first knew in my own family. Our sibling summer of reading as young adults was a chosen return to a pattern we had learned in childhood. My parents read to us morning and night, we read novels before bedtime, we read devotions in the morning, and we read picture books or adventure tales in the afternoon. The culture of our home was shaped in large part by the stories we shared, and my parents saw this as one of the formative ways in which they created a ground for us to know each other not just as siblings but as friends.

That pattern of shared story and relationship is one whose power I have experienced throughout my adult life; it is one of the relational tools that my introverted self knows can always create space for friendship in whatever new place I sojourn. In my time at Oxford, I've watched as a poetry group started by my tutor turned a group of shy theology students into talkative friends who revealed astonishing things about their own lives in their comments on the luminous poetry we read aloud together. I've watched a group of disparate students—young professionals, singles, and couples, all dogged by the hurried loneliness of the academic or working life—coalesce as a community over a shared weekly meal and read-aloud surprise in our home, each member taking a turn to bring something to read to the group. And let's be honest, I knew that things with my husband-to-be might just work out when I saw books by Tolkien, C. S. Lewis, Peter Kreeft, and Chaim Potok on his bachelor shelves. We had been dating only two weeks when I got the chance to peek at his books. I knew it would be telling: student rooms in Oxford are so tiny, there's room for only a few absolute favorite or necessary titles—if, of course, you are the kind of person who loves your books enough to lug them with you all over the world. And what if Thomas wasn't? The door opened, and my eyes shot toward the shelves. There in splendid promise stood a fat volume of The Lord of the Rings, with a slim copy of Lewis wedged close by and a bevy of other familiar titles stacked beside them. I sighed in relief. He'd passed the test—on several levels. (And our two copies of The Lord of the Rings, one in Dutch and one in English, now have pride of place on our living room bookshelves.)

While reading is something you must choose as an individual,

Joy Clarkson

Beloved, built-in best friend–sister who also happens to be a brilliant student of art, literature, and virtue and a reader whose insights open all sorts of worlds to me every time we talk. We text each other quotes and borrow each other's books and revel together in the world of words. It's sheer delight to have such a sister and to list her favorites here.

Favorite Books: One Fiction, One Spiritual, and One Nonfiction

- *Peace like a River* by Leif Enger. This is a book that has stuck in my heart. Enger's writing is sumptuous and delightful. Interspersed throughout the books are moments of the miraculous tucked into ordinary life. Even as the characters walk through the darkest days of their lives, there is a playfulness and a humor, all aided by the fact that the story is told from the perspective of a child. With frankness, depth, and lightness, the book swims in themes of forgiveness, love, theodicy, exile, and the miraculous. I couldn't put my finger on exactly what it is that gripped me about this book, but perhaps you'll have to read it to know what I'm going on about.

- *Walking on Water* by Madeleine L'Engle. This book is full of wisdom for the artist, the Christian, and anyone who lives in both of those worlds. Reading it was both inspiring for me as a creative person and as a Christian pursuing depth in my relationship with God. It pushes readers toward a greater sense of meaning and excellence in our work, showing how the creative capacity isn't simply a rhetorical tool for conveying Christian messages but a reflection of God's image as a Creator-God in us. I highly recommend it for the Christian and the creative.

- *The Abolition of Man* and *The Weight of Glory* by C. S. Lewis. *The Abolition of Man* is a collection of Lewis's lectures concerning education, but it touches on many other topics as well. The main thrust of the argument is that a truly educated person is not only a receptacle of knowledge but someone whose loves and desires are oriented around the good; he or she wishes that we would love our neighbor, praise beauty, and disdain evil. According to Lewis, the educator's job is to "inculcate just sentiments." Written for a very different audience, *The Weight of Glory* is a suitable companion to *The Abolition of Man*. Originally a sermon preached in Oxford, it speaks about heaven as the foundation of all our desires and about how we will live best if we live with heaven in mind. Lewis somehow manages to make heaven conceivable and helps the reader see the world as charged with meaning and pointing to something beyond itself. Together these reads are intellectually enlightening and imaginatively stimulating.

it is also something that I hope will bring you, as a book girl, into rich community with others. This book is, itself, rooted in my own companionship with other readers, crafted by conversations, by quotes texted to me by my mom and my sister, by book lists sent by friends. My hope is that even as you begin the life of reading, you will find yourself brought into a new realm of relational possibility by the books you read and the conversations they open. Chapter 2 covers a little more about what it might look like to craft and cultivate that fellowship. At this point, though, we'll simply explore the two ways by which the sharing of books deepens our capacity to relate: through shared consciousness and deepened compassion.

One of the most fascinating things I've learned in the years that I've studied language is that words form the way we look at the world and each other. We almost literally *see* things differently from other people based on the language we have been given to describe the reality around us. Consider how powerfully language enters into modern debates on ethical issues such as personhood, death, or even what human life is—when it begins, what it's worth, how we ought to protect it. The words each side uses describe vastly different realities. Owen Barfield, a twentieth-century British philosopher whose thinking about language and consciousness influenced C. S. Lewis, writes in *Saving the Appearances* about the way we humans experience and know the world:

> I do not perceive any *thing* with my sense-organs alone,
> but with a great part of my whole human being. Thus,
> I may say, loosely, that I "hear a thrush singing." But in
> strict truth all that I ever merely "hear"—all that I ever hear
> simply by virtue of having ears—is *sound*. When I "hear a
> thrush singing," I am hearing, not with my ears alone, but
> with all sorts of other things like mental habits, memory,
> imagination, feeling and (to the extent at least that the act of
> attention involves it) will.[2]

Before you could hear a thrush sing, someone had to teach you what singing is and had to show you a certain bird and teach you its name and even had to tell you that you could use your will to stop and listen to the song of a bird because it is something beautiful. In each step in this marvelous progression, words play a central role in identifying and naming the experience of hearing a thrush sing. Every time we read, the words we encounter are teaching us what to pay attention to, how to perceive it, and what value to place upon it. Imagine, then, the power of reading in fellowship—the insight and the strength of conviction created when stories are shared, when friends have a common way to describe the world or a shared vocabulary to describe what is good, beautiful, and true.

Right before I began the writing of this book, I spent three years studying church history and doctrine, and one of the things that amazed me was the way the early church was formed by words. The Gospels and the Epistles were read aloud in the young churches, memorized by new believers, carried by hand from church to church as Christian doctrine and belief were formed. The letters of Paul, each one opening with a powerful reminder of his readers' identities as saints, or the Gospels, those central stories of Jesus that weave every believer into the same epic story, were the powerful words shared by the early church, read aloud and woven into a common language of faith. The early Christians drew such power from this shared vision that the gospel spread throughout the Roman world within decades.

Words make worlds, and when words are shared, communities, movements, and revolutions form around them.

But another aspect of shared reading is the way it teaches us to look beyond our own view of the world. Reading changes our consciousness on the most personal level by challenging us to consider the way someone else might experience life, and this is where compassion often begins. I was fascinated when I began the research for this book to discover that scientists now believe reading a novel can help a reader to expand what researchers call a person's "theory of mind" or, in simpler terms, a person's capacity to understand that other people think and feel differently.[3] Reading actually helps us to tune in to someone else's emotion or point of view, and the better the writing, the more insight we are given.

A recent series of studies looks at the different levels of empathy or emotional insight shown by people who were given different things to read.[4] Those who had been given nonfiction or genre fiction (plot-driven stories with little character development) and then asked to identify the emotional expressions on the faces of people in a series of photographs had little luck. But those who read literary fiction (character-driven stories that explore the inner worlds or thoughts of multiple characters, exposing the reader to different ways of seeing) scored significantly higher. What this suggested to the researchers is that reading allows us to place ourselves in another's shoes, seeing the world through another's eyes, empathizing with views different from our own.

Further, when scientists looked at brain activity during such reading, they found that they could actually see imaginative empathy from a neural or biological point of view. In a study that looks at the way a novel impacts the brain and lingers in the mind, researchers found that when people read a description of action in a good book, the part of their brain that receives language was still active and awake long after they had finished their reading. The reading seemed to signal the part of the brain that processes motion. Just as thinking about walking can actually stimulate your brain and muscles to remember the feeling of walking, reading a book stimulated the brains of readers in such a way as to suggest they were imaginatively "feeling" the story as something real.

Imagine the power that gives us to feel the pain of another, to understand someone else's struggle, stubbornness, or need. The kind of compassionate insight offered by a perceptive story is one that drives us toward connection. We are given the insight both to understand and to reach across the barriers of confusion or suspicion that so often separate us from the people we might come to know as friends, or even those who stand in need of our offered presence.

The memory that sprang to mind when I read this research was of two little girls, myself and my soon-to-be best friend, Katrina, sitting silent, stubborn, and shy in the back seat of a car on a hot summer's drive twenty years ago. Our mothers were friends and had determined that we should be too, but for some reason now beyond recall, we didn't feel like complying. We had an hour's weekly drive to a shared lesson, and for the first few weeks we sat side by side without talking, convinced of the other's hostility. Until Katrina brought a book. One week she opened a novel and began to read. I tried so hard not to look, but curiosity and boredom made me steal a glance, then a longer look, until I was surreptitiously reading whole pages over her shoulder. When she finally caught me, we both blushed and stared. And then she moved the book a little in my direction. I took the page in hand. I can't remember how many more hours it took before one of us made a comment about a character, but once that conversation began, a friendship was born. It lasts, threaded by other books we love, hundreds of handwritten letters, and more than twenty years, to this day.

I've found this kind of book-bred empathy to be powerful as an adult, too, particularly in the realm of my faith, as I've wrestled with theological ideas—and people—I disagree with. To think about theology at all is to enter a debate that's been going on since the Garden of Eden, and from the moment I arrived in Oxford and delved into doctrine, I was surprised to find how quickly the battle lines of opinion and belief got drawn between the students in my first-year doctrine class, myself included. There we were, a group of passionate people who were in that place precisely because of our shared commitment to the core tenets of the Christian faith. Yet there we were also, week by week, increasingly divided by our different understandings of what Scripture *really* said, what grace *really* looked like in action. I found that one student in particular said the opposite of what I thought every time he spoke. He hit all my sore points, embracing the very aspects of God that I found threatening. I found that even as I grew quickly friendly with the larger group, I avoided him and his "lot" (as they say in England). The fact that grace (that oh-so-important topic) was quickly draining from our larger interactions as a class, or even that our reactions with each other often reached to the roots of our own backstories of struggle and belief, was lost in the heat of opinion that burgeoned that first year . . . until one of the tutors started a weekly reading group for our class.

Two particular points made the optional class unique. First, we gathered to discuss an excerpt from a classic book that all of us had already read, so we began from the common ground of the author's time-proven thought. Second, there was space for real discussion, as it rose from the words we read in company for the work of questioning and listening, which is so different from the defensive quickness of debate. I was amazed at how quickly understanding, insight, and respect bloomed within the circle of those early morning classes as our common reading became a way of reaching toward each other. As we read the quotes we loved and argued about the passages we didn't, we began to ask each other "Why?" *Why* do you love that line? Because that's the one I hate. *Why* do you think about grace in that way? *Why* do you think this aspect of judgment is so important?

Slowly but surely, we entered into the way the other saw the world, allowing us both to understand how different people had come to their beliefs and also to inhabit a different way of viewing God. The fact that the one student who drove me nuts was also the quickest to be frank, to admit fault, to ask the direct question forced me to a begrudged respect that became deep and genuine as I encountered his stark, unquestioning belief, his uncompromising faithfulness to hold himself accountable to Scripture—a way of believing very different from my own wrestle and dance of faith, often marked by questions and shaped by my love of paradox. Our reading became a way of reaching out to the other, beginning the journey toward understanding, which is the work, I think, of love, of the God who acts unceasingly to renew our communion with himself and each other.

The fact that love uses books to do that is a wonder . . . and our gift.

May the books you encounter in this chapter startle you with just that kind of unexpected reconnection, that startled friendship. May you, bookish girl, in whatever circle you find yourself—that of new friendship, of difficult siblinghood, of opposing faith, of marriage, or of a strange new home, find yourself able to connect through the relational power of words, by the possibility of love and friendship that always opens when a good book is shared.

The Books We Shared:
My Family's Favorite Read-Alouds
(OR, BOOKS TO KNIT HEARTS TOGETHER IN FRIENDSHIP)

Ask me for a single memory or image that captures my family culture growing up, and I will no doubt describe a moment of reading aloud (or eating—my family is very talented at feasting, but that's another story). My core family image is of us siblings curled in various corners of the couch (or sprawled on the floor with Legos, if you were my brothers), dusk out the window, hot chocolate very possibly in hand, as one of my parents read aloud from our latest novel. This scene could shift in countless small ways—set on the porch on a warm afternoon, in a local café, or with all of us crammed in the car for a road trip, peaceful for just as long as the riveting audiobook played. What is core is the stories we shared, the worlds in which we were immersed together by the enchanted habit of reading aloud.

The books on this list are the ones we still remember, the stories whose imagery and characters, quotes and quips slip into our conversations to this day. We might describe someone as "brave as Bilbo" or tease each other by mimicking the cool, suave disapproval of the ever-proper butler Jeeves. They are the kinds of books whose characters seem to leap off the pages, with voices that beg for dramatic interpretation even by the introverts (it's no accident that my brother Joel now reads professionally for audiobook companies), with plots that keep even the extroverts in expectant hush (we are evenly split in this personality department), and with twists and turns that sate our never-ending hunger for the next adventurous tale.

In sharing these books with you here, I hope the delight continues.

The Man Who Was Thursday: A Nightmare by G. K. Chesterton

I read this in high school with a merry and opinionated bunch of siblings and friends. Half of us thought it was Chesterton's unofficial masterpiece; the others thought he must have been high on something wild when he wrote it. The plot sounds ludicrous: a policeman tasked with exposing a group of anarchists in Victorian London decides to impersonate one himself in order to probe the depths of the anarchist's inner circle, headed by an enigmatic leader called by the code name Sunday. It's a wild tale of topsy-turvy pursuit, disguises, double identities, and bewilderment, but it's also a symbolic romp, I contend—Chesterton's bid to help us embrace the wild goodness and bewildering nature of faith in a fallen world. I can't say much more without giving the story away, but the key line in the book for me is this one, spoken by the hero Gabriel Syme:

> "Then, and again and always," went on Syme like a man
> talking to himself, "that has been for me the mystery of
> Sunday, and it is also the mystery of the world. When I see the
> horrible back, I am sure the noble face is but a mask. When I

see the face but for an instant, I know the back is only a jest. Bad is so bad, that we cannot but think good an accident; good is so good, that we feel certain that evil could be explained. . . .

"Shall I tell you the secret of the whole world? It is that we have only known the back of the world. If we could only get round in front . . ."

Also by Chesterton:
- *The Napoleon of Notting Hill*
- The Father Brown Mysteries

The Dark Is Rising Series by Susan Cooper

Drawing deeply on Arthurian legend, this is the tale of Will Stanton, the "seventh son of a seventh son" who discovers that he is one of the "old ones," servants of the Light, tasked with protecting the world from the forces of the Dark. Set amid the history and beauty of Wales, with an intricate plot and characters of real depth, this story captivated my whole family as we listened to it aloud on a long road trip.

(Caveat: the underlying symbolism of Light and Dark in this series is more dualistic than Christian. I include the books because I think them to be a riveting depiction of good fighting against evil and of personal courage, and a rich immersion in the Celtic, Norse, and Arthurian myths shaping British culture. And it's just plain fantastic reading.)

Peace Like a River by Leif Enger

I have read this book twice aloud and once on my own, and wasn't bored once. Neither were my brothers (the first group to hear it aloud), nor the hardworking gap-year students I mentored to whom I read it aloud in the evenings. Considering they had between four and six hours of lectures or reading a day, it's a wonder they wanted another hour, but this novel is the sort that rivets its readers: a tale of murder and miracles, of love as inexorable as death, and characters quirky and brave and laugh-aloud funny. It's the tale of Jeremiah Land, a South Dakotan janitor who speaks with God; of Davy, the teenage son with justice gnawing at his heart; of Swede, little sister and cowboy poet; and Reuben, the asthmatic boyish narrator who feels he was kept in the world to bear witness to it all. The word craft of this book is superb, the wry observations of various humanity some of the best I've read. Its capacity to communicate an almost Old Testamental sense of awe before the Almighty is a wonder. I can't wait to read this aloud, yet again, to my future children and let them come to the paradoxical gleam of its final passage:

> I breathe deeply, and certainty enters into me like light, like
> a piece of science, and curious music seems to hum inside
> my fingers.
>> Is there a single person on whom I can press belief?
>> No sir.
>> All I can do is say, Here's how it went. Here's what I saw.
>> I've been there and am going back.
>> Make of it what you will.

Oliver Twist by Charles Dickens

My siblings and I listened to this classic tale on tape (no, really, it was tape in those days) during a period of our lives that required frequent long drives to piano lessons and Awana evenings through the rural back roads of Texas. We lived with my grandmother in Texas Hill Country, forty-five minutes from the nearest decent grocery store, and regularly had to pile in the car—four children under the age of twelve—for *another* half hour of driving. We were shockingly eager for this time in the car because it meant we could find out a bit more of what had befallen Oliver, the pitiable young orphan cast on the mercy of cruel orphanage keepers and the terrifying Bill Sikes. When Oliver escaped, would he follow the Artful Dodger in a career of pickpocketry, or would he maintain his innocence even at the sly hands of the con man Fagin? Dickens is at his famed best in this tale of intertwined lives, the dark side of London, and unexpected grace.

The Big Fisherman by Lloyd C. Douglas

This was one of our epic reads, a book I read aloud to my siblings that took a good few months. We stuck with it, though, for the vivid way in which it brought the historical era of Jesus' coming and ministry to life. By weaving the tale of Fara, a young Arabian girl set on revenge, with that of Peter, the new disciple of Jesus and the "big fisherman" of the title, this story immersed us in the color and tension of Jesus' world, helping us to imagine what it might have been like to encounter the startling man who called himself God's Son.

Cheaper by the Dozen by Frank B. Gilbreth Jr. and Ernestine Gilbreth Carey

I don't know how many times we listened to this book when I was growing up, but I added to the count by sharing it with my husband on our first American road trip together. It is a dear, laugh-out-loud funny, historical, and heartwarming tale of a family with, yes, a dozen children. Set in the years around World War I, this hysterical memoir recounts the escapades of a family headed by a father who happened to be a motion-study expert and was intent upon applying those systems to the raising of his own brood. (If you want to listen to this as an audiobook, be sure to get the version read by Dana Ivey.)

The Complete James Herriot: All Creatures Great and Small by James Herriot

My family had an hour dedicated to high tea and read-alouds every Sunday afternoon, and Herriot's charming accounts of life as a Yorkshire country vet were often requested. Stories both tender and funny, they evoke English country life with soul-warming insight into the workings of the human (and country) heart.

A Wrinkle in Time by Madeleine L'Engle

A children's book, a fairy tale, and a symbolic science-fiction romp through space and time—L'Engle's beloved novel could be classified as all of these. It opens with the classic mystery line "It was a dark and stormy night," amid whose bluster we are swiftly introduced to Meg, myopic, stubborn, and fiercely protective of her gifted little brother, Charles Wallace, and her brilliant scientist mother. Meg's father, a respected scientist, has been missing for a year, and that night she is summoned to an intergalactic search for him by the midnight visit of the mysterious Mrs. Whatsit, who blusters clumsily into the Murray kitchen, demanding, "Have you ever tried to get to your feet with a sprained dignity?" Thus begins a quest, in the company of the marvelous threesome Mrs. Who, Mrs. Which, and Mrs. Whatsit, to rescue Mr. Murray, who is imprisoned on a distant planet by the evil power of It. In her whirlwind story, L'Engle immerses Meg and us in both the glory of the universe and the evil that must be combated and resisted, not just by strength but by holy foolishness, by the death-defying, beauty-making power of love as enacted even amid Meg's faults and fallibility.

The Giver by Lois Lowry

This perceptive and challenging dystopian novel for young adults was a fascinating read-aloud for my family. We kids were mostly teenagers by the time we encountered this provocative tale of a society in which pain and strife had been eliminated . . . as had most of what we would consider necessary for a rich life: emotion, memory, pain, and joy. But Jonas, a young boy ready for the assignment of his societal role, soon discovers these basic aspects of humanity when he is appointed as the next "Giver," the single person in a generation who is given the task of remembering pain, beauty, love, and fear, receiving and bearing these difficult emotions on behalf of the community. A fascinating exploration of what it means to be human.

Rainbow Valley by L. M. Montgomery

This is the seventh book in the Anne of Green Gables series (reviewed on page 54), and while I have read them all countless times, this was the one we siblings read aloud and loved—boys and girls alike. A story weaving together the adventures of Anne's own lively brood of six with that of the motherless Merediths, children of the local Presbyterian minister, the tale is full of Montgomery's usual flair for recounting the comical mishaps of village life as they tangle with the high drama of childhood imagination. But there is also romance, as the Meredith children seek a new mother, and the forging of bonds between the Blythes and the Merediths that will last through the Great War hovering on the horizon of their childhood.

The Heaventree Trilogy by Edith Pargeter

When my friend Ruth recommends a book, I generally order it whenever I next have space in my reading list. She was right about this one; this superb historical novel, set in the contested Welsh borderlands of the thirteenth century, traces the fate of the young and loving Harry Talvace, an architect of loyal heart and high ideals. Contracted to the powerful and difficult Lord Isambard to build a cathedral on his land in the Welsh borders, Harry finds himself entangled in the intrigues of politics, unrequited love, and the dictates of his own tender conscience. This is one of those stories that just feels like a pleasure to read with others, the kind that makes you forget the passing of time. There's worth here, of course; I love Harry's vision in creating his cathedral, the care with which he brings stone to such life that it echoes with the life of God. I love his loyalty to the peasant boy he claims as his brother. I even love his frailty, the sensitive heart that leaves him so vulnerable to the powerful and cruel. But there's also the pleasure of a rollicking good story of lyrical narration, lively characters, and a powerful evocation of the danger and beauty suffusing the medieval world.

Just David by Eleanor H. Porter

By the famed author of *Pollyanna*, *Just David* is the story of a young boy, newly orphaned, whose gift of music and guileless heart combine to startle a whole town to new life. A lovely, idealistic novel that combines mystery (who *is* David, who was his mysterious father, and why have they lived in solitude in the mountains?) with the tale of the grieving older couple who takes him in, *Just David* is steeped in innocence and beauty, and their power to restore.

Kidnapped: Being Memoirs of the Adventures of David Balfour in the Year 1751 by Robert Louis Stevenson

A daring tale of high adventure and a kidnapped young boy who wends his way through the Scottish Highlands, this classic novel was the first I read aloud as a teenager to all my siblings . . . and the one my brothers never balked at reading. We were riveted by Davy's plight at the hands of a mercenary old uncle and his journey to reclaim his lost inheritance.

The Hobbit by J. R. R. Tolkien

You knew I couldn't let this list go without at least one title by Lewis or Tolkien. This is the shorter and homier novel that opens the future adventures recounted in The Lord of the Rings. Bilbo Baggins was the first hobbit to go on a grand journey, a timid soul chosen as the "burglar" to aid a band of dwarves in defeating a dragon and reclaiming their gold. This novel subtly probes themes of courage, greed, and fellowship, stirring our own hearts with a little of Bilbo's feeling as we read that "something Tookish woke up inside him, and he wished to go and see the great mountains, and hear the pine-trees and the waterfalls, and explore the caves, and wear a sword instead of a walking-stick."

Right Ho, Jeeves! by P. G. Wodehouse

My brothers will still sometimes slip into the nasally, posh accent of the upright butler Jeeves when they have something particularly hysterical to say. There's nothing quite like Wodehouse for a certain kind of British narrative humor and nothing like the escapades of Bertie, a foppish young gentleman of the twenties who must be continually rescued by the long-suffering but often self-righteous Jeeves. We listened and laughed to this audiobook on many a road trip throughout my teen years.

"What! You Too?": The Firsthand Accounts That Remind Me I'm Not Alone
(OR, MEMOIRS THAT FEEL LIKE FRIENDS)

I'VE ALWAYS LOVED that C. S. Lewis was the one who described friendship as being born the moment at which two people say to one another, "What! You too? I thought that no one but myself . . ."[5] because he was the author who provided that sense of camaraderie for me. When I first read his description of joy—the feeling of delight and desire that welled up for him in the reading of old stories, in looking into the tiny world of a child's garden, in glimpsing the far-off hills—I felt as if someone had looked into my mind to give words to the wonder and yearning I could not, in my teenage angst, express. Lewis was fundamental in teaching me to understand my own flashes of joy—in music, in story, in glimpsing the landscape out the window on a long road trip—not as distractions from spiritual growth but as glimpses of God's expressive goodness, meant always to draw me deeper into his reality.

Memoirs are a special genre. They are gifts of particular and personal generosity in which an author allows a reader to inhabit his or her own memory, that journey of image and imagination by which we arrive at the truths that shape the way we live. Biographies recount the outward facts of a life; memoirs tell the story from the inside. What I have realized is how often the following books have offered shelter to me as I am forming my own tale. By dwelling in Madeleine L'Engle's Crosswicks Journals, I have managed to keep hold of God's goodness when discouragement might have made me lose my grip. The refuge of Buechner's *The Sacred Journey* helped me to discover afresh that grace is present even in the moments when we come face-to-face with our own mortality. Lewis helped me to translate beauty into God's own invitation. One of Andrew Peterson's songs ("Shine Your Light on Me") recounts the way his friends once were "singing out my song / when the song in me had died," and I often feel that this is the grace of memoirs. They sing and speak what needs expression, and sometimes rescuing, within us.

As you travel through the titles below, may you, too, find strength for the story forming in your soul as you dwell in the narratives of those who have traveled before.

The Sacred Journey: A Memoir of Early Days by Frederick Buechner

In this account of a moment in his childhood that shifted his experience of time, Buechner delves into the heart of what it means to discover our own mortality, to realize that we are under the power of time, with the clock ticking toward death. That might sound dark, but this is a luminous book, recounting a child's innocence and the way grace restores the trust that our first encounter with death strives so hard to take from us.

The Supper of the Lamb: A Culinary Reflection by Robert Farrar Capon

This book is a revelry in the "taste and see" goodness of God by a talented chef and Episcopalian priest who finds grace in the midst and making of feasts. I first heard it read aloud as a contemplation before a feast at a conference celebrating creativity, fellowship, and creation. Most of us were teary before dinner began. A delicious book replete with recipes, it is a joyous, immersive experience exploring the hunger of our souls and the rich satisfaction found in the person of Christ and the supper of the Lamb.

Pilgrim at Tinker Creek by Annie Dillard

Part nature memoir, part meditation on the beauty and violence of the natural world, part theological discussion, part lyrical essay, this memoir considers the profound beauty of the world and its fallenness as glimpsed in the quiet of the solitary year Dillard spent in a rustic cabin. Wry and poignant, humorous and wise, with insights like this to startle you awake: "The world is wilder than that in all directions, more dangerous and bitter, more extravagant and bright. We are making hay when we should be making whoopee; we are raising tomatoes when we should be raising Cain, or Lazarus."

The Crosswicks Journals by Madeleine L'Engle

You've seen L'Engle in my lists a couple of times before, but this time it is for her Crosswicks Journals, her contemplation of her life in different phases: as a wife, as a daughter, as a mother. Drawing on childhood memory, theology, and literature, L'Engle's musings always lead readers to a deeper engagement with the beauty of the world and the people who so richly make its story. She asks hard questions, and she makes honest observations about herself, her husband, and her children, but she writes in such a way that the asking is a way of walking forward in hope, in seeking beauty. These books also inspired me to follow L'Engle's example of keeping a dictionary next to the dining room table—you never know when a certain word will come up in family debate! In this series:

- *A Circle of Quiet*
- *The Summer of the Great-Grandmother*
- *The Irrational Season*
- *Two-Part Invention: The Story of a Marriage*

Surprised by Joy: The Shape of My Early Life by C. S. Lewis

It might begin to seem that I'm trying to fit Lewis into every book list in this book, and that might just reflect the scope of his insight and influence on me! This autobiography is the account of Lewis's conversion from atheism to Christianity, but it is much more than simple testimony. This is Lewis's exploration of joy—the feeling that for him evoked "an unsatisfied desire which is itself more desirable than any other satisfaction." The sense was kindled in him by mythic stories, by the beauty of nature, by moments in his childhood, and by a longing so poignant he eventually came to believe that "if I find in myself a desire which no experience in this world can satisfy, the most probable explanation is that I was made for another world."[6]

The Old Ways: A Journey on Foot by Robert Macfarlane

I found this memoir on a book table of a rambling bookstore in England. Macfarlane's account of his journeys on foot, this book is part poem, part natural history, part history, part contemplation on the pilgrim nature of human existence, written in the contemplative, watchful voice of a writer who lives in profound and affectionate attention to the world around him. I'd read any of Macfarlane's books for pure education and literary pleasure.

Also by Macfarlane:
- *Mountains of the Mind: Adventures in Reaching the Summit*
- *The Wild Places*
- *The Lost Words*

Blue Like Jazz by Donald Miller

A postmodern memoir of faith; traced through the shifting lens of art, music, and culture; a book whose honest doubts and open pursuit of God give voice to the spiritual hunger and pilgrim identity of many young believers. This memoir, tracing the slow growth of faith, is funny ("I always thought the Bible was more of a salad thing, you know, but it isn't. It's a chocolate thing"), honest ("the most difficult lie I have ever contended with is this: Life is a story about me"), and poignant in recounting Miller's acceptance of a God who, like jazz, doesn't always resolve.

The Cloister Walk by Kathleen Norris

Norris's memoir about a season spent in a Benedictine monastery, "immersed in a liturgical world" that sated a deep hunger in her soul, this is a beautiful, poetic exploration of the life of liturgy, ritual, contemplation, and prayer. It gave shape and articulation to my own deep desire for a sense of meaning and rhythm in the life of faith.

Also by Norris:
- *Amazing Grace: A Vocabulary of Faith*
- *The Quotidian Mysteries: Laundry, Liturgy, and "Women's Work"*

CHAPTER 8

Books Can Open Your Eyes to WONDER

Unlocking the Beauty All around Us

In a world where thrushes sing and willow trees are golden in the spring, boredom should have been included among the seven deadly sins.

ELIZABETH GOUDGE, *THE ROSEMARY TREE*

THE SUMMER I WAS TEN, I stalked through my backyard, intent upon naming the trees, the rocks, the nooks and corners of my world. I had a battered copy of *Anne of Green Gables* in my hand, as it was this red-haired sprite of a story-world friend who had inspired me to such action. Anne sees a "lake of shining waters" in a duck pond and a "white way of delight" in an apple orchard, and after a summer morning immersed in her story, my own sight seemed to shimmer with her imagination. I suddenly perceived the vivid personhood of the world around me—grandfather trees and playful flowers, the tiny world of my backyard made suddenly rich with the mystery of a creation that came to me like the presence of a friend. In trying to describe my own world in Anne's imaginative terms, I began to see it differently. The world began to mean something in its beauty. I touched a pine tree, and the bark became toughened skin on a wise old soul. And the light—what should I call it? It was like my mother's hand on my face.

To be a woman who reads is to be a woman who wonders.

Words liven us to the vast, vivid, bustling world around us, kindling us to see sky and tree, child and friend afresh as gift, as mystery. Anne's engagement with the world taught me to encounter the stuff of life not as a collection of atoms or something to be taken for granted but as real treasure, a gift I was made to ponder and love. Little did I know while reading *Anne of Green Gables* that twenty years later in college I'd read Alexander Schmemann's *For the Life of the World* and realize that embracing Anne's wondering view of creation allowed me a glimpse of the sacramental life—a belief that, as Elizabeth Barrett Browning puts it, "earth's crammed with heaven, / And every common bush afire with God." A woman who reads sees the fire and stops to stare in wonder.

One of the great gifts of reading comes to us in the renewed vision of strong, good words. Language, as philosophers continue to learn, has the power to shift our consciousness, to make us freshly aware of the world, to enable us to see things we just didn't notice before. Owen Barfield, philosopher and friend of C. S. Lewis, writes particularly of the way imaginative words in a work of poetry or fiction have the power to give us a "felt change of consciousness."[1] When we read a well-crafted novel, encounter a startling combination of words in poetry, or read a psalm praising the Creator for his creation, we encounter not just beautiful or descriptive language but a fresh view of the world. The words we use on a daily basis teach us to see the physical world in a certain way. The way we (and the books we read) describe our homes, our families, and the stuff of ordinary life actually teaches us to value and understand it. A scientist shows us how to look out the backyard window and describe a magnificent old oak tree as a *Quercus* (Latin name), while the songwriter and poet Rich Mullins speaks of an oak in spring (in his song "The Color Green") as a creature who "lifts up his arms in a blessing for being born again." And then there's Tolkien, who turned trees into people and called them Ents.

In reading descriptions like these, we look along a writer's words into his or her view of the world so that sometimes what is familiar to us becomes wondrously strange. L. M. Montgomery, the author of the Anne books, once wrote that "it has always seemed to me, ever since early childhood, that, amid all the commonplaces of life, I was very near to a kingdom of ideal beauty."[2] She took that sense and wove it into her description of Anne's world so that her readers could look through her words and see not just an apple tree in blossom or the sun glinting off a pond but a living mystery, something whose beauty could reawaken a reader to the presence of love at the back of the universe. To see in such a way is to wonder, and to wonder is to have a mind and eyes awake and engaged with the world in its mystery and splendor.

We need our vision rekindled by writers like Lucy Maud or C. S. Lewis or Elizabeth Goudge (whose books are, I think, the slightly more grown-up and very English older sisters of the Anne series), people who looked at the world and understood that it has something to tell us about ultimate reality. We need words to reenchant the world, partly because we have inherited a disenchanted way of seeing. We live in a culture shaped by materialism, by the belief that the physical world has no spiritual meaning and can be entirely explained by the language of science. Even if we believe that God is the creator of the cosmos, we tend more and more to describe it in terms of atoms and inches and measurements rather than in the language of mystery. Like Eustace in *The Voyage of the Dawn Treader*, the character who embodies what C. S. Lewis considered the worst habits of the modern world, we could easily describe a star just as "a huge ball of flaming gas."

Like Eustace, we need the sparkle-eyed correction of the much wiser Koriakin, who quickly replies, "That is not what a star is but only what it is made of."

An encounter with someone like Koriakin in a story or a reading of Psalm 19, with its claim that the heavens actually "declare the glory of God" (verse 1), or the discovery of a few lines of Gerard Manley Hopkins's poem with its enthusiastic burst—"Look at the stars! look, look up at the skies! / O look at all the fire-folk sitting in

Ruth Moon Mari

Ruth is the friend I turn to for poetry, the reader whose insight and good taste are a source of constant enrichment in my reading life. She's also a dear, kindred-spirited friend whose list of poems I'm delighted to include here.

Poems I Love

- **"There Are Birds Here"** by Jamaal May. I love this poem for the way it captures the feeling of frustration when people refuse to acknowledge the real complexity, including beauty, that is present even in tragic or sad or depressing situations. It reminds me of Chimamanda Adichie's TED talk on the danger of a single story (which I also love but is not poetry).

- **"Disgraceland"** by Mary Karr. A real-feeling poem about how someone stumbles across faith.

- **"Fairy-tale Logic"** by A. E. Stallings. I like the imagery and how the twist at the end links the Christian faith with a fairy tale—it gives me a fresh perspective on the reality of how weird and marvelous our faith tradition is.

- **"Thanks"** by W. S. Merwin. This poem captures for me the feeling of holding in tension the world's brokenness and beauty, and seeking to be thankful for the beautiful while not ignoring the terrible.

- **"Patience"** by Kay Ryan. I like the revelation of this poem—"Who would have guessed it is possible that waiting is sustainable"—and that there are so many lessons to be found there.

- **"Hopeful Angel"** by Keith Ratzlaff. I like this for the artistic element (it's an ekphrastic poem based on a fairly abstract drawing/painting set by Paul Klee) and the embodiment of imperfection—trying hard, not quite getting it right, and trying again.

- Two poets I like in general are Christian Wiman and Robert Bringhurst.

the air!"—heals our dulled eyes and brightens them to perceive that our world is a realm of startling and daily wonder. We look afresh on stars and trees, on the stuff of home and garden, and even on the ordinary people who bother and bug us every day as beings of mystery, whose freedom and beauty speak to us of the Creator whose image they bear. For as C. S. Lewis wrote in his splendid sermon "The Weight of Glory," "The dullest, most uninteresting person you can talk to may one day be a creature which, if you saw it now, you would be strongly tempted to worship, or else a horror and a corruption such as you now meet, if at all, only in a nightmare."

We also need good, strong words to liven our wonder because, let's be honest, we're just a bit too busy and distracted to notice the gift that existence really is. We live in an age of screens that blink and beep at us unceasingly. We live increasingly in the patterns of an online world that never sleeps. We live with so many distractions—so many things to buy, so many places to go—that we barely have time to sleep, let alone stop long enough to recognize that the smallest moments of the everyday are rich in beauty, steeped in God's creative presence.

We need to have our attention restored, that holy capacity to be fully present to the moment in which we find ourselves. We need to be summoned back from the many tasks we have yet to do, the endless scroll of the online world, the frantic pace that nips at our heels like a pesky dog. We need to be halted in our frenzied steps and called back to *this* moment in its possibility, to *this* day in its shifting seasonal beauty, to *this* person, irreplaceably precious. The written word, the great works of literature and essay—if we will only engage them for a few moments—have the power to arrest us in this way, to demand our attention, to set us back down in the present with a quieter mind and more attentive eyes.

I learned this afresh at Christmas during the final six months of my three-year degree. My first year in Oxford I had walked the streets in a daze of grateful exultation. There I was, a student at glorious old Oxford, a university I had dreamed of attending all my life. I wandered old English gardens, walking with the pleasant ghosts of Lewis and Tolkien, following them in the long study hours of discovery that brought me to the kind of understanding that was deepening my faith and widening my grasp of grace. But somewhere along the way, the study load, then a part-time job, then the wondrous (but exhausting) business of falling in love and planning a wedding, then the ceiling in our newlywed house falling in, then the back-to-work busyness of the fall shifted me out of that sense of blessedness. There was still so much to enjoy and enjoy to the full—a marriage sweeter than I could have imagined, a new cottage (with a garden!), life in a cobblestoned corner of Oxford—but there was so much work to be done, so little time in which to do it, and so much that exhausted me that I walked my glorious Oxford streets with downcast eyes and a harried heart.

Until I encountered a poem. A radiant poem by a poet who struggled throughout her life with a depression that voided her world of beauty but who managed, in rare, sweet moments, to come to attention, and thus to wonder. Through her hard-fought words, she called me back to attention and to gratefulness, too. I read the poem with a group of women at my college. We had started an Advent poetry group that met once a week for a bit of reading and discussion, our attempt toward creativity and quiet in the midst of our harried lives. We savored that poem, reading Sylvia Plath's words with thought and care, and as we did, these verses leaped out to grip my mind, describing the way that light can fall, briefly, on a

> . . . *kitchen table or chair*
> *As if a celestial burning took*
> *Possession of the most obtuse objects now and then—*
> *Thus hallowing an interval*
> *Otherwise inconsequent*[3]

I left our discussion with the sudden feeling that Plath's "incandescent" light suddenly burned in my own eyes; I looked upon the "inconsequential" elements of my own existence in a newly awakened way. I felt as if I had somehow been living in a tired, dark place in my mind, far away from the actual presence of my ordinary moments. That poem summoned me to attention. I saw my cottage, my husband, my own intense work, the women round me at the table in the light of that "celestial burning." How precious, how precious the tiniest moments of this life in its love and creativity, its ordinary splendor of home-cooked meals and the growing partnership of new marriage. How precious those moments spent in the study that would shape the rest of my life. How precious my very walk home, under leaves whose gold was a fire on the dark branches of the trees, a flicker of flame in the rainy air.

Through that poem, my attention was restored, and with it, my thanks. I realized that day that gratitude is in large part the shift of conscious attention that helps me to see miracles in their tiny glory all about me, and then to praise. My Advent season was spent in a much calmer state because in the words of that poem, my sight had been "set . . . on fire" (Plath again). In the rainy weather; in the frequent text fests with my precious, scattered family; in the arms of my husband; and in the work of my last papers, I was able to take joy in the present moment, attentive to the wonder of my own life in its ordinary grace.

What I recovered through that poem was wonder.

J. R. R. Tolkien once wrote that the reading of a fairy tale allows us a "recovery" of vision.[4] We think we have entirely understood our own world; it comes to us in the "drab blur of triteness or familiarity" that makes us think we have mastered it and know it entirely, the very assumption that comes to us in the frenzy and distraction of the modern world. But when we step aside into the world of story and encounter "the centaur and the dragon," we learn to see our own world in a new light. We emerge from a story to behold the equally startling reality of "sheep, and dogs, and horses—and wolves."[5] A story jolts us out of boredom with the familiar, out of distraction and carelessness, so that we are able to rediscover "the wonder of things such as stone, and wood, and iron; tree and grass; house and fire; bread and wine."[6]

I said earlier that *Anne of Green Gables* was my first taste of a sacramental viewpoint, but what I have realized is that every good book I have read, from The Lord of the Rings to the poetry of Sylvia Plath to the epics of the human heart by George Eliot, has been teaching me, through words, to see the world as a gift and to recognize the loving presence behind it. As Alexander Schmemann, a theologian I love, so joyously puts it, "All creation is the sign and means of God's presence and wisdom, love and revelation."[7] The gift of great books, of well-crafted words is that they liven us to this reality again and again. A woman who reads is one who sees that every common bush is afire with God. A book girl is one who takes off her shoes, and wonders.

"A Little Poetry Every Day": The Poems That Opened My Eyes to Wonder

(OR, A POETRY LIST FOR BEGINNERS, BY A BEGINNER)

WHEN I STUDIED at Wycliffe Hall in Oxford, I took part in one of the weekly fellowships that brought together students from various courses for a morning meeting of prayer, friendship, and discussion. My first year there, we each took turns leading the group in exploring a topic that interested us. Somewhat to my own startlement, I decided to lead the group in an exploration of poetry and prayer. I found this surprising because in the wild and wondrous realm of poetry, I am but a novice. Poetry is something that both fascinates me and bewilders me in the way it distills scenes of beauty and moments of deep emotion or powerful narrative into sparse yet compelling words that help me to perceive the whole subject anew. At times, poetry also befuddles me. I don't always find it easy or clear, and I tend to seek out anthologies that help me by giving some context or explanation.

Maybe it was that need for communal input that made me dare to try a bunch of poetry out on my generally introverted fellowship group. The result was a delight as the poems worked upon us like light on a prism, each person glimpsing a different refraction, a different depth of meaning in the words. Our observations deepened our understanding of the poem and also our insight into each other. That's why I include a section here, but it's also why this chapter is a list for beginners written *by* a beginner.

I've included a brief list of anthologies and collections by contemporary poets that I've found immensely helpful in my first voyages of poetic discovery. You can journey much further by searching out more poems online or in individual collections by the poets you particularly enjoy from the following compilations. The point is simply to begin. I love the Goethe quote "A man should hear a little music, read a little poetry, and see a fine picture every day of his life" for many reasons but particularly for that phrase "a little poetry." That's how I've discovered poetry—bit by bit, pursuing the snippets and single poems that strike my fancy. I'll admit, I don't usually sit down to read poetry for hours at a time, but I keep a book or two of it around, and when I have time, I take a moment to savor the woven language and startling imagery that somehow rekindles a glad light within my eyes. Robert Frost, great poet that he was, opined that "a poem . . . begins as a lump in the throat, a sense of wrong, a homesickness, a lovesickness."[8] May you taste a bit of that aching beauty as you explore.

The Best Poems of the English Language: From Chaucer through Robert Frost by Harold Bloom (Editor)

A superb immersion into the greatest poems of the English language, compiled by Harold Bloom, the eminent literary critic and scholar. With key selections from six centuries of great American and British poetry (most headed by Bloom's knowing commentary) and an essay entitled "The Art of Reading Poetry," this anthology is an excellent place to begin if you want a survey of the best-loved English poetry.

Sounding the Seasons: Seventy Sonnets for the Christian Year and Waiting on the Word: A Poem a Day for Advent, Christmas and Epiphany by Malcolm Guite

Priest, poet, literary scholar, folk-rock musician, rider of motorcycles, and defender of imagination, Guite sometimes seems to embody poetry as well as write it. But write it he does, in sonnets of verve and spiritual insight, written to celebrate the feasts and seasons of the church year. You can find these in the lovely volume *Sounding the Seasons*, as well as more of his original poetry in *The Singing Bowl*. Guite is also well known for his seasonal anthologies of poetry in celebration of Lent and Christmas. In *Waiting on the Word: A Poem a Day for Advent, Christmas and Epiphany* and *Word in the Wilderness: A Poem a Day for Lent and Easter*, he selects luminous poems, accompanying each with a short essay contemplating their particular insight or power. I've used these collections in my personal devotions as well as in hosting an Advent poetry group.

Drawn to the Light: Poems on Rembrandt's Religious Paintings; The Color of Light: Poems on Van Gogh's Late Paintings; and In Quiet Light: Poems on Vermeer's Women by Marilyn Chandler McEntyre

Combining McEntyre's own hushed poetry with the great art of a few beloved artists, these books are a combination of written and painted beauty from which I have drawn great comfort and joy.

A Book of Luminous Things: An International Anthology of Poetry by Czeslaw Milosz (Editor)

A unique collection, with poems from around the globe and across the centuries curiously juxtaposed in this "luminous" volume of poetry by Milosz (a Nobel laureate poet himself). A collection in which you will encounter poets you might not discover otherwise, themed around universal ideas such as epiphany, nature, travel, and the moment, this anthology offers a glimpse into the varied splendors of poets around the world.

Poetry for Young People Series by Sterling Publishing

A series of mini-collections of poems by the world's great poets, each picture book is based on a single poet and illustrated to match the mood and tone of the selected work. A vivid, beautiful way to engage with classic poetry a little at a time with the aid of unique and fitting illustrations.

A Sacrifice of Praise: An Anthology of Christian Poetry in English from Caedmon to the Mid-Twentieth Century by James H. Trott (Editor)

A rich, historical survey of Christian poetry from the seventh century to the present, drawing on works from Protestant, Catholic, Reformed, evangelical, and contemporary poets. Comprised of hymns, poems, prayers, and meditations, this over-eight-hundred-page book was a rich resource for me in both my devotional life and my poetic exploration. There are also brief, helpful introductions to the various poets.

The Golden Books Family Treasury of Poetry by Louis Untermeyer (Editor)

I didn't stumble upon this collection until I was a teen, and though it is technically a children's anthology, I pored over its whimsical illustrations and excellent selection of classic poetry, old and new, and packed it as one of the first books to be carted across the ocean to Oxford.

Startled Awake:
Novels That Kindled My Delight in Existence

(OR, BOOKS TO MAKE THE WORLD COME TO LIFE)

I TEND TO MEET deadlines in a writing vortex: I eat, breathe, sleep, and think the book to completion, and all else falls by the wayside until the moment the thing *has* to be sent off. I must admit to submitting the first draft of the book you hold in your hands at three in the morning. My faithful husband sat nearby plying me with water and gummy bears (you'd be surprised at how effective these can be in maintaining mental strength), with all the candles in our little living room lit to keep me awake and inspired.

One might assume that after such a late evening, the next day would find me too groggy to have any eye for the autumn beauty of Oxford. But I found my vision heightened instead of dimmed, an experience that felt like a fresh revelation to me. I strolled through water-cool air under a sapphire sky, watched leaves flicker like golden flames in a friendly wind, and felt profoundly grateful as my feet pounded these old Oxford cobbles. What I realized as I walked was that my kindled vision came from the many books I had read afresh during the writing of this manuscript.

Throughout the long months of writing, I daily immersed myself in rereading the novels that first taught me to love the beauty of God's good earth, to revel in the gift of existence. Their words lingered in my mind that morning as I encountered the turning trees and remembered Anne's joyous proclamation, "I'm so glad I live in a world where there are Octobers" (from *Anne of Green Gables*). I chuckled at the many characters on the street with the hilarity of Juliet's letters in the back of my mind (from *The Guernsey Literary and Potato Peel Pie Society*). I made my tea and cake that afternoon steeped in the pert and delicious observations of Prudencia, who found the many teatimes of her new home excessive . . . at first (in *The Awakening of Miss Prim*).

Silly as it may seem, I was startled to realize how richly reading had reshaped my vision. It's the very thing I argue for, but ah, the gift of it as it comes afresh continues to amaze me. And it is a *gift*. For one of the things I have come to realize in composing this book is the fact that novels like the ones on the following pages are acts of generosity. Each is an offering rooted in the author's sense of responsibility and gratitude for some goodness or truth deeply perceived.

In writing about wonder in *Book Girl*, I have become deeply aware of the fact that I write and live from what I have been generously given. I am a lover of books, a learner, keen for new adventures because so many people before me—my parents, my favorite writers, the friends who pressed good books into my hands, the tutors at Oxford who were faithful to communicate what they had discovered—were generous with their words. They spoke me into wonder. They startled me awake. They took me by the metaphorical hand and pointed at the rainbow just out the window. Consider the list below my way of passing on their grace.

Remembering by Wendell Berry

I can't recommend this as the first Berry novel you should read, and it might seem an odd choice on a list of novels to kindle delight because it opens (very purposefully) by evoking the deep sense of disconnection and disorientation known by Andy Coulter, a middle-aged farmer who is injured, depressed, and estranged from his family in a San Francisco hotel room. As a reader, I felt profoundly disturbed. But that was exactly what I was supposed to feel, because this is a novel of pilgrimage, exploring the isolation and loneliness of life in the modern world. We walk with Andy as he is drawn out of anonymity and back into belonging, as he is "held, though he does not hold" (one of my favorite lines in literature) by the memory of those who were faithful before him, by the knowledge of those who wait in faith back home. In remembering, Andy and the reader are drawn together out of isolation and into the belonging formed by our love of both person and place. The description of gratitude toward the end, where Andy discovers the "blessedness" he has "lived in . . . and did not know" is one of my favorite descriptions of thanks in literature.

Also by Wendell Berry:
- *The Memory of Old Jack*
- *A Place on Earth*
- *Jayber Crow*
- *Fidelity: Five Stories*

All the Light We Cannot See by Anthony Doerr

"It's embarrassingly plain how inadequate language is," says one character in this arresting novel, but Doerr puts language to work in a way that conveys the height and depth of the world in its splendor. It's not a happy book, its central characters a reluctant, orphaned recruit to the Nazi army and a blind girl whose village lies in the path of war.

But it's a book that glories in the richness of the world—its beauty, its intricacy, and our own capacity to behold it and be connected through it even amid the atrocities of war.

The Awakening of Miss Prim by Natalia Sanmartin Fenollera

Miss Prim is a neat, modern woman; a competent librarian; and a principled feminist who still considers herself old fashioned. But when she is immersed in a small town where feasts accompany the smallest town meeting, children sprawl in the library reading Latin, and the third item on the agenda at the Feminist Society is to find her a husband, she finds her ideals and assumptions turned on their head. A delightful, slightly tongue-in-cheek critique of the modern age so dotted with accounts of good teatimes I usually feel the urge to bake a cake halfway through a chapter.

A City of Bells by Elizabeth Goudge

Henrietta, the heroine of this novel set in the sleepy city and hidden beauty of Wells Cathedral, is one of those characters who makes me feel that the author has glimpsed my soul; Henrietta is touched by the beauty of the world, determined that people should be whole and happy, and also a bit impatient with the processes of redemption. She embodies all this in a story of a tragic and missing poet, a grandfather who is a workaday saint, a mischievous small boy, and her experience of a cathedral world shot through with love.

The Keeper of the Bees by Gene Stratton-Porter

Jamie is a wounded veteran of World War I, with an open wound that won't heal and a heart in about the same state. Unwilling to spend his final days in a tuberculosis ward, he hobbles onto the open road in California for a last taste of freedom. To his shock, he soon finds himself the startled caretaker of a stricken beekeeper's cottage and discovers that he may not be quite ready to die after all. Porter is in her usual glory here as a strong storyteller for whom God's good creation is as much a character as the people it challenges, restores, consoles, and slowly heals, like Jamie, whose interest in life intensifies after his meeting with a troubled and mysterious young beauty.

The Guernsey Literary and Potato Peel Pie Society by Mary Ann Shaffer and Annie Barrows

This is the book I read when I'm in the mood for sheer delight: in books, in friendship, and in the kind of beauty that can endure even amid Nazi vagary. "Reading keeps you from going gaga," puts one colorful character succinctly, and this is the story of a few brave and imaginative souls on Nazi-occupied Guernsey who talk a friend out of a tight spot by inventing a book club on the spot . . . and decide to make it real. It's also the story of Juliet, the wry, quirky, book-loving columnist who discovers the tale of the Guernsey Literary Society after the war and decides to write their story. Written entirely as a series of letters between Juliet and various delightful (and maddening) correspondents, this hysterical, dear tale draws both Juliet and the reader into the windswept beauty of Guernsey, into the grief of loss, and into the power of friendship, imagination, and kindness to remake and heal the world. It's almost an effortless read, but poignant—the kind whose world I hate to have to leave at book's end.

The Enchanted April by Elizabeth von Arnim

The second word in the title gives it all away—this book is a tale of enchantment, not by inexplicable forces of magic, but by the sheer power of beauty. The charming tale of the downtrodden but determined Lottie, who, upon glimpsing an advertisement for a Tuscan villa to be let for the month of April, decides on the spot to take it, convincing three other reluctant and prim British women to join her. Beauty—in house and weathered vine, in golden days and quiet hours—thus begins its transformative work.

The Journeyman by Elizabeth Yates

I love this story of a young artistic boy in Colonial times, misunderstood by his family but given the gift of an apprenticeship to a journeyman painter. It's the kind of book that lingers in imagination and conversation for years. As a young reader, I was deeply intrigued by Jared, a boy gifted differently from those around him who used his remarkable skill to bring beauty into the simple houses of early New England farmers and homesteaders, using his craft to brighten their walls and liven their souls. A story about art and the different strengths by which we may shape the world around us.

Beauty Speaks Truth:
Books about the Arts
(OR, WHY CREATIVITY IS VITAL TO FAITH)

FROM THE TIME I was a little girl, I experienced moments of beauty in which I *knew* that God was real and that he loved me (there were moments of terrifying darkness, too, but that is a longer story to tell). In glimpsing the fire of a Texas sunset, in hearing the strains of a Celtic folk song, in reading about Mary Lennox's discovery of her secret garden, I knew a thrill of what I can only call assurance—a deep, abiding knowledge of God's goodness and the sense that his mystery was reaching out specifically to me. As a child, I accepted this grace without question because it was so clearly a gift. It was only as a teenager that I began to question and wrestle with the truth that beauty seemed to tell me. What did it mean that beauty spoke to me? Why did stories help me to understand God in a way theology sometimes didn't? Was it all right to love art and music, to see creativity as a holy vocation?

It was in reading the following authors that I was finally able to come to an understanding of the way image and artistry, song and story, participate in the Incarnation, helping to reveal and speak out the reality of Christ to the world. The writers of the books in the following list explore the way that we as humans participate in the creativity of God and understand him through it. Through their words, I have found a striking articulation of the power of beauty to speak forth truth, to help us daily to taste and see that the Lord is good (Psalm 34:8). I have found celebration, as the artists speak of the way Christians, through the act of creating, participate in bringing the Kingdom of God to bear in the world. I have found a fierce and lovely embrace of beauty as a holy defiance of death, despair, and meaninglessness.

The following is an eccentric collection; there's theology, there are essays or works on aesthetics, and there are essays by Christian artists. There are also beautiful books of photography and art that richly affirm the power of beauty to communicate truth. I include them all here because we live in a pragmatic, scientific age that measures reality by what can be observed, listed, and analyzed, and sometimes this mind-set creeps into our spiritual thinking as well. We see some activities as provably holy (church, Bible reading, practical service, financial responsibility), while we see others, such as creativity, music, hospitality, or creation as peripheral to our faith, even frivolous. My goal in including these books is simply to pass along the writers who helped me to see afresh, to embrace beauty as a gift, something we are all called to perceive and create. As you read, may you, too, find joy in a "taste and see" immersion in God's goodness.

Imaginative Apologetics: Theology, Philosophy and the Catholic Tradition by Andrew Davison (Editor)

As you might have gathered from earlier parts of this book, imagination has mattered deeply to me since childhood, largely because it helped me to love and understand a God who both drew me and frightened me, whose beauty I yearned to touch, whose holiness

I did not know how to imagine. I often found Aslan more approachable than Jesus. This marvelous collection of essays helped me to understand why and gave me the vocabulary I needed to defend the spiritual relevance and apologetic power of imagination in story and poem, song and painting to awaken both Christian and seeker to a feeling of "homesickness for the ultimate truth."

The Evidential Power of Beauty: Science and Theology Meet by Thomas Dubay

I stumbled upon this book on the shelf of a friend in China. I was captivated by the rising, symphonic quality of this writer's exploration of the beautiful and the fact that in science, truth is often recognizable by its beauty. The most elegant equation is often the correct one. A book that affirms beauty as integral both to the structures of creation and to the nature of God's revelation, it richly illuminates the Von Balthasar quote on its cover: "Every experience of beauty points to infinity."

The Art of God by Ric Ergenbright

Saint Augustine described the world as a book, and it is in this spirit that photographer Ric Ergenbright presents us with the language of beauty as spoken by the whole of creation. A book that richly affirms the way creation reveals the nature and presence of God, this was a favorite in my home when I was a child. I spent hours poring over the gorgeous images. To this day, I deeply appreciate the splendor of his photography and the depth of his contemplation.

Refractions: A Journey of Faith, Art, and Culture by Makoto Fujimura

Fujimura, a contemporary artist, author, and founder of the New York City–based International Arts Movement, has composed this collection of essays, prayers, and reflections on the nature of art and the call of the artist to capture the attention of a world hungry for God. This book has nourished and ministered to many of my friends—some artistic, some just interested in how to bring beauty into faith—helping them to a vision and a vocation as creators.

Walking on Water: Reflections on Faith and Art by Madeleine L'Engle

This book has been for me, as for many Christian creators, one of the most encouraging, insightful, and vocationally affirming books I've read on the spiritual value of creativity and beauty. L'Engle sees creativity not as limited to works of "official" art but as a way to express and embody the life of Christ. Her fascinating comparison of the creative Christian to Mary, the mother of Jesus, as he or she is asked to become a bearer of the work of the Holy Spirit, has encouraged and strengthened me in the vocation of writer as well as that of homemaker, friend, and wife, for as L'Engle so luminously affirms, "In a very real sense not one of us is qualified, but it seems that God continually chooses the most unqualified to do his work, to bear his glory."

The Lost Words by Robert Macfarlane and Jackie Morris

This is a recent glory of a picture book written to help modern children reengage with the fading language and ever-present mysteries of the natural landscape. Drawing on a list of words that researchers discovered are absent from the vocabulary of modern children, *The Lost Words* is a luminous, lyrical book of illustrations that evoke the movement and essence, the ordinary miracle of things like *dandelion*, *otter*, *bramble*, and *acorn*, drawing its readers into a worldview freshened by wonder and marked by gratitude.

Seeing Salvation by Neil MacGregor and Erika Langmuir

A book crammed with some of the greatest depictions of the life of Christ in art, the images in this book were taken from a famed art exhibit of the same title, while the text is a contemplation on the work of the artists who sought to capture the truth of the Christian story. A fascinating glimpse into the way that art has, throughout history, shaped the way we see the work of God.

Noah's Ark by Rein Poortvliet

When my parents discovered that this book was going out of print, they bought a copy for each of their children and saved them for wedding gifts. Mine now sits in an honored spot in my living room, just as it did in my childhood home—a world of a book created by an artist whose humorous, poignant, vivid insight into creation is imaged in a collection of paintings centered on the story of Noah's ark. The kind of book that is mesmerizing to young children . . . and the adults looking over their shoulders.

The Gift of Music: Great Composers and Their Influence by Jane Stuart Smith (with Betty Carlson)

A rich and varied collection of short biographies of some of the world's greatest composers, with a particular emphasis on the faith that drove and irradiated their music. A book that celebrates the gift of creativity, it also offers an introduction to classical music for readers ready to delve into that world.

The Private World of Tasha Tudor by Tasha Tudor and Richard Brown

Tasha Tudor is one of my heroines: a doughty New England soul who decided she much preferred the clothes, manners, and lifestyle of the early nineteenth century to the vagaries of the modern world. Her home, her clothes, her skill in house crafts of all sorts, and her value for heritage all reflect this proclivity and make her life an object of fascination. But what draws me again and again is the way she rejoices in the beautiful, making the work of the ordinary an art in and of itself, whether with elevenses for tea or in the planting of an extravagant garden. This is a quiet, wry, insightful record of her life as captured by a photographer who was allowed into her lovely world and realized the worth of her way of seeing.

Theological Aesthetics: God in Imagination, Beauty, and Arts by Richard Viladesau

This is definitely the more academic of the books in this list, a title I studied at Oxford when exploring the way the arts communicate doctrine. I list it here because if you want to delve more deeply into the theological underpinnings of beauty, this is an excellent place to begin. I wish I had found it earlier; Viladesau looks at beauty as a source of revelation and argues for God's good reality as the only way we could have beauty at all. By exploring the way different theologians have interacted with the work of great artists, he illuminates the way beauty teaches us about the nature and reality of God.

CHAPTER 9
Books Can Deepen Your SOUL

The Gift of Pondering

In a world of noise, confusion and conflict it is necessary that there be places of silence, inner discipline and peace. In such places love can blossom.

THOMAS MERTON

IN THE MISTY GLOOM of an early winter's eve, I was scuffing up a chill Oxford street after a day of lectures and library time. It was four o'clock in England, which meant shadows stretched like great black hands over the streets and curtains were pulled tight over all the little windows I passed. The tug toward home in that darkling hour usually would have turned my feet, but that day I had a special book in my bag and a heart in search of an hour's contemplation. I tucked myself into a corner table at a marvel of an old café, a domed glass building piled in and out with luxuriant potted plants and lit by globe lights strung from the ceiling. It's a once-a-year kind of place, expensive and exceptional, but at four o'clock on a Wednesday afternoon in January, it was wondrously deserted, and those magical orbed lights glimmered in the dusk like small moons and stars. It was this space and this hour of enchanted quiet I wanted in which to carry out my January tradition of reading Anne Morrow Lindbergh's *Gift from the Sea*.

I sat. I breathed. I opened the pages of this slim friend of a book and read afresh the words that gripped me with calm as the new year opened at my feet, helping me to halt the run of my frantic thoughts, the rush of my steps, to begin the journey back to what the wise Lindbergh calls "a central core to my life." This comforting mentor, mother of six children, and wife of a world-famous pilot reminded me that "women need solitude in order to find again the true essence of themselves." I savored her words as night fell. I let the hush of that empty café surround me. I read a psalm and opened my journal, and in Anne's quiet company, I looked at my life anew in its goals and dreams, its rhythms and stresses, and began to learn all over again to "be still," as the psalmist puts it (Psalm 46:10), or to "live 'in grace,'" as Anne describes it. My writing was a prayer, and peace came into my bones.

In that moment I remembered again that a woman who reads is a woman who ponders, who knows the holy secret of time spent in quiet, the power that comes from stepping back from the madness of screen and email, schedule and headline, to seek an inner place of hush in which she may know her own heart and the voice of the Holy Spirit afresh. A woman who reads is a rebel, defying the pace of the instant at which the modern world gallops from dawn till dusk. Her mind is her own, formed not by a scroll down the social-media feed or the frantic scurry of too much to do but by her daily decision to walk in company with the wise, those authors who help her to step back, to listen, to pray, and to ponder. Like Mary, the mother of Jesus, tangled up in the greatest task and story the world has yet seen, she knows that she must step back from even the holiest drama to ponder, to treasure in her heart (Luke 2:19) the things that are good and slough away the needless things that keep her from peace.

The first woman who modeled this life for me was my mother. The form of her curled in the corner of the couch in the half-light of dawn, with a Bible, her journal, and a book of theology or devotion nearby, lurks in the sweet shadows of my earliest memories. I sensed from little girlhood that those moments centered my mother in grace; I knew the quiet into which I crept was somehow sacred (though that certainly didn't keep me from breaking it with morning chatter). By the time I was a teen, I'd copied that practice as well as her habit of a dawn-light walk. During the years that we chatted and tromped in the mornings, I began to notice the way my mother was shaped by her walk with the words of wise authors. "This morning I was reading . . ." It might have been Philip Yancey or Dallas Willard, Edith Schaeffer or Amy Carmichael, but what she read led her to reflect, giving her the strength of an independent mind rooted in the gathered wisdom of those who had traveled before her.

As I began to follow in her footsteps, I stumbled (quite literally) across a book in my late teens that deepened my understanding of what those times of quiet and reading accomplished. During an introverted ramble through a big, old bookshop in Nashville, I managed to catch my foot on the jutted corner of a bookshelf, thereby upsetting both my balance and the excellent cappuccino I held. A mere drop of coffee splashed onto the page of the small book I was perusing, but oh, it looked very large and dark on the clean, creamy paper. There was nothing to do but to buy it. What grace that I did! That book, so humbly written, was *Interior Castle* by the inimitable Saint Teresa of Avila. I came to love the wise, compassionate, and profoundly realistic voice of this spunky medieval nun who wrote about prayer as the soul's journey back to the center of one's being where God, whom she called the Beloved, always dwells, ready to be ever more known. Teresa saw the cultivation of quiet as the journey to which every soul is called out of the madness of life (medieval or modern) and back to the ground of the love that keeps us in life.

The part reading plays in that journey is that of companion and guide. Words—in novel, poem, or devotion—are often the road

I walk in my journey toward prayer, on my way toward a centered and gracious peace. The more authors I have explored, particularly in my devotional life, the more I have come to notice that those whose words most help me toward maturity share a common theme: the pursuit of quiet as the choice to listen not to the countless and

Kimberlee Conway Ireton

A writer and friend whose creativity and encouragement have kindled my heart and sparked my imagination many a time. You can find Kimberlee's lovely *The Circle of Seasons* listed on page 219.

Desert Island Books for Grown-Ups

- **The Bible.** The older I get, the more I appreciate my favorite book's epic scope and braided story lines, the way its seemingly disparate parts fit together so beautifully—mirroring, reflecting, and refracting one another's light.

- **The Book of Common Prayer.** My own words are so paltry sometimes, so not enough. A good prayer book gives me other words, better words, words tested by time and trial and faith.

- **Pride and Prejudice** by Jane Austen. I've read this book close to a dozen times and named two of my children after the main characters. If I'm going to languish on a rocky beach somewhere in the middle of the ocean, I may as well bring Mr. Darcy with me.

- **Till We Have Faces** by C. S. Lewis. Beautiful, multivalent, and provocative, this novel is hands-down Lewis's best book. You have to read the whole thing, though. Trust me, you will want to quit before the end. Don't do it; the end changes everything.

- **Jane Eyre** by Charlotte Brontë. I once heard that Mr. Rochester is the number-one hunky hero of literature for gals in the UK. I don't get that myself. But I adore Jane—her integrity and nobility of soul inspire me—and since she loves Mr. R., for her sake, I've learned to appreciate him (even though I think she deserves way better).

- **Middlemarch** by George Eliot. Eliot's compassion, even for her villains, is deep and wide, authentic and convicting. The characters in this book are among the most noble, fallen, beautiful, and alive of any novel I've read.

- **Diary of an Old Soul** by George MacDonald. A poem a day, each one wrestling with God or self with such transparency that I find myself wanting to highlight almost every word.

- **The Scent of Water** by Elizabeth Goudge. This is the novel I want to write: simple and beautiful, with glimmers of history and mystery shining through the thin places. It captures the beauty and pathos of the ordinary, which when transfigured by love, turns out not to be ordinary at all.

clamoring voices of the world but to the still, small voice of love within. Their words hold me up and help me to that listening when my own strength is small. In the early mornings, when my brain was weary and my heart sore, words kept me on that road of quiet reflection that leads toward peace—the words of Thomas Merton urging me to "learn to be alone"[1] or the poetry of George Herbert telling me of the way "love bade me welcome"[2] or the writings of C. S. Lewis, with his humble and humorous common sense, telling me that we must "lay before Him what is in us, not what ought to be in us."[3]

But reflection is something I've had to fight for in the last several years, and I think it's a battle faced by countless women in the modern world. We live in an age of profound and constant distraction, a way of existence increasingly centered on screens that accompany us from dawn till dusk, fragmenting our attention and driving us into restless and constant activity. The older I get and the more my hours of work and rest have become entangled with the online or virtual world, the more I have noticed a restless anxiety growing in my heart. The longer I've spent on social media, the more I notice the frantic leap of my mind, from this opinion to that as my fingers click restlessly in search of the next best thing. I think this is a restlessness common to the modern mind.

Is online reality wrong? Of course not. It is the space in which I work, the community to which I often write, with my laptop as my daily tool. Social media has connected me with friends and peers, with good work and life-changing insights. My phone connects me to family and friends scattered around the world. But what concerns me is the way the incessant activity of the virtual world increasingly invades the whole of my daily experience, reshaping my patterns of thought, filling my moments of quiet. I recognize myself in Dana Gioia's research as one of the people whose long habit of thoughtful reading is being replaced by my time on the screen. To an extent, this is contemporary life. But when I found, a few years ago, that I could no longer even rise in the dawn light without fighting the impulse to check my phone or read for an hour without the need for distraction, I decided to take a break from the online world to see what state my mind would be in after a few weeks away from the online bustle and back in the slower pace of books.

Of course at first the habit of checking phone or screen felt like an itch that I longed to scratch. And the loneliness of my quiet moments cut a good bit deeper in the long silence of writing afternoons or solitary evenings. But I stuck out the weeks by sheer stubbornness, and in the long spaces of quiet, I began to read in earnest. I read a biography of the Brontës (fascinating women). I delved into *Island of the World*, a novel whose quiet beauty and bared grief left me sitting in a long, long quiet at the end of each chapter. I tried a bit of poetry. I got my early mornings back into their old rhythm, and I read a lot more of my Bible in those quiet times and began the massive undertaking of Evelyn Underhill's *Mysticism*. What I found was that the echoed words of wise authors helped me to prayer, led me by the hand into silence, and left me there to ponder.

At the end of my break, I checked back in to the world of screens, but I found that they did not grip my attention in the same way. I had a renewed capacity to choose what I would skim or click, to stop when my mind grew weary. In the end, as I evaluated the quiet that seemed to reign again in my thoughts, I realized that my time away from the online world and in the presence of good books had allowed me to reclaim the sovereignty of my own mind. The words I read in slow quiet helped me to regain the direction, rhythm, and source of my thoughts. And that single fact has made me unashamed of standing on soapboxes when it comes to the priceless value of reading and reflecting as activities we must continue to cultivate even amid a world driven by and turning on the presence of screens.

Nicholas Carr, author of *The Shallows: What the Internet Is Doing to Our Brains*, writes that "the Net is, by design, an interruption system. . . . It seizes our attention only to scatter it." But how do I apply a scrambled attention to the command to "pray without ceasing" (1 Thessalonians 5:17, NASB)? How do I reconcile the constant mental activity online with God's ringing directive to "be still, and know that I am God" (Psalm 46:10)? How do I choose the one thing needed of sitting at the feet of Christ (Luke 10:42), listening, while giving my brain to the thousand articles and opinions paraded online? These were the questions that prompted my break in the first place. They are the questions that continue to drive my resolve to seek times of reflection and that strengthen my belief in the power of a book in the hand, binding my attention to the unclickable presence of its physical pages, requiring my silence and my fixed attention to help me back toward peace.

That step toward a pondering heart so often begins with reading. I've seen this in the life of just about every woman I respect. If there is a single factor common to the people I want to be like when I grow up, whose lives are marked by wisdom, creativity, independence of thought, and centered peace, it is their daily and dogged pursuit of quiet, reading, and prayer. Gwen, my *tante*, in whose home I have spent countless special days, begins each morning of my visits with fragrant coffee in china cups, an open Bible, and a pile of books from which she can't wait to read me the wonders she has recently discovered. Phyllis, my mentor and adopted grandmother, greets me each time I visit with a table set for tea and a Bible on the arm of her chair. "Look at this, Sarah," she'll say, pointing out some quote or verse, alert to its power to shape and change our lives.

The women my own age whom I admire are the same: Mari, my brilliant academic friend and kindred spirit, reads me snippets of Mary Oliver as we walk in the sprawling parks of Oxford between her speaking engagements; Jenny, my former housemate and bosom friend, read me Wendell Berry love poems at my bridal shower; and

Katrina, that best and oldest friend, sends quotes in her letters from all the old books we love even as her tiny daughter squirms nearby.

These are my models of women who ponder, women whose souls are rooted in the wise words and quiet they have grown in their chosen hours of reading. I know that in my yearly sojourn with Anne Morrow Lindbergh, I'm keeping company with a bevy of book girls who are on their way to what Anne describes as the "state of inner spiritual grace from which I could function and give as I was meant to in the eye of God."[4]

The Holy Way:
Books That Taught Me to Pray
(OR, SUMMONED TO ATTENTION)

MY FIRST YEAR at Oxford—when I was living on the top floor of the oldest building at Wycliffe, with the chapel cross out my window—I often rose early on Sundays. The college was so quiet then, the bustle of the week and the usual friends absent, and the space felt somehow holy. I felt summoned to attention, to prayer. Sometimes I felt awed and expectant, but sometimes I just felt lonely, and one such morning I wandered to the library in search of something to help me move past my weariness and loneliness. I found a slim, battered, brick-red book by Thomas Merton stuck between several academic tomes. In so many other seasons of my life, Merton had been my mentor in prayer, a friend who showed me the way to God's presence when I felt that I had forgotten how to walk. That morning the book felt like a gift specifically to me, and perhaps it was, for

I went back to my room and pondered Merton's words in the gray dawn light that pooled and shimmered around me. The light made my small, square room a still, expectant space, and Merton's words shaped the room of inmost self as well:

> Our discovery of God is, in a way, God's discovery of us. We cannot go to heaven to find Him. . . . He comes down from heaven and finds us. He looks at us from the depths of His own infinite actuality, which is everywhere, and His seeing us gives us a new being and a new mind in which we also discover Him.[5]

In that moment, those words were gift and guide, leading me into the prayer I could not find by myself.

When it comes to prayer or even quiet, I am of the spiritual temperament that begins with excellent intentions and ten minutes later snaps out of a daydream (or, let's be honest, a consideration of what I should have for breakfast) in bewildered frustration, wondering when I stopped praying. My mind leaps here and there, I wonder if God can hear me, and I yearn for a deep sense of peace and quiet in my heart, but I find the journey to that place so very difficult. I am convinced that I must, like Mary, choose the "one thing . . . necessary" (Luke 10:42, NASB) of sitting at the feet of Jesus. I yearn to hear his voice amid the clamor of the wider world. But listening is a discipline, a grace that requires work. It's not God's displeasure I worry about so much as my own incapacity to focus, to hush, to let all else fall away so that I can begin to listen to the Holy Spirit.

I think this is why I am so profoundly grateful for the following books. Over the years I've found that when I walk toward prayer in the company of these wise and patient guides, I am far more able to grow in the silence and focus for which I so long. The prayerful, tender words of these writers have often acted upon me like the hand of a friend who catches you when you're about to fall, speaking a bit of encouragement just at the moment you might give up. The love of God, the life of prayer—these are practices we often need to be taught. The following books, like Merton's words on my hushed Sunday morning, have been my mentors and teachers in the holy way.

The Practice of the Presence of God by Brother Lawrence

"We ought not to be weary of doing little things for the love of God, who regards not the greatness of the work, but the love with which it is performed." So wrote the humble Brother Lawrence, a medieval monk who worked in the kitchen and the garden and who saw the whole of his life as prayer, lived in conversation with God. "He is nearer to us than we think," Brother Lawrence writes, challenging the believer to simply remember God amid the work of the ordinary—the cooking and cleaning, the quiet so intricately part of the everyday. This book helped me to form a theology of the ordinary as its words livened idealistic me to the possibility of remembering and reveling in God's presence, not merely in a soaring quiet time, but amid dishes and deadlines, the rush of work and the hush of exhaustion.

The Rest of God: Restoring Your Soul by Restoring Sabbath by Mark Buchanan

This contemplative, creative, and very scriptural explanation of the role of rest as a spiritual discipline in the life of faith has shaped my convictions about taking a Sabbath day as a day of actual rest, a cessation of work. By helping his readers to understand that rest is not so much about not doing things as it is about trusting in God to be our ultimate source and provider, he offers a mode of discipleship very different from the hurry-up culture in which we live.

Love's Immensity: Mystics on the Endless Life by Scott Cairns

A gentle, luminous collection of the writings of the church's most beloved mystics, set in lyrical verse by Cairns, a contemporary poet. I found a daily dose of these poems to be an influence of quiet on my heart, their words ringing in my imagination throughout the day.

My Utmost for His Highest by Oswald Chambers

One of the greatest and most enduring devotionals, composed of Chambers's heartfelt sermons to soldiers and students on the devout life of the believer, this inspirational book is divided into a year's worth of daily readings. It's questions like these that have made it a spiritual classic for generations:

> Sanctification is not a question of whether God is willing to sanctify me—is it my will? Am I willing to let God do in me everything that has been made possible through the atonement of the Cross of Christ? Am I willing to let Jesus become sanctification to me, and to let His life be exhibited in my human flesh?

Celtic Daily Prayer by Northumbria Community

This book has been a daily resource to me for over a decade. Compiled by the Northumbria Community, a fellowship working in the stream of "new monasticism" by living in community on the ancient and holy island of Lindisfarne, this book was my introduction to a more liturgical mode of prayer. With morning, midday, and evening liturgies composed mostly of Scripture, and with daily meditations and readings drawn from a plethora of excellent Christian authors who focus on Celtic themes of pilgrimage, reconciliation, beauty, and contemplation, this book has become the basic devotional resource I use to continue my daily quiet times even amid a hectic schedule. To pray the canticle daily is a gift:

> *Christ, as a light illumine and guide me.*
> *Christ, as a shield overshadow me.*
> *Christ under me, Christ over me,*
> *Christ beside me on my left and my right.*

A Book of Comfort: An Anthology by Elizabeth Goudge

You've already met Goudge as one of my most-beloved novelists, but I deeply prize her devotional work as well in this collection of excerpted poetry, theology, stories, essays, and devotions. As the daughter of a cathedral dean, raised in the great churches of Oxford, Wells, and Ely, she offers great breadth in this selection. Her attention to both beauty and theological profundity makes this a perennial spiritual resource, something I turn to in order to quiet my mind and deepen my prayer life.

Also by Goudge:
- *A Book of Peace*
- *A Book of Faith*

No Man Is an Island, New Seeds of Contemplation, and Bread in the Wilderness by Thomas Merton

I have such trouble choosing a single Merton title, so here you have three. The first two are the contemplative classics for which Merton is best known, books that confront the restless discontent of the contemporary world with an invitation to find rest and satisfaction in the heart of God. In *No Man Is an Island*, Merton summons his readers both to detachment—from self-interest, from worry—and to a refreshed recognition that "we may be the object of God's love precisely because of [our] shortcomings." Only in this standing can we be confident, not in illusions of our goodness, "but in the endless, unfailing mercy of God." In *New Seeds of Contemplation*, Merton writes a guide to the contemplative life in response to the countless letters he received from those in the wider world hungry for silence, for a sense of God's reality, for peace. "Hurry ruins saints as well as artists," he writes. Finally, *Bread in the Wilderness* is Merton's exploration of the Psalms as the central liturgy of the monastery, the bread that feeds the souls of those who pray them day in and day out, leading them into the presence of Christ.

The Singer Trilogy by Calvin Miller

The story of the Gospels retold in a lyrical poem recounting the life of a Singer whose Song could not be silenced and whose love would not be stopped. A gentle, allegorical reading that speaks the gospel afresh into a weary heart.

The Interior Castle by Saint Teresa of Avila

"This Beloved of ours is merciful and good. Besides, he so deeply longs for our love that he keeps calling us to come closer." When my eye fell upon those words in the small golden book I'd picked up to browse in a bookstore, I felt the tug of yearning. How could I come closer to that Beloved? *The Interior Castle* is in large part an answer to that question, the humble and spunky Saint Teresa's medieval exploration of prayer as the way by which we journey to the inner room of our hearts, where Christ dwells, ever present, our own Beloved. It's the plainspoken, almost humorous realism of this book that makes it approachable: "The devil frequently fills our thoughts with great schemes, so that instead of putting our hands to what work we can do to serve our Lord, we may rest satisfied with wishing to perform impossibilities." (Take that, idealistic Sarah!)

But it's the tenderness, the real belief in the love of God always beckoning to us, inviting us to prayer, that makes this book such a companion to devotion. I'm still not sorry I spilled my coffee on it and was forced to shell out twenty dollars. It's been worth every penny and more.

The Letters of Evelyn Underhill by Evelyn Underhill

If *Mysticism* (see review on page 118) is too much to tackle, consider Underhill's chatty, practical letters, written to seekers around the world who flocked to the advice of this clear-eyed, realistic spiritual mother. Underhill's mission is obvious in this book: to help others deepen their life of prayer and their experience of Christ's real, present love.

The Celtic Way of Prayer: The Recovery of the Religious Imagination by Esther De Waal

I've been entranced by Irish music and Celtic tales since childhood, so when I discovered the remarkable collection of ancient Celtic prayers collected in the nineteenth century and published as the *Carmina Gadelica*, I was caught. The beautiful blessings and songs of worship, with their powerful imagery ("Behold the lightener of the stars / On the crests of the clouds, / And the choralists of the sky / Lauding Him"), express an awareness of God's power and beauty in creation that I yearned to better understand. De Waal's book was my answer, one that introduced me to the world of early Celtic monasticism on whose rhythms of prayer and praise the earliest Celtic blessings were composed. What I love here is De Waal's exploration of what makes Celtic prayer so potent; she deeply examines the joy the Celts took in the natural world, the oral and lyric traditions in which they operated, and their rich sense of praying in the company of all the angels and saints, the kin and kingfolk of heaven.

The Divine Conspiracy: Rediscovering Our Hidden Life in God by Dallas Willard

What difference does salvation make to life in the here and now? How do we draw the life and grace of Jesus into every day of our lives? These are some of the questions Willard seeks to answer, and he does so with such eloquence and compassion that his book is now a modern classic. His hope is to "gain a fresh hearing for Jesus, especially among those who believe they already understand him. Very few people today find Jesus interesting as a person or of vital relevance to the course of their actual lives."

Silence and Honey Cakes by Rowan Williams

I hadn't heard much about the desert fathers until I moved to Oxford, when I was assigned an essay on Athanasius and his biography of the first desert hermit, Saint Antony. Suddenly I was plunged into the vivid desert world of early Christianity in which some Christians left the temptations of the world to dwell in the wilderness, combating sin and Satan, pursuing purity for Christ. Their "sayings" are pithy stories or statements of wisdom and spiritual instruction for which pilgrims would journey long. (If you're interested in finding out more, Benedicta Ward's *The Sayings of the Desert Fathers* is a good place to start.) This brief contemplation on those sayings by Rowan Williams, an Anglican theologian, considers the psychological and spiritual relevance that those words have for us today as we examine ourselves, as we strive to live in community, as we wrestle with prejudice or fear, and as we confront the demons whose source is so often our own sin.

The Gift of Sacred Time:
Books for the Church Year
(OR, FINDING A SPIRITUAL RHYTHM)

I LIVE TO THE CADENCE of church bells now. Elizabeth Goudge called Wells the "city of bells," but that description could easily describe Oxford; you can hear a chorus of them striking at the oddest times. Sometimes a single dramatic toll to mark the hour; sometimes great, waterfalling crescendos ringing through the streets. Now, though, with my front-room window facing the golden brick of a church tower and the bells humming out on the quarter hours from 6:45 in the morning to 11:00 at night, the bells are personal to me, deep old voices warbling a call to prayer, singing my every day into a kind of structured music.

In a way, those bells and the cadence with which they frame my hours are part of the larger rhythm I've learned during my time in Oxford as I've increasingly (if erratically) adopted the practice of morning and evening prayer and the marking of the year by the seasons of earth and church. There is a clear sense in British culture and in my church here of both time and space as realities you mark and claim, made sacred by the way you see them, the words with which you frame them, the actions with which you fill them.

I encountered communal evening prayer my first month in Oxford, and as I began to attend regularly, hearing Scripture and prayer at a set time each day, I found the liturgies forming my thoughts, comforting me in stressed moments, giving me a cadence of worship in which to live the crazy rounds of my days. Then I found the glory of the church year, with its high days centered on the core events of Christ's life: not just Christmas and Easter, birth and death, but Ascension and Pentecost, feasts that remind me of Christ's return to the Father to prepare a place for all who love him, and of the Holy Spirit coming among us. What these prayers and feasts, these liturgies offer me is not only a mind formed by reverence but a deepened sense of identity, a fuller knowledge of who Christ is and the hope and glory to which he is drawing me.

What the church year and its liturgies have allowed me is the sense of my life, my one story of faith, my ordinary moments as caught up in the great narrative, the ceaseless coming of God. In an age where time and season are increasingly lost to the unsleeping pace of the internet era, the church year has helped me to draw my own days back into a rhythm of prayer, thanksgiving, wonder, and hush: a rhythm of grace by which I am learning to recognize God's reality in every aspect of my life.

Even if you (like me) did not grow up experiencing the practice and beauty of liturgy or thinking much about time itself as sacred, I encourage you to peruse the following books. Several of them have been helpful to me as introductions to the whole topic of liturgy; others are companions to certain seasons (Advent or Lent); others are imaginative and poetic in their interaction with the church year.

What is common to all is the way they have enriched and deepened my worship.

The Rhythm of God's Grace: Uncovering Morning and Evening Hours of Prayer by Arthur Paul Boers

This was one of the first books I read that introduced me to the idea of daily, fixed-hour prayer. The simple explanation and persuasion of this book was immensely helpful to me as a beginner in the realm of liturgy as it explains the ancient rhythms of the church and how common prayer is a way of joining my voice with Christians all over the world.

Heavenly Participation: The Weaving of a Sacramental Tapestry by Hans Boersma

A contemporary theologian who works in the evangelical tradition and draws deeply on the writings of the early church, Boersma has made it one of his main goals to revive an understanding of "sacramental ontology," what he considers to be the profoundly Christian way of perceiving the created world and our embodied selves as participating in the life of God. His book *Heavenly Participation* has been crucial in helping me to understand the significance of beauty, liturgy, and tradition.

The Circle of Seasons: Meeting God in the Church Year by Kimberlee Conway Ireton

A book by a writer I count as a friend, this is an introduction to the world of the church year. Winsome and personal, woven through with stories, explanations, and ideas that illuminate the theology driving each season, this is an excellent introduction if you are new to the liturgical arena.

Every Moment Holy: New Liturgies for Daily Life by Douglas Kaine McKelvey

Years ago, I was delighted to discover that the early Celtic Christians had liturgies for everything from the coming of spring to the laying of a hearth fire. I loved the way their shared prayers reveal God's grace amid the ordinary, the way the prayers join us, in the glory and grit of our ordinary days, with the movement of heaven itself. This book is crafted in that lively tradition and pointed toward the modern reader, offering prayers such as "A Liturgy for the Morning of a Medical Procedure" and "A Liturgy for Feasting with Friends" and even, happy thought, "A Liturgy for the Ritual of Morning Coffee." Accompanied by marvelous woodcut illustrations, this is a book to treasure and savor.

You Are What You Love: The Spiritual Power of Habit by James K. A. Smith

An insightful book arguing for a definition of humans as "desiring creatures" rather than "thinking things." Using examples such as the liturgical structure of a shopping mall (read it and be amazed), Smith demonstrates our need to consider the way in which our moral character and our beliefs are shaped, not just by thought or doctrine, but by what we love and learn to love through habit, ritual, and liturgy.

The Divine Hours Series by Phyllis Tickle

Tickle's collections of prayers and Scripture passages draw novice disciples into the rhythm of fixed-hour prayer so integral to medieval monastic rhythm. Creating a book of hours for the modern reader, Tickle draws on the Anglican *Book of Common Prayer*, as well as the writings of the early church fathers, to help modern believers enter the ancient rhythm of daily prayer.

Watch for the Light: Readings for Advent and Christmas and *Bread and Wine: Readings for Lent and Easter* by Plough Publishing

This is one of my favorite resources, a collection of daily readings designed to accompany a reader through the two great seasons of the church year, Advent and Lent. With entries by many of my most-loved writers, ranging from early church fathers and medieval poets to contemporary theologians, these books invite readers into a soulful journey, into that excavation of the heart that is one of the gifts of the Advent and Lenten seasons.

God with Us: Rediscovering the Meaning of Christmas and *God for Us: Rediscovering the Meaning of Lent and Easter* by Greg Pennoyer and Gregory Wolfe (Editors)

Another set of favorites whose beauty I have savored for years, these books provide daily readings along with daily works of art for the four weeks of Advent and the season of Lent. With reflections written by recognized theologians and Christian authors, they offer a rich, thoughtful, often challenging immersion into the yearning and beauty of these seasons.

CHAPTER 10

Books Can Impart HOPE

The Final Word Belongs to Love

*"Hope" is the thing with feathers— / That
perches in the soul— / And sings the tune
without the words— / And never stops at all.*

EMILY DICKINSON, "'HOPE' IS THE THING WITH FEATHERS"

I SAT IN THE RAINY half-light of my tiny English living room, in the
blank silence of the loss of my first child, a "little bean" I would never
meet. The world had gone so quiet. My heart was so, so cold. I found
I could not command my feelings, either of sorrow or of hope. Grief
felt like the suspension of normal life—as if my entire being had been
tossed up into the air and I was waiting to see what would crash to
the ground and what was still safe. The old things I loved—cooking,
walking, writing—there was no help or joy in those for now. I simply
sat. But reading was so deeply a part of my habits that I found myself
skimming a book brought by a friend before I really thought about
what I was doing. In that gray light I read about Julian of Norwich's
vision of something that looked small as a hazelnut but was actually the whole world, cradled in the palm of God's hand, and her

knowledge that "God made it. . . . God loves it. . . . God preserves it." I remembered that my baby was about the size of a hazelnut when he died. I read on and found Julian's luminous affirmation, chanted down through the war-torn ages, that because of the love of God "all shall be well, all shall be well, all manner of things shall be well." And I began to weep as my mind filled with the image of my own lost babe, held like the hazelnut of the world in the palm of God's hand—not lost, but found, and waiting for me.

And in that moment I lived afresh the truth that a woman who reads has learned how to hope. She understands that the grief of the present—small sorrow or searing pain that it may be—is not the final word. "Love," as Chris Rice croons in his ballad, "has the final move," and the best stories teach a woman who reads how to frame her sorrow within the larger tale of both human endurance and divine redemption. A good story, a piece of true theology, a radiant poem help us to look beyond the darkness of the present toward what Tolkien called "joy, joy beyond the walls of the world,"[1] the light that endures beyond all pain and one day will invade our broken world to "wipe every tear from [our] eyes" (Revelation 21:4). A woman who reads has heard what Alfred Delp called the "first notes as of pipes and voices"[2] that signal the radiant fulfillment to come, even as she dwells in what C. S. Lewis called "the shadowlands"[3] of earthly life.

But a reading woman is also a realist; she lives in this broken place, and she grapples with the daily stuff of life in a fallen world. Broken bodies, shattered relationships, a world in which wars and flat tires and miscarriages are daily realities—this is her story, and the great works of fiction and theology show her what redemption looks like in ordinary time. I find it ironic that the reading of novels is sometimes criticized as an escapist activity, because some of the novels I love best are the ones that have taught me how to accept and survive the most grievous facts of my life. It was Alan Paton's *Cry, the Beloved Country* that first made me honest enough to admit the way personal pain made me doubt God's goodness or the way grief made ordinary life feel pointless. But it was that same book that showed me the possibility of a creative, stubborn faith that could endure even in total tragedy. Set in South Africa, in the era of apartheid, with two fathers grieving two sons, Paton's story confronted me with this conversation:

— This world is full of trouble, umfundisi.
— Who knows it better?
— Yet you believe?
Kumalo looked at him under the light of the lamp.
I believe, he said, but I have learned that it is a secret. Pain and suffering, they are a secret. Kindness and love, they are a secret. But I have learned that kindness and love can pay for pain and suffering. There is my wife, and you, my friend, and these people who welcomed me, and the child who is so eager to be with us here in Ndotsheni—so in my suffering I can believe.

I needed those words. I first encountered them in my early twenties when I was in the early days of my wrestle with a diagnosis of obsessive-compulsive disorder, a mental illness that I knew would be present for the rest of my life. As I dealt with the reality of a brain I considered "broken," I had to confront my own limitations, my inability to live a "normal" life (whatever that really means), to have a body within my control, or even to respond in an optimistic way. I wanted my prayers to bring about instant relief, and when they didn't, the discouragement felt overwhelming, making ordinary life seem useless. My impulse was to just retreat into a dark room. But novels like Paton's came into my anger and hurt, showing me that "the tragedy is not that things are broken, the tragedy is that things are not mended again."

Those words were the first in a series of novels that helped me to understand and see in character and plot that redemption isn't something zapped down upon us but rather is rooted in the "deeper magic"[4] (in Aslan's terms) of God with us in the broken place, bearing our sorrow and turning death backward. In the vision of Sam Gamgee, exhausted and alone in the deserts of Mordor, I learned that hope isn't found in the absence of suffering but in glimpses of "light and high beauty" that help us to believe that "the darkness is a small and passing thing."[5] Through the works of George Eliot and her tale of an abused and desperate wife who discovers God's love through a preacher's compassionate words, I learned that my small sorrows don't leave me unable to help in "the blessed work of helping the world forward,"[6] if only I will choose to act, to hope, to work. Her words that "the real heroes of God's making"

Sally Clarkson

You already know her as the marvelous, matchless, imaginative mother who read to me while I was still a babe in the womb. She is also a splendid writer herself, one whose books have shaped the hearts of countless women, whose wisdom, creativity, and joy in learning have shaped me every day of my life. You can read her in her own right in *The Mission of Motherhood*, *Own Your Life*, *The Lifegiving Home* (which we wrote together), *Different*, and *The Lifegiving Table*. But here you get her own list of best-loved reads, the books she most deeply savored in her own reading journey.

Favorite Books as a Youth	*My Favorite Books as an Adult*
- *Where the Red Fern Grows* by Wilson Rawls	- *The Keeper of the Bees* by Gene Stratton-Porter
- *Christy* by Catherine Marshall	- *The Chronicles of Narnia* by C. S. Lewis
- *A Wrinkle in Time* by Madeleine L'Engle	- *Christ Plays in Ten Thousand Places* by Eugene Peterson
	- *The Jesus I Never Knew* by Philip Yancey
	- *A Circle of Quiet* and *Walking on Water* by Madeleine L'Engle

come into their action "by long wrestling their own sins and their own sorrows"[7] were a rallying cry to me, a challenge to rise from discouragement and learn to love, work, and hope again. Those novels taught me that I had the power to choose a gentle and holy defiance. I could resist despair by choosing instead tiny, daily acts of creativity, kindness, beauty, and prayer, acts that were rooted in "the greater love that holds and cherishes all the world,"[8] as Wendell Berry puts it.

I read a lot of Berry just before my own marriage. The months leading up to my late-summer wedding held an interesting tension for me—on one side, the pure radiance of this love that I had been given in my husband-to-be, of the Oxford wedding to come, and of the new life in a little English cottage about to begin. On the other side was a summer remarkable in my memory for the daily headlines of death and destruction—the war in Syria, political unrest in the US and the UK, nightclub shootings, sniper killings in Dallas—and the way those greater sorrows niggled at my own more private fears. What would suffering look like in marriage? Could our love weather loss? Would my husband truly be able to cope with OCD, my own small, daily battle with darkness?

On the morning of a bridal planning day organized by my sister and anticipated by us both for weeks, we woke to news of the Bastille Day terrorist attack in Nice. We sat in my room, cups of tea in hand, feet propped on my battered old armchairs, and wondered what to do. The joy of that bridal and sisterly day seemed insignificant next to the immensity of pain throbbing in the world. How could we shop or laugh or even plan a menu when people were dying? We weren't quite sure how to act, and when my sister left me for a few minutes, I found the old darkness and doubt suffusing my thoughts as the larger grief of the world niggled to life the fear I bore as I journeyed toward one of the largest commitments of my life.

But bless my sister, she returned with freshened cups of tea and poetry books in hand. No matter what, she said, we were going to begin this day with good, strong words to revive our souls. I blinked back tears. First on her list of bridal delights was the savoring of love poems. We sat there as the light out the window gathered strength and took turns reading: Shakespeare's assertion that "love . . . looks on tempests and is never shaken," Elizabeth Barrett Browning's declaration that she loved "to the depth and breadth and height" her "soul could reach when feeling out of sight," and Yeats's radiant assurance to his love that "one man loved the pilgrim soul in you" (oh, I love that line).

And then we came to Wendell Berry. It wasn't a romantic poem exactly, considering the title included the words "The Mad Farmer Liberation Front." But it was about love: fierce, exultant, enduring love as clothed in the acts of the everyday, defying the death and grief and distraction of the modern world. His rallying cry was to "love the Lord" and to "love the world," to daily do "something that won't compute" with the dour expectations of the fallen world. "Laugh," wrote Berry. "Laughter is immeasurable" (and my sister began to giggle). "Be joyful / though you have considered all the facts." And soon the words began to blur through our tears as we saw our own moment on a Colorado morning in its beauty and took comfort in each other and in our love despite the headlined facts of that morning. We read aloud with shaky but joyous voices down to the last, radiant line: "Practice resurrection."

I suppose that line could mean many different things depending on the reader, but in that moment, for me, it was clear. To practice resurrection meant to take joy in the gift of my upcoming marriage, in the precious camaraderie of my long sisterhood; to not allow those marvelous gifts of love to be diminished by darkness. It meant to let our hearts be joyful in the face of "the facts," to let the happiness of picking out wedding shoes and planning little gifts for the guests proclaim a different reality from that of destruction. To practice resurrection that day for me meant also to trust—in the presence of God to sustain us in that moment, to root my marriage, to keep us safe, even from the foibles and vagaries of OCD.

Very soon after that day, I came across a line in *Hannah Coulter*, the Berry novel I was reading at the time, that helped me to understand that my choice to rejoice in love that day with my sister was a small model of the hope that the whole of my marriage was meant to image. When Hannah, a young farmwife, marries Nathan Coulter, a survivor of the same war that took her first husband, she states her belief that her new marriage stands for

the possibility that among the world's wars and sufferings two people could love each other for a long time, until death and beyond, and could make a place for each other that would be a part of their love, as their love for each other would be a way of loving their place. This love would be one of the acts of the greater love that holds and cherishes all the world.

That love, holding and cherishing all the world, is exactly the love I glimpsed afresh in Julian's words in the rainy half-light of that Oxford morning as I mourned the loss of my first little babe. Little did I know, when I read that passage before my wedding, that my husband and I would confront our first deep sorrow within a year, holding hands as we stared at the still little form on the doctor's screen. Little did I know what grief like that would feel like, voiding light and joy from the rest of the world. But little also did I know that my husband's cherishing of me in my grief would indeed be startling, creating for me a space in which I tasted that greater, divine love that I had glimpsed in the Berry passage.

Words like Berry's have sheltered and strengthened me throughout the sorrowing moments of my life. They have been a silvered thread weaving the broken fragments of my heart and my hope back together, helping me to trust that nothing is ever lost in the great hands that hold all of our lives like a tiny hazelnut, cradling us in a love that "contains all the world" and yet throbs also in the center of our hearts, leading us toward a great and coming redemption. Such words have come to me countless times through the gift of good books, and I believe that they come to every woman who reads, agents of strength and comfort that take us bookish girls by the hands and teach us not just to feel hope but to live it, to clothe it, to "practice resurrection" every day of our lives.

Not Escapism: Novels That Helped Me Cope with a Broken World

(OR, BOOKS THAT COMFORT THE SOUL)

"HUMANITY can be roughly divided into three sorts of people—those who find comfort in literature, those who find comfort in personal adornment, and those who find comfort in food," opined Elizabeth Goudge. While I do in some part identify with each of the types above, I usually turn to books first in times of distress, discouragement, or general disillusionment with life. Some of the novels I love with an abiding and grateful affection are the ones in whose vision of the world I have dwelled as in a shelter. These are the books that acknowledge pain, both of body and mind. They make no bones about the reality of loneliness or loss, the way some wounds and some relationships will never be whole this side of heaven. I will warn you: a few of the books on this list are outright tragedies. But I include them here because they tell the truth of the world's sorrow, something we sometimes need to hear affirmed, even as they allow us a glimpse of the hope that is always working to make our suffering the ground of a new beginning.

Tolkien made quick, scornful work of critics who accused readers of fiction of "escapism." The critics, huffed Tolkien, confuse "the escape of the prisoner with the flight of the deserter,"[9] for we often read novels not to escape reality but to engage with it afresh. When our capacity to see or our ability to hope has been diminished by exhaustion, grief, or boredom, it's books like the following that help us to gird up our loins and keep the story of our own lives going.

A Place on Earth by Wendell Berry

When Gwen and I discussed this novel years ago, we decided that one of the best words we could think of to describe its quality was *hush*; the story is hushed in the way our own lives, lived in the circle of our own days, is hushed. When I enter the world of a Berry novel, I'm not whisked away to an exotic land or a romantically unrealistic setting. Rather, I'm immersed in the workaday thoughts of people who eat and love and work pretty much like me, and in this case, who carry on with normal life in the face of a rising grief. In this novel we walk in thought with Matt Feltner; Margaret, his wife; and Hannah, his daughter-in-law (whose life is fully explored in *Hannah Coulter*, review on page 47) as they endure the slow loss of their son and husband, who has been declared missing in World War II. The tale of grief is told slowly, following its rise in dark evenings and its slight waning in the normalcy of working days and old friendships. It's an ordinary tragedy, but one richly imaging the grace that can rise amid hard work and a community that, while never denying grief, seeks to move through it into a fragile hope. I have found it to be deeply sustaining, a steadying hand in times of struggle.

Silence by Shusako Endo

A novel that is a narrative contemplation on the nature of suffering and God's silence within it, this story considers the life of a persecuted Jesuit missionary in seventeenth-century Japan and the two young priests who go in search of him who are unwilling to believe reports of their mentor's apostasy. The story delves deeply into suffering when idealism is stripped away, when right and wrong appear confused. An aching but honest story of faith, probing the heart of Christ's presence with us in the broken place.

The Remains of the Day by Kazuo Ishiguro

Narrated by Stevens, the proper and upright butler who is dedicated to the service of Lord Darlington, this story considers Stevens's relationship with Miss Kenton, the housekeeper who both frustrates and draws him, the woman whose significance to his life it takes him a novel's length of narration to realize. This is a story that deals with the sorrow of unexpressed love, in which we recognize with Stevens only too late the way that "there was surely nothing to indicate at the time that such evidently small incidents would render whole dreams forever irredeemable." A tragedy, but one that teaches the urgency, the irreplaceable preciousness of love. (Even if you had a difficult time with the film—considered something of a classic, starring Anthony Hopkins and Emma Thompson—give this book a chance, as I felt the story works so much better when you are allowed to get inside Stevens's thoughts.)

Rilla of Ingleside by L. M. Montgomery

I was riveted by this final book in the Anne of Green Gables series and its heroine, Rilla (named after the famed Marilla), Anne's youngest daughter. Idealistic, innocent, with an excellent sense of humor and a penchant (like her mother) for awkward moments, Rilla comes of age at the opening of World War I, watching her brothers, her childhood friends, and the boy she is just beginning to think she loves leave for the brutalities and griefs of the battlefield. I love this book for its daily, down-to-earth account of tragedy and uncertainty as those who remain faithful at home endure and are transformed. For Rilla is left behind to watch and wait, and this is the chronicle of the loving maturity she reaches through loss, through faithfulness, and through the deep hope and rooted humor she fights to keep in the face of pain. It's a triumphant and aching story that helped me to take courage for my own small battles.

Cry, the Beloved Country by Alan Paton

This was the novel that first helped me to understand what faith and a grieved, loving faithfulness can look like in the midst of devastation. It's a tragedy, set in South Africa and centered on the character of Stephen Kumalo, a native African priest. The story explores the racial abuses and tensions that led to apartheid, weaving those evils with the long, grieved account of Stephen's search for his beloved and lost son, Absalom. There is no lessening of social or personal guilt here; the effects of poverty and the consequences of hatred are clear. But so is hope; its quiet presence is unabated by the reality of grief, and that is the gift this novel gave me. Through this book, I came to the realization that hope does not mean the cancellation of grief or fear; it is rather present right in their midst, denying death the ultimate word. In Kumalo's words: "For it is the dawn that has come, as it has come for a thousand centuries, never failing."

Also by Paton:
- *Too Late the Phalarope*

The Chosen by Chaim Potok

This is the kind of novel that draws you into its narrative and characters so fully you don't realize until the end that in the reading you have come to fundamental understandings about faith or suffering or friendship, or in this case, silence. This is a tale of fathers and sons, and their competing ideals of faith as lived out in the lives of two Jewish boys, one a devout but secular Jew, the other the son of a Hasidic rabbi. Reuven Malter and Danny Saunders are both growing up in Brooklyn against the backdrop of World War II, but Danny, brilliant and analytical and hungry for education, is destined to follow in his father's footsteps as leader of their Hasidic sect. The two boys become close friends as Reuven comes to observe the strange and grievous fact of Danny's life: he has been raised in silence. His father will not speak to him unless they are studying the Torah. This story of friendship, of fatherhood, and of what silence may communicate is one of my favorite novels (and my husband's, too, I might add).

> You can listen to silence, Reuven. . . . You have to want
> to listen to it, and then you can hear it. It has a strange,
> beautiful texture. It doesn't always talk. Sometimes—
> sometimes it cries, and you can hear the pain of the world in
> it. It hurts to listen to it then. But you have to.

Also by Potok:
- *My Name Is Asher Lev*

The Yearling by Marjorie Kinnan Rawlings

I didn't expect to like this book. I picked it up as an adult, feeling that I must dutifully skim it for a children's book list I was compiling. I knew it was about a boy and his adopted fawn and was generally a coming-of-age tale. I was bored before I even started. But I obediently began, and ah, I was captured. I met myself afresh in this story that is indeed about a boy and his fawn and the difficulties of maturity, but one that aches with the beauty of a child's innocent affection, of the world when it is still unmarked by suffering. It is a novel that deals in grief, the shattering of heart that comes to each person when that glorious, unbounded innocence is lost. This novel is one of those that taught me how to sorrow, how to live in the fallenness of the world and still to see the "fineness" of its beauty and to go on despite the darkness. For as the wise and gentle Penny Baxter tells his son:

> You've seed how things goes in the world o' men. . . . You've seed ol' Death at his tricks. . . . Ever' man wants life to be a fine thing, and a easy. 'Tis fine, boy, powerful fine, but 'tain't easy. Life knocks a man down and he gits up and it knocks him down agin. I've been uneasy all my life. . . . I've wanted life to be easy for you. . . . I wanted to spare you, long as I could. But ever' man's lonesome. What's he to do then? What's he to do when he gits knocked down? Why, take it for his share and go on.

(Though this isn't a book recommendation, Andrew Peterson has created a beautiful album of music themed around *The Yearling* called *Light for the Lost Boy*. I can't recommend it highly enough as a companion to this story.)

Home by Marilynne Robinson

You'll know from my review of *Lila* (see page 56) how much I respect Robinson's skill in untangling the self-deceptions and suffering of the human heart. *Lila* and *Gilead*, the other books in this loose trilogy, also deal deeply in the consequences of evil and pain, the trust it takes to hope. *Lila* is definitely a book I would include in this list, but Robinson is equally powerful and particularly poignant in this story of the Reverend Boughton (best friend of the old man in *Lila*), his prodigal and maddening son, and the bereft daughter watching their last days together. A novel that masterfully shows the way that the secret sorrows we bear frustrate and separate us, this is also the story of love's frustrated, dogged, inexorable power to try once again for connection.

Also by Robinson:
- *Gilead*
- *Lila*

The Silmarillion by J. R. R. Tolkien

If you think I'm trying to sneak a bit of Tolkien into as many lists as I can, you're right. I am fascinated by the origin story Tolkien wrote for his imagined world, one that directly examines the entrance of sin and suffering into a good creation, in the terms of an ancient epic. I think this was Tolkien's theodicy—his defense of God's goodness—written after his time in the trenches of World War I. The creation account of God's creative song as joined by legions of angels is matchless.

The Hawk and the Dove by Penelope Wilcock

Quiet and wry, a novel centered on the medieval Benedictine abbey of St. Alcuin, this story considers the arrogant and impatient Father Peregrine as he wrestles with his soul while seeking to be a faithful abbot to his community. This is the first book in the series, with the later books describing the deep faith required when Father Peregrine must come to terms with illness and infirmity, a process both agonizing and humorous, and requiring as much grit for the suffering as any more obvious persecution.

God Is Big Enough:
Spiritual Books That Helped Me through Seasons of Struggle
(OR, LITERARY COMPANIONS FOR CRISES OF FAITH)

MY FIRST REAL CRISIS of faith came when I was seventeen, and it wasn't so much about God's reality so much as his goodness. I didn't think there was much tangible evidence of it. (We'll leave aside teenage absolutism for the moment.) My family was making a difficult cross-country move, I had my own small host of troubles, and in that terrifying insight that comes to children at one point or another, I realized that my parents had no control over our painful circumstances. I remember sitting with my mom late one evening (my mother says that all her children waited to have their spiritual crises until far past bedtime), almost spitting out my doubt and fear, my sense of betrayal. I also remember the keen sense of knowing that came to me when I finished and we both sat in the silence and I realized that my mom couldn't answer. There was nothing she could say to settle my questions or make things better in that moment.

What she did say probably saved my faith.

"God is big enough for your questions. Don't be afraid to doubt, but go to him to do it."

What those words helped me to do was struggle *with* God instead of away from him, and the books in the following list are the ones that came alongside me in the next decade and taught me to struggle well, to fight toward hope, toward a renewed grasp on God's love as it comes right into the heart of our brokenness. These books are the ones that helped me to form an understanding of suffering, of daily struggle, even of the restlessness that comes amid happiness, not as something zapped down upon me or watched without care by a distant God, but as the ground Christ himself invades, the place where by his life and power, beauty grows afresh. Some of the authors, like Buechner, I discovered as a teenager. Some, like Von Balthasar, I first encountered in a college library. But all the faithful writers below did exactly what my mom encouraged me to do: they wrestled with God and, in so doing, equipped me to live out my hope in God's redemption right in the middle of a broken world.

Letters and Papers from Prison by Dietrich Bonhoeffer

I must be honest. I wrestle with Bonhoeffer. I read his *Discipleship* in my teen years and felt challenged by his idea of "costly grace" but also intimidated by the stark, uncompromising nature of his theology. But when I had to study him for a year as part of my degree, I came to respect him for what is one of the driving elements in his writing: his uncompromising and total devotion to Christ. He was a remarkable man: a German philosopher, a theologian, a Lutheran pastor who was put to death by the Nazis. It was in reading his *Letters and Papers from Prison*—the record of his anguish and his unfaltering faith, but also his growing conviction that Christ invades the very heart of the world's suffering—that I discovered the voice of a mentor I will return to throughout my life. To know Christ—to encounter him in the grief or joy of each moment, to embody his self-giving life—was the core of Bonhoeffer's theology, one that captivated me in this book. Be sure to get an edition that includes the poems Bonhoeffer composed in prison, poems in which he expresses both his hope and his anguish, his self-doubt and his confidence:

> *Who am I? This or the Other?*
> *Am I one person today and tomorrow another?*
> *Am I both at once? A hypocrite before others,*
> *And before myself a contemptible woebegone weakling?*
> *Or is something within me still like a beaten army*
> *Fleeing in disorder from victory already achieved?*
> *Who am I? They mock me, these lonely questions of mine.*
> *Whoever I am, Thou knowest, O God, I am thine!*

Speak What We Feel: Not What We Ought to Say by Frederick Buechner

Buechner is a theologian and a pastor, but he is also a poet and a novelist. His frankly beautiful writing, with its questioning, honest tone, has been a companion to me in many seasons of struggle, loneliness, or change, but this contemplation on the way suffering sometimes helps us to speak truth is one of his books to which I most often return. *Speak What We Feel* takes its title from King Lear's famous statement in the moment of his undoing ("The weight of this sad time we must obey, speak what we feel, not what we ought to say"). In it, Buechner examines four writers—Gerard Manley Hopkins, Mark Twain, Shakespeare, and G. K. Chesterton—whose times of greatest darkness forced them beyond the bounds of popularity or reason to speak, in story or poem, the deepest and hardest truths they knew. A beautiful account of the way that suffering can sometimes reveal hope in a depth and quality we have never touched before.

Also by Buechner:
- *The Sacred Journey: A Memoir of Early Days*
- *The Hungering Dark*
- *The Magnificent Defeat*
- *Listening to Your Life: Daily Meditations with Frederick Buechner*

The Pilgrim's Progress and Dangerous Journey: The Story of Pilgrim's Progress by John Bunyan

You no doubt know of the classic *The Pilgrim's Progress*, but I'll recommend the somewhat simplified and arrestingly illustrated retelling of it in *Dangerous Journey*. This classic allegorical account of the Christian's journey to heaven, with its vivid images of Vanity Fair and the Slough of Despond, rings remarkably true to the daily struggles of discipleship.

The Doors of the Sea: Where Was God in the Tsunami? by David Bentley Hart

To wrestle with doubt is, I believe, integral to a real and healthy faith. My doubt has centered mostly not on the existence of God but on his goodness. How can we hold to a loving and powerful God in a world so devastated by violence and sin? This slim, wordy (it must be admitted), but eloquent book, written in response to the devastating 2004 tsunami in Asia, has helped me to a clear, aching grasp of God's incredible love as it invades the sorrow and shattering of the world. It's a "quick" read, originally an article in the *Wall Street Journal*, that draws on history, theology, and writers like Dostoevsky to defend the overwhelming love and redemptive will of God.

At the Scent of Water: The Ground of Hope in the Book of Job by J. Gerald Janzen

I first discovered Janzen's work on Job in the dawn light of my college library, the day before my Old Testament essay was due. I was supposed to be collecting last-minute quotes for a project on Job. Instead, I found myself immersed in a commentary on one of the most mysterious books in the Bible that startled me with this assertion: "Why is the man so pious and so upright? Is it only because he is so blessed and so prosperous? The question which is raised in heaven is not answered there but is given into the hands and heart of the man to answer in the context of manifold suffering."

What became clear to me in Janzen's compassionate and frankly poetic prose is that the story of Job is an affirmation not merely of God's sovereignty in suffering but of humankind's capacity to respond in loving, mature trust. This is what Job declares before the assembled powers of the world: a conscious, radical affirmation of the enduring goodness and real justice of his Creator. This is the theme slightly more personally explored in *At the Scent of Water*, a book combining academic observation with a delightful amount of poetry and an account of Janzen's own battle with pancreatic cancer to demonstrate the deep hope that lies at the root of Job's strange story. (If you're interested in the commentary as well, it's called *Job: Interpretation: A Biblical Commentary for Teaching*.)

Thoughts to Make Your Heart Sing by Sally Lloyd-Jones (illustrated by Jago)

This may seem an unlikely title to include in a list of books meant to help with great grapplings of faith. It's a children's devotional, created as a companion to the wildly popular *The Jesus Storybook Bible*. What I love about it—and the reason I include it here—is that in times of my spiritual exhaustion, it isn't necessarily another brilliant defense of God's goodness that enables me to keep believing. It's a single word, an image of beauty, a promise of his faithfulness to which I can cling, and that's what this book offers in devotional thoughts that focus on a single Scripture or promise, accompanied by luminous illustrations that bring each promise to life. This book is created to nourish the heart of a child, which is what I often become in times of struggle. I have found these devotions to be surprisingly potent—and radiantly lovely—contemplations in times of weariness.

A Grief Observed by C. S. Lewis

This is C. S. Lewis's deeply personal account of his grief at the death of his wife, Joy. After losing her to bone cancer just three years after their marriage, Lewis scrawled out his anger and terror, his sense of futility, his inability to grasp hope, in poignant fragments in a few notebooks. The angst he expressed was so raw that the book was at first published under a pseudonym. But for all its tortured grapple with pain, this is also one believer's account of his wrestle with God, one that drew him inexorably back to faith. I have loved this work in times of struggle because of its honesty and fearless doubt. Lewis is a writer who says what we all wish we could find the words to express (and are sometimes afraid to say), and this book of grief offers the gift he so generously gives in his other works: the image of a faith not lost but deepened in its encounter with question, sorrow, and desire.

The Return of the Prodigal Son: A Story of Homecoming by Henri J. M. Nouwen

Some books speak to the part of us that yearns for glory; some kindle our strength; some touch the secret places of our sorrow, helping us to open what is grieved, guilty, and lost to the touch of Christ. Nouwen, for me, is the third: a writer who helps me to face what is most broken in myself not with renewed effort but with a run into the arms of my Father. In this aching and beautiful exploration of the ways in which we all, whether addicted or yearning or depressed, live the life of the prodigal, Nouwen leads the reader to this realization: "I am the prodigal son every time I search for unconditional love where it cannot be found." Centering his contemplations on Rembrandt's painting of the prodigal's return, Nouwen draws us into a recognition of our need and of the grace that waits to receive us, for "when I look through God's eyes at my lost self and discover God's joy at my coming home, then my life may become less anguished and more trusting."

Also by Nouwen:
- *Life of the Beloved: Spiritual Living in a Secular World*
- *The Way of the Heart: The Spirituality of the Desert Fathers and Mothers*
- *The Wounded Healer; Ministry in Contemporary Society*
- *Love, Henri: Letters on the Spiritual Life*

A Long Obedience in the Same Direction: Discipleship in an Instant Society by Eugene H. Peterson

Perhaps one of the foremost books on what Christian discipleship really looks like for the modern believer, this classic of spiritual formation reiterates Peterson's long-term message that the gospel isn't about a quick fix for happiness or a token for self-fulfillment or a zapping remedy for sin. Rather, it is "a long obedience" requiring us to walk a few more steps every day in the company of Christ. Written around the beautiful psalms of ascent, it is a realistic and encouraging challenge to contemporary believers.

Also by Peterson:
- *Christ Plays in Ten Thousand Places: A Conversation in Spiritual Theology* (reviewed on page 117)
- *Tell It Slant: A Conversation on the Language of Jesus in His Stories and Prayers*
- *Eat This Book: A Conversation in the Art of Spiritual Reading*
- *Run with the Horses: The Quest for Life at Its Best*

Theo-Drama: Theological Dramatic Theory (especially volume 4) by Hans Urs von Balthasar

I haven't included *too* many academic-type books, but I'll set this here for those whose curiosity is piqued. Von Balthasar is one of my favorite theologians, a brilliant, respected systematic theologian who called for a renewal of "kneeling theology," the kind only accomplished by a life of prayer. He seems almost incapable of writing anything short (*The Glory of the Lord: A Theological Aesthetics*—his systematic theology based on a contemplation of beauty, truth, and goodness—is seven thick volumes long), but I waded through his *Theo-Drama* and understood more about sin and evil, human choice and divine freedom than I have from any other source. His theology is epic in scope—he is a visionary who sees the larger picture of redemption and strives to communicate every detail of its intricate plot and particular beauty. But his tone is one of warmth and wonder, a brilliant consciousness formed by prayer. Try his *Credo: Meditations on the Apostles' Creed* for an easy first taste.

Own Your Life: Living with Deep Intention, Bold Faith, and Generous Love by Sally Clarkson

Ask any of the Clarkson siblings what one phrase our mom used over and over again when we were growing up, and you'll get the answer in chorus: "You have a choice to make." If there was one thing my mom wanted us to grasp, it was that we kids (no matter how we felt) had the capacity to choose: love, forgiveness, gentleness, joy. As an adult, I am so grateful for that deeply formative message because it helped me early on to see myself as capable, responsible, able to change the world around me simply by my capacity to choose. How interesting, then, that one of the most fascinating ideas I stumbled across in my theological studies was how vital it is for people to understand themselves as agents, able to shape their own stories, to *choose* to create, resist evil, or fight for the good. It's what God communicated to Israel throughout the Old

Testament, it's what I think Gandalf was trying to tell Frodo, and it's what my mom communicated to us every day of our young lives. *Own Your Life* is my mother's personal exploration of what it means to be an agent, to own the story God has given you with grace, purpose, and chosen joy. I pass it on to you now. *You, too, have a choice to make.*

Also by Clarkson:
- *The Mission of Motherhood: Touching Your Child's Heart of Eternity*
- *The Ministry of Motherhood: Following Christ's Example in Reaching the Hearts of Our Children*
- *The Lifegiving Table: Nurturing Faith through Feasting, One Meal at a Time*
- *The Lifegiving Home: Creating a Place of Belonging and Becoming* (with Sarah Clarkson)
- *Different: The Story of an Outside-the-Box Kid and the Mom Who Loved Him* (with Nathan Clarkson)
- *Dancing with My Father: How God Leads Us into a Life of Grace and Joy*

Reaching for the Invisible God: What Can We Expect to Find? by Philip Yancey

Yancey was one of the authors who most helped me to live out my mom's directive to struggle with, rather than away from, God. The book deals in questions: How do we relate to a God we're never sure is there? Where is God in pain? How do I know my prayers are heard? All these are questions that have shaped my own wrestle with faith. With his usual mix of story, anecdote, research, and personal reflection, Yancey helps me to realize that doubt is not a threat to faith, that it is part of the journey we walk in belief, in trust, as we reach in faith for the "invisible God."

Books Are Meant to Be PASSED ALONG

The Ongoing Legacy of the Reading Life

My best friend is the man who'll
get me a book I ain't read.
ABRAHAM LINCOLN

THERE ARE DAFFODILS in the vase by my window as I write, and my belly is just about too big for comfort as I sit here in the Saturday quiet of my little Oxford living room. I wrote the opening to this book when the first autumn leaves flecked the grass and the sky was just beginning to darken with the long winter nights that come so early here in England. Back then, my little book girl was my secret, barely visible joy. Now she kicks as I write so that I squirm on the couch. The light grows every evening, the days stretch along with my belly, and we stand on the cusp of spring. As this journey through the gifts of the reading life comes to a close, I am rich in the knowledge that I will soon meet the little book girl to whom this book is dedicated.

In preparation for her coming to our tiny Oxford house, we have kept our baby shopping to a list of the absolute essentials, including, of course, an ever-growing stack of our favorite books. It should come as no surprise that half of the gifts I open for this little one are books—baby books, children's classics, picture books—the ones beloved of my friends, the stories they hope will enrich and liven our days together. Amid these treasures are three special books that make my heart both ache and exult every time I see them. They are worn, even ragged, their illustrations from a different era. But they are precious, the image I want to leave you with as we complete our journey together through the reading life.

These picture books were a gift from an elderly woman in my church. I first knew Alice and her tall, friendly husband as one of the beaming older couples who took real delight in welcoming Thomas and me into the parish church. As we planned our wedding there, I discovered that she, too, had come to that church as a bride. Their wedding gift to us was an antique etching of the church sanctuary that she had treasured for decades, and I felt a sense of deep camaraderie, of shared strength as I walked down the aisle on my wedding day and saw her there with her husband, their marriage and kindness so rich a source of life and joy to those in the church, and to me.

One year later, she stood as a widow where I had so recently stood as a bride, and I sat where she had, watching as her beloved was laid to rest after a brief, grieved fight with cancer. But there was no bitterness in her face. There was peace, a gentle quality I'd witnessed in her often as her husband's life faded and she began the process of sifting through their home and marriage, cleaning things out, letting things go, and—great gift to me—passing things on. For Alice had been a teacher, one who loved children's books and pored over the old guides to literature with the same fervor that I do in preparation for my baby. We quickly recognized each other as kindred-spirited book girls, and when it came time to pass on the books that had shaped her as a teacher and companioned her as a young mother, she brought them to me. Her face, even in that time of grief, was so bright and sure as she put the stacked books into my hands.

"I know you'll love them—and *use* them," she said. "And I know you'll pass them along in your time."

Alice is my image of what a book girl grows to become: a giver.

One who, out of the richness of her reading life, out of a soul made quiet with wisdom, passes on the treasure she has found. In closing *Book Girl*, I hope that you will do the same with all you have discovered in this book. The reading life is, I'm convinced, a form of love, a way of encountering the world in its splendor and drama. The reading life comes to us as a gift and, as it fills us, drives us to fresh generosity. As you read and imagine, learn and grow in the company of great books, I hope you, too, will find that joyous urge that comes of a heart grown rich to hand out books to the children in your life, to pass on novels to your best friends, to press a good story into the hands of a struggling teen.

It's what my mother did for me, what I hope to do for my daughter, and what I hope you have experienced in reading this book. If I could press a few of my best-loved old novels into your hands, I would. I wish I could set my battered copy of *Pilgrim's Inn* in your hands or pass along my bent-edged *Miss Rumphius*. I'd give it to you with the same joy and surety I saw in Alice's eyes, the same sparkle-eyed, kindred-spirited camaraderie of the book-girl fellowship. Since I can't do that, consider the whole of this book my way of passing along the glory. I'll end by saying to you what Alice said to me: I know you'll *love* these books in their beauty and imagination. I know you'll *use* them—to learn and grow, to gain hope, to battle well. And I know that when it's time, when another book girl just on the edge of discovery comes into your life, you'll *pass them along*.

And the book-girl story will begin in joy all over again.

Lists for the Growing Book Girls in Your Life

Years ago, when I was in a phase of fascination with Scottish history and legend (prompted by the discovery of Scottish heritage in my family ancestry), I came across an intriguing set of historical figures called *seanachís*. These were the cultural descendants of the early Celtic bards whose vocation was to be the storytellers, the legend keepers for their people; to memorize and recite the love poems and haunting songs, the battle-forged epics of history, the stories in whose brave deeds the identity and history of a people were rooted. Seanachís were documented well into the twentieth century, often traveling village to village, keeping the old tales and songs alive with evenings of song and story by the fire in the local pub. People came away thrilled and heartened by the tales they heard, and children were quickened to life with new dreams of courage or creativity, sparked by the stories woven around them by the gifts of the seanachí.

After many years of thinking about books, researching reading, and writing about the power of story to shape the way we understand ourselves, I am convinced that our world needs adults willing to be seanachís in the lives of the children they love. In a world of confusing headlines and worldviews, amid the countless distractions of technology, children need adults who will draw them into the gift and wisdom of great stories. They deeply need imaginations formed by beauty, vocabularies big enough to articulate their dreams. One of the most powerful ways that you as a book girl can be a giver, passing along the gift of the reading life, is by cultivating reading in the life of the children in your care. Whether you are a parent, determined to make the reading life a rhythm and a joy in the everyday structure of your home; or a teacher, with a whole bevy of curious minds in your daily care; or a mentor, a friend, or an auntie to a few budding book girls, you have the power to give the powerful and soul-forming gift of reading. The research is clear on the power of reading to drive education, to widen possibility. But beyond that, books offer children the chance to enter life itself as a story, to see themselves as heroes and heroines with great adventures and battles and loves just beginning. That is an irreplaceable gift.

As we close, here are a few lists to help you in that wondrous project of passing along the reading life.

Picture Books

When I delved back into all my favorite picture books from childhood (a delightful task) for my first book on books, I came across a collection of illustrated fairy tales that I suddenly remembered was a treasure to me in little girlhood. It was the book I'd take into my room on a long Sunday afternoon or a rainy day so I could pore over the intricate images, the whimsical tales. When I rediscovered the book as an adult, I was intrigued to realize that the illustrator was Michael Hague, an artist whose work I'd long admired for its intricacy, detail, and depth, for the way it reflected the qualities of the classical masterpieces of art I loved as a teen. As I stood there flipping through the old pages, I realized that this was no coincidence. The more old picture books I rediscovered (by illustrators such as Barbara Cooney, Thomas Locker, and Trina Schart Hyman), the more I became aware that those picture books exposed me to beauty in a way that formed my appetite and trained my imagination to exult in good art as an adult. Those picture books, in their small way, prepared me to enjoy the works of Monet and Vermeer, Caravaggio and Fra Angelico, just as their carefully crafted scripts readied me for Dickens, L'Engle, and Lewis.

I am thus very passionate about picture books, because these little treasures shouldn't be seen as a substitute for "real" art and literature; rather, they shape the way a child sees the world, the art she craves, the beauty she learns to love. Picture books are the lovingly crafted, child-sized packages of art and literature through which little ones first encounter the intricacy of the written word and the realm of art. These slim books, the bedtime tales read over and over, the birthday gifts, the well-paged companions of every day are the missives of beauty and humor forming the hungers and delights of their little readers with every word and vivid illustration. With that in mind, the following is a list of the picture books I've stacked ready for my own little book girl. I can't wait to watch her eyes come alight.

- *Roxaboxen* by Alice McLerran and Barbara Cooney
- *Miss Rumphius* by Barbara Cooney
- *The Relatives Came* by Cynthia Rylant
- *The Boy Who Held Back the Sea* by Thomas Locker
- *My Mama Had a Dancing Heart* by Libba Moore Gray
- *Saint George and the Dragon* by Margaret Hodges
- Brambly Hedge series by Jill Barklem
- *Wilfrid Gordon McDonald Partridge* by Mem Fox
- *Fritz and the Beautiful Horses* by Jan Brett
- *The Bear That Heard Crying* by Natalie Kinsey-Warnock and Helen Kinsey
- *Alphabears* by Kathleen and Michael Hague

Children's Classics

Children's books, I was fascinated to discover, are a relatively recent invention. Until about the Victorian era, there were few books written specifically for children and even fewer (if any) written just to delight and entertain (rather than provide moral instruction). A fascinating milieu of cultural trends combined with the vivid imaginations of a few early writers (such as George MacDonald and Lewis Carroll) to abruptly shift the terrain of the publishing world and bring the children's book into being. That began what is now known as the golden age of children's books, a time that lasted pretty much through the publishing of *Winnie-the-Pooh* and World War I. The books in this list were written in an era that prized childhood for its wonder and innocence, that sought to celebrate a child's more compact view of the world, that appealed to the oh-so-elusive quality of childish innocence . . . and insight.

These books are timeless in their appeal and would easily suit the individual reading of a child around eight years old or older. While they fit a general category of late elementary/middle-school reading, they also make excellent read-alouds, with plots and characters that keep adults riveted as much as young children. I have to admit to an old-fashioned opinion that every child should grow up with these classic books. To that end, I may have started collecting my own leather-bound editions one by one—a good dozen years before I met my husband. Luckily, he was doing the same with Dutch classics of his own.

- *Peter Pan* by J. M. Barrie
- *The Wind in the Willows* by Kenneth Grahame
- *The Little Princess* by Frances Hodgson Burnett
- *The Secret Garden* by Frances Hodgson Burnett
- *The Complete Tales of Winnie-the-Pooh* by A. A. Milne
- *The Tale of Peter Rabbit* by Beatrix Potter
- *Little Women* by Louisa May Alcott
- *Little Men* by Louisa May Alcott
- *Kidnapped* by Robert Louis Stevenson
- *Treasure Island* by Robert Louis Stevenson
- *The Water-Babies* by Charles Kingsley
- *The Railway Children* by E. Nesbit
- *The Story of the Treasure Seekers* by E. Nesbit
- *Heidi* by Johanna Spyri

Children's Fiction

This list could go on for pages, for the books on this list are the ones I look back upon as the stories that broadened my idea of the world. They're the sorts of novels that met me in those formative middle years of childhood (roughly ages eight through thirteen), expanding my dreams for what I could do or try or become. Each bookish world I encountered, each character I met enlarged my understanding of peoples, cultures, crafts, and callings. They expanded my vocabulary. They opened new rooms of dreaming in my thought and introduced me to eras in history I had only begun to imagine. They helped me to come to a sense of self and purpose even before I reached the angst of the teenage years.

In the middle-school years of education, children are often already beginning to figure out their answers to what philosophers see as the fundamental human questions: Who am I? Why am I here? What is a good life? What is a good love?

The books in the list below are the ones that equipped me to answer and enjoy those questions as my own story opened at my feet:

- Little Britches series by Ralph Moody
- *The Mysterious Benedict Society* by Trenton Lee Stewart
- *The Penderwicks* by Jeanne Birdsall
- *All-of-a-Kind Family* by Sydney Taylor
- *Caddie Woodlawn* by Carol Ryrie Brink
- *Winter Cottage* by Carol Ryrie Brink
- *Johnny Tremain* by Esther Forbes
- *The Good Master* by Kate Seredy
- *Carry On, Mr. Bowditch* by Jean Lee Latham
- *Ellen* by E. M. Almedingen
- *Across Five Aprils* by Irene Hunt
- *I, Juan de Pareja* by Elizabeth Borton de Treviño
- *Mother and Me: Escape from Warsaw 1939* by Julian Padowicz
- *The Trumpeter of Krakow* by Eric Kelly
- *The Wolves of Willoughby Chase* by Joan Aiken
- *Because of Winn-Dixie* by Kate DiCamillo

Fairy Tale and Fantasy

I think all children should come early to the great fantastical titles that follow mostly because I think every child needs to learn early how to hope, and hope with a great, joyous will. Hope has a lot to do with imagination, with our capacity to imagine a brave act or a happy ending beyond what we can see. Children are small philosophers, encountering the goodness and the darkness, the joyous and the grievous in their experiences with an intensity we sometimes forget as adults. Because of this, they need stories that deal in ultimates—stories whose images make a window into all that waits beyond the walls of the world, into the love that is always present to them, even in their fear. They need fantastical tales of knights and dragons, kings and castles, epic quests and fairy-tale love. They need books of wild, holy imagination, rich with hints of eternity on every page. They need fairy tales. They need myth. They need fantasy, because fantastical yarns and epic tales help children to picture a happy ending, to act bravely, to believe that beauty is possible. The books below are also simply some of the most intriguing page-turners I remember loving from my own little girlhood. They delight . . . and they nourish the deepest rooms of the soul.

- The Chronicles of Narnia by C. S. Lewis
- The Green Ember series by S. D. Smith
- The Wingfeather Saga series by Andrew Peterson
- *Henry and the Chalk Dragon* by Jennifer Trafton
- A Series of Unfortunate Events by Lemony Snicket
- *The Princess and the Goblin* by George MacDonald
- *At the Back of the North Wind* by George MacDonald
- *The Lost Princess* by George MacDonald
- Harry Potter series by J. K. Rowling
- Tales of Hans Christian Andersen
- Redwall series by Brian Jacques
- *Dangerous Journey: The Story of Pilgrim's Progress* by John Bunyan

Acknowledgments

ONE OF MY FAVORITE quotes comes from a Wendell Berry novel, when a character arrives home after a long absence of both body and heart. Upon entering his home, realizing the love that has always been waiting to embrace him, he comes to a full realization of the "blessedness he has lived in." He walks from room to room, "saying over and over to himself, 'I am blessed. I am blessed.'"[1]

I have often felt the same in the writing of this book as I walked through the rooms of my memory, realizing the gifts of reading and imagination given to me as a child and by the friends and mentors I've known since. I've felt that sense of blessing in encountering the kindred-spirited book girls at Tyndale Momentum, whose work and vision made this book possible, and in the care of my husband and family as I pounded out this manuscript.

In particular, I would like to thank:

Jan Long Harris and Sarah Atkinson for their enthusiasm for this project and their vision for creating a book for book girls. To work with you has been a privilege and a kindred-spirit delight.

Stephanie Rische for being not just an editor with profound insight, lovely humor, and the kind of radiant encouragement that kept me on my writerly feet, but for making the work of revision a delighted conversation between friends.

Jillian Schlossberg and the Tyndale Momentum design team for their artistry and infectious enthusiasm in designing the *Book Girl* look.

My mentors and companions in the reading life who contributed their own book-girlish lists to this book. I've learned and rejoiced so deeply in your company.

My parents, for giving me the gift of the reading life when my own story was just beginning, for supporting the dreams sparked by all those stories we read aloud, and for being the generous givers that all great readers become.

My mom, for reading aloud to me in the womb and for being my bosom friend ever since.

My husband, Thomas. Oh, love. How can I put my thanks for the whole of our life and story into a single sentence? Thank you for loving, supporting, and believing in your book girl. I'm so glad I'm yours.

Notes

INTRODUCTION: BECOMING A BOOK GIRL
1. Barbara Cooney, *Miss Rumphius* (New York: Penguin Books, 1982).

CHAPTER 1: ON THE CRAFTING OF BOOK LISTS
1. Mortimer Adler and Charles Van Doren, *How to Read a Book: The Classic Bestselling Guide to Reading Books and Accessing Information* (New York: Touchstone, 1972), 337–54.
2. Suzy Platt, ed., *Respectfully Quoted: A Dictionary of Quotations Requested from the Congressional Research Service* (Washington, DC: Library of Congress, 1989).
3. C. S. Lewis, *An Experiment in Criticism* (Cambridge: Cambridge University Press, 1961), 140–41.
4. Wendell Berry, *Hannah Coulter* (Berkeley: Counterpoint, 2004), 83.
5. Rowan Williams, *Dostoevsky: Language, Faith, and Fiction* (London: Bloomsbury, 2008), 169.
6. G. K. Chesterton, "The Red Angel," *Tremendous Trifles* (The Project Gutenberg ebook #8092, 1909).
7. C. S. Lewis, *The Weight of Glory* (New York: HarperCollins, 2001), 45–46.

CHAPTER 2: BEGIN AT THE BEGINNING
1. "Reading 'Can Help Reduce Stress,'" *Telegraph*, March 30, 2009, http://www.telegraph.co.uk/news/health/news/5070874/Reading-can-help-reduce-stress.html.
2. Ellis Peters, The Chronicles of Brother Cadfael.
3. Eugene Peterson, *Eat This Book: A Conversation in the Art of Spiritual Reading* (Grand Rapids, MI: Eerdmans, 2006).
4. Louis L'Amour, *Education of a Wandering Man* (New York: Bantam Books, 1990), 93–94.

CHAPTER 3: BOOKS CAN BROADEN YOUR WORLD
1. Robert Louis Stevenson, "The Celestial Surgeon."

2. Sebastian Wren, "The Brain and Reading," Balanced Reading, http://www.balancedreading.com/brain.pdf.

3. Janet Fulks, "Reading May Be the Key to Unlocking Basic Skills Success," Academic Senate for California Community Colleges, April 2010, https://www.asccc.org/content/reading-may-be-key-unlocking-basic-skills-success.

4. C. S. Lewis, *An Experiment in Criticism* (New York: Cambridge University Press, 2012), 3.

5. Madeleine L'Engle, "Do I Dare to Disturb the Universe?" in a speech delivered to the Library of Congress on November 16, 1983.

6. From a letter to Francois d'Albert-Durade, 1859.

7. From a letter to Charles Bray, July 5, 1859.

8. From a letter from G. B. Smith to Tolkien, quoted in John Garth, *Tolkien and the Great War* (New York: Houghton Mifflin, 2003), 105.

CHAPTER 4: BOOKS CAN SHAPE YOUR STORY

1. Samantha Ellis, "Ten Things Anne of Green Gables Taught Me," *Guardian*, May 19, 2017, https://www.theguardian.com/books/2017/may/19/10-things-anne-of-green-gables-taught-me.

2. Richard N. Ostling, "Religion: Merton's Mountainous Legacy," *Time*, December 31, 1984.

3. Philip Yancey, *The Jesus I Never Knew* (Grand Rapids, MI: Zondervan, 2002), 144.

CHAPTER 5: BOOKS CAN STIR YOU TO ACTION

1. Rowan Williams, *Dostoevsky: Language, Faith, and Fiction* (London: Continuum, 2009), 169.

2. Evelyn Underhill, "What Do We Mean by Prayer?" *Renovaré*, September 21, 2016, https://renovare.org/articles/what-do-we-mean-by-prayer.

CHAPTER 6: BOOKS CAN CULTIVATE THE IMAGINATION

1. J. R. R. Tolkien, *The Lord of the Rings: Deluxe Illustrated Edition* (New York: Houghton Mifflin, 1991), 894.

2. Alison Milbank, "Apologetics and the Imagination: Making Strange," *Imaginative Apologetics: Theology, Philosophy and the Catholic Tradition*, ed. Andrew Davison (Grand Rapids, MI: Baker Academic, 2011), 33.

3. C. S. Lewis, *The Voyage of the Dawn Treader* (New York: HarperCollins, 1994), 247.

4. James K. A. Smith, *Desiring the Kingdom: Worship, Worldview, and Cultural Formation* (Grand Rapids, MI: Baker Academic, 2009), 24, 57.

5. C. S. Lewis, *Surprised by Joy: The Shape of My Early Life* (New York: Harcourt Brace, 1955), 220.

6. Lewis, *Surprised by Joy*, 172–75.

7. C. S. Lewis, *On Stories: And Other Essays on Literature* (Orlando: Harcourt Brace, 1982), 90.

8. Owen Barfield, *Poetic Diction: A Study in Meaning* (Middletown, CT: Wesleyan University Press, 1984), 50.

9. Malcolm Guite, *Faith, Hope, and Poetry: Theology and the Poetic Imagination* (Farnham, UK: Ashgate Publishing Limited, 2012), 5.

CHAPTER 7: BOOKS CAN FOSTER COMMUNITY

1. C. S. Lewis, *The Four Loves* (San Diego: Harcourt Brace, 1960), 113.

2. Owen Barfield, *Saving the Appearances: A Study in Idolatry* (Middletown, CT: Wesleyan University Press, 1988), 20.

3. Alison Flood, "Literary Fiction Readers Understand Others' Emotions Better, Study Finds," *Guardian*, August 23, 2016, https://www.theguardian.com /books/2016/aug/23/literary-fiction-readers-understand-others-emotions-better -study-finds.

4. David Kidd and Emanuele Castano, "Different Stories: How Levels of Familiarity with Literary and Genre Fiction Relate to Mentalising," *Psychology of Aesthetics, Creativity, and the Arts*, 11, no. 4, 474–86.

5. Lewis, *The Four Loves*, 113.

6. C. S. Lewis, *Mere Christianity* (New York: HarperOne, 2001), 136–37.

CHAPTER 8: BOOKS CAN OPEN YOUR EYES TO WONDER

1. Owen A. Barfield, "A Felt Change of Consciousness," *A Barfield Reader: Selections from the Writings of Owen Barfield* (Hanover, NH: University Press of New England, 1999), 78.

2. From a series of autobiographical articles by Montgomery, published in installments in 1917 in *Everywoman's World*, gathered into a book titled *The Alpine Path: The Story of My Career* (1974).

3. Sylvia Plath, "Black Rook in Rainy Weather," *Best Poems Encyclopedia*, https:// www.best-poems.net/sylvia_plath/black_rook_in_rainy_weather.html.

4. J. R. R. Tolkien, *On Fairy-stories* (London: HarperCollins UK, 2014), 77.

5. J. R. R. Tolkien, *Tales from the Perilous Realm* (Boston: Houghton Mifflin Harcourt, 2012).

6. J. R. R. Tolkien, *Tree and Leaf* (London: HarperCollins UK, 2012), 58–69.

7. Alexander Schmemann, *For the Life of the World* (Crestwood, NY: St. Vladimir's Seminary Press, 2004), 8.

8. Robert Frost and Louis Untermeyer, *The Letters of Robert Frost to Louis Untermeyer* (New York: Holt, Rinehart, and Winston, 1963), 23.

CHAPTER 9: BOOKS CAN DEEPEN YOUR SOUL

1. Thomas Merton, *New Seeds of Contemplation* (Boulder, CO: Shambhala Publications, 2003), 82.

2. George Herbert, "Love III" in *George Herbert and the Seventeenth-Century Religious Poets* (London: W. W. Norton, 1978).

3. C. S. Lewis, *Letters to Malcolm, Chiefly on Prayer* (London: HarperCollins, 2017).

4. Anne Morrow Lindbergh, *Gift from the Sea* (New York: Knopf Doubleday, 2011), 17–18.

5. Thomas Merton, *New Seeds of Contemplation* (New York: New Directions Books, 1961), 39.

CHAPTER 10: BOOKS CAN IMPART HOPE

1. J. R. R. Tolkien, "On Fairy-Stories" in *Tree and Leaf* (London: Harper Collins, 2001), 68.
2. Alfred Delp, "The Shaking Reality of Advent," in *Watch for the Light: Readings for Advent and Christmas* (Walden, NY: 2001), 94.
3. C. S. Lewis, *The Last Battle* (New York: HarperTrophy, 2000), 198.
4. C. S. Lewis, *The Lion, the Witch and the Wardrobe* (New York: HarperTrophy, 1994).
5. J. R. R. Tolkien, *The Lord of the Rings: Deluxe Illustrated Edition* (New York: Houghton Mifflin, 1991), 957.
6. George Eliot, *Scenes of Clerical Life* (Ware, UK: Wordsworth Editions, 2007).
7. Ibid.
8. Wendell Berry, *Hannah Coulter* (Washington, DC: Counterpoint, 2004), 68.
9. J. R. R. Tolkien, *Tree and Leaf* (London: HarperCollins UK, 2012), 61.

ACKNOWLEDGMENTS

1. Wendell Berry, *Remembering* (Berkeley, CA: Counterpoint, 2008), 98–99.

Discussion Questions

1. In the introduction, the author describes how she came to be a book girl. When did you realize you were a book girl? What people or circumstances contributed to your love of reading?

2. In the introduction, the author identifies what she sees as the top three gifts of reading: it fills our hearts with beauty, gives us strength for the battle, and reminds us that we're not alone. What gifts have you encountered from the reading life?

3. In chapter 1, the author offers some guidelines about how to choose books and how to discern what constitutes good reading. How do you choose what book to read next? Are there people in your life whose recommendations you particularly resonate with?

4. Have you ever found yourself in a reading slump? How did you get out of it? Are there certain books or types of books that help you when you've gotten out of the rhythm of reading?

5. In chapter 2, the author gives suggestions for reading in fellowship. Do any of these recommendations resonate with you? Are there any that you'd like to begin to implement?

6. In chapter 3, the author says, "We understand our worlds through the words we are given." Can you think of a time when a passage from a book gave you empathy for or a deeper understanding of a person or situation in your life?

7. The author gives her "Beloved Dozen" list in chapter 3. What titles would you include on your must-read list?

8. In chapter 4, the author says, "A great book meets you in the narrative motion of your own life, showing you in vividly imagined ways exactly what it looks like to be evil or good, brave or cowardly, each of those choices shaping the happy (or tragic) ending of the stories in which they're made." In what ways have books shaped the story of your life?

9. In chapter 5, the author describes the role literature played in making her faith her own: "Tolkien's story helped me to recognize Scripture as *my* story, the one in whose decisive battles I was caught, the narrative that drew me into the conflict, requiring me to decide what part I would play: heroine, coward, lover, or villain." What impact have books had on your faith and your discovery of self? Are there particular books or passages that have been especially meaningful to you on your spiritual journey?

10. In chapter 7, the author describes how books gave her mutual ground on which to connect with her siblings. Have you ever had a similar experience of appreciating someone or identifying with them as a result of a shared reading experience?

11. What mentors fostered a love of reading for you? Who are you passing along the gift of reading to?

12. What books on the author's books lists do you love too? What additional titles would you include? What books have you added to your to-read list after finishing this book?

About the Author

SARAH CLARKSON is an author, a blogger, and a student of theology. She graduated from Wycliffe Hall, Oxford University, with a bachelor's degree in theology, where she also spent a proud year as president of the Oxford C. S. Lewis Society. She's the author of *Read for the Heart* (a guide to children's literature) and *Caught Up in a Story* (on the formative power of story), and the coauthor of *The Lifegiving Home* (on creating a place of belonging). Through blogs, books, and her current research, she explores the theological significance of story, the intersection of theology and imagination, and the formative power of beauty. She writes regularly about her adventures at www.sarahclarkson.com and is at slow work on a novel. She can often be found with a cup of good coffee in one of the many quaint corners amid Oxford's "dreaming spires," where she lives in a red-doored cottage with her husband, Thomas, and their own tiny book girl.

THE *Life* GIVING HOME

FROM THE CLARKSON FAMILY

THE *Life* GIVING HOME

CREATING A PLACE OF
belonging & becoming

SALLY & SARAH CLARKSON

978-1-4964-0337-7

Every day of your family's life can be as special and important to you as it already is to God. In *The Lifegiving Home*, you'll embark on a new path to creating special memories for your children, establishing home-building and God-centered traditions, and cultivating an environment in which your family will flourish.

Online Discussion *guide*

TAKE *your* TYNDALE READING EXPERIENCE *to the* NEXT LEVEL

A FREE discussion guide for this book is available at bookclubhub.net, perfect for sparking conversations in your book group or for digging deeper into the text on your own.

www.bookclubhub.net

You'll also find free discussion guides for other Tyndale books, e-newsletters, e-mail devotionals, virtual book tours, and more!